Louis Graveraet Kaufman

Praise for *Louis Graveraet Kaufman*

"Lurking behind the creation of the Empire State Building and General Motors was an acute and fabulously successful banker from the woods of Michigan. Louis Graveraet Kaufman's wealth also paid for a top-drawer life of glamorous parties, triplex apartments, private railcars, and America's largest log home. Ann Berman unearthed this forgotten titan's story through years of old-fashioned digging and turned the surprising facts into a wonderful book that crystallizes the doomed prosperity of the pre-Crash years into a great American saga."

—Raymond Sokolov

"Michigan's 'Forgotten Tycoon' is no longer overlooked. Ann Berman's comprehensive biography of Louis Graveraet Kaufman fills a gap in the history of American banking and that of the Upper Peninsula of Michigan. From the rural woodlands of the Great Lakes to the urban canyons of New York City, Kaufman's dramatic rise and fall left marks on our modern world today."

—Beth Gruber, research librarian, Marquette Regional History Center

"With vivacious prose, Ann Berman brings to life Louis G. Kaufman, banker, financier, and visionary. From his magnificent lodge on Lake Superior to the Court of St. James, this sweeping story is pivotal to the history of banking, the automobile industry, Upper Michigan, and the New York skyline."

—Tyler R. Tichelaar, PhD, award-winning author of
The Mysteries of Marquette

"Michigan's Upper Peninsula is known for waterfalls, rock formations, and the Mackinac Bridge. But as Ann Berman's marvelous biography *Louis Graveraet Kaufman* makes clear, the Upper Peninsula should also be famous as the birthplace and longtime home of the Zelig-like Jazz Age figure who conquered Wall Street and built the Empire State Building. It's a fascinating business history but also a richly detailed social history of private train cars, debutante balls, and George Gershwin's piano. Who could ask for anything more?"

—Joanne Kaufman, writer

"Ann Berman's biography of Louis Graveraet Kaufman is an engaging read. Berman deftly brings to life the story of an influential financier who has largely been forgotten by history. Born to a Jewish peddler in the Upper Peninsula of Michigan, Kaufman made his fortune on Wall Street during the Roaring Twenties and, along the way, bankrolled the Empire State Building. Berman weaves a fascinating rags-to-riches story."

—Jason M. Barr, author of *Cities in the Sky: The Quest to Build the World's Tallest Skyscrapers*

"Once one of the most innovative and influential financiers in the country, Louis Graveraet Kaufman has been almost entirely forgotten—until now. Ann Berman's extraordinary research and narrative skills bring long-deserved recognition to this unlikely figure's remarkable life."

—Daniel Okrent, author of *The Guarded Gate* and *Last Call*

Louis Graveraet Kaufman

THE FABULOUS MICHIGAN GATSBY WHO CONQUERED WALL STREET, TOOK OVER GENERAL MOTORS, AND BUILT THE WORLD'S TALLEST BUILDING

ANN BERMAN

A PAINTED TURTLE BOOK
DETROIT, MICHIGAN

© 2025 by Ann Berman. All rights reserved. No part of this book may be reproduced without formal permission.

ISBN 9780814348154 (paperback)
ISBN 9780814348161 (ebook)

Library of Congress Control Number: 2024943263

On cover: Louis Graveraet Kaufman, ca. 1916. Collection of Peter Kaufman. Cover design by Philip Pascuzzo.

Grateful acknowledgment is made to the Bertha M. and Hyman Herman Endowed Memorial Fund and the Leonard and Harriette Simons Endowed Family Fund for the generous support of the publication of this volume.

Wayne State University Press rests on Waawiyaataanong, also referred to as Detroit, the ancestral and contemporary homeland of the Three Fires Confederacy. These sovereign lands were granted by the Ojibwe, Odawa, Potawatomi, and Wyandot Nations, in 1807, through the Treaty of Detroit. Wayne State University Press affirms Indigenous sovereignty and honors all tribes with a connection to Detroit. With our Native neighbors, the press works to advance educational equity and promote a better future for the earth and all people.

Wayne State University Press
Leonard N. Simons Building
4809 Woodward Avenue
Detroit, Michigan 48201-1309

Visit us online at wsupress.wayne.edu.

CONTENTS

Introduction	1
1. How It All Began	7
2. The Kaufman Family Conquers Marquette	35
3. Louis Graveraet Kaufman Conquers New York	57
4. Granot Loma Rising	89
5. West Egg in the Upper Peninsula	119
6. The Sweets of Success: Power, Money, and High Society	145
7. The Beginning of the End	167
Epilogue: After LG	207
Acknowledgments	219
Author's Note	221
Notes	225
Bibliography	235

INTRODUCTION

was hunched over a library table piled high with books, deep into research for a magazine article on American rustic furniture, when I first saw the name: Granot Loma. The unfamiliar assemblage of letters on the page was oddly compelling, as was the author's assertion that the greatest Adirondack-style furniture ever made was created for Granot Loma lodge in Michigan. I am a Michigan girl, born and bred, and with many years of cultural journalism under my belt I fancied myself quite the expert on things artistic and architectural in the Wolverine State. Yet I had never heard of this lodge with the wonderful furniture and the oddly spelled name. I held up my right hand, palm facing in, to form the mitten map familiar to every Michigander and traced a finger "from lake to lake" as I wondered if Granot Loma still existed and, if so, where it might be.

A quick internet search revealed that Granot Loma, built between 1919 and 1923, was still standing in Michigan's Upper Peninsula on the south shore of Lake Superior, just west of the city of Marquette. There were photos too, and they were startling: I had been expecting to see a rambling, low-slung camp like so many built by wealthy nineteenth-century families on Adirondack lakes, but what I was looking at was more like a palace. Its many facades—constructed of huge, closely set logs, crenelated with bays, and set with hundreds of glistening windows—soared two stories high, rising from massive stone foundations to slate roofs dappled with chimneys of the same stone. Opposite the lodge, a small, forested island created a focal point for the eye, like a folly in an English landscape. Photographed from above, Granot Loma's own landscape was extensive, encompassing endless acres of woodland, a mile of lakeshore, and, in an inland clearing, a cluster of picturesque farm buildings that resembled a worn Disney attraction.

I sat for a long time wondering how this castle in the woods had come to be and, more personally, why its discovery was of such interest to me. During the decade I'd spent documenting great houses and collectors, nothing had ever attracted me in quite this way. I wanted to see Granot Loma as soon as possible and thanks to my métier, I knew how to arrange a visit. I got on the telephone to my editor at *Architectural Digest* and then called Granot Loma's current owner, a bond trader from Chicago named Thomas Baldwin. As I had expected, *AD* loved the house and Baldwin was thrilled to have his lodge featured in a national magazine. A few weeks later, I was on a plane to Green Bay, Wisconsin (the nearest airport with jet service), where, as the sun began to set, I picked up a rental car and headed east toward the Upper Peninsula under gloomy October skies.

I could hear waves breaking and felt a cold wind on my face as, tired from the drive, I stumbled out of the car in the darkness outside Granot Loma. Then the door opened, and I was suddenly awake. I was entering a rustic fairyland where every mantel, balustrade, newel post, and chandelier in its palace-sized rooms was enlivened with tree trunks and branches that curved and swirled in the characteristic shapes of the Adirondack style—part Art Nouveau, part woodland glade. Light bulbs plugged into knot holes or peeping from hollow tree trunks cast a mellow light over the hand-hewn wrought-iron serpents that connected each door to its casement; acres of gleaming wooden floors dotted with flat-weave, geometric rugs rushed up to giant windows that by day would showcase dramatic lake views. My head swiveled wildly as I glimpsed a stone fireplace big enough to camp in, and another encased by a large plaster teepee. In an octagonal sitting room, logs were set in complicated patterns that echoed its eight sides. The place was extravagant—unreal—and like nothing I had seen before.

The next morning, notebook in hand, I toured the lodge and property with Tom Baldwin, trying to write and gawk at the same time. I quickly learned that while he had restored the rotting logs on the lodge's exterior and spruced up the kitchen, little else had changed here since the 1920s. The original giant chandelier made from a huge pine root and carved with animal shapes was still suspended over the great room, and the bathroom lined with birch bark and paved with small round lake stones was original to the lodge. In the basement, 1920s white tiled massage and water therapy rooms shared space with capacious his and hers liquor vaults dating from Prohibition. I trailed Baldwin down long corridors lined with guest bedrooms (so many that they had to be numbered) and around outbuildings that once housed visitor overflow, servants, and the family's pair of Rolls Royces. A deserted children's playhouse was garlanded with spider webs that echoed the web-like wood and twig decoration on its front porch. Down the road at the lodge's "gentleman's farm," a silver Tiffany clock could be seen in the cupola atop the main barn, there were gently shredding blue ribbons from county fairs in the dusty manager's office, and in the empty hayloft illuminated by a shaft of timely sunlight, a large, upholstered sleigh emblazoned with the name "Buick."

I was practically vibrating with images by the time Tom Baldwin sat me down to provide some backstory on the lodge. Granot Loma, he told me, was built by Louis Graveraet Kaufman (1870–1942), a local man with a Jewish father and part Anishinaabe mother who married a wealthy Chicago girl, went to New York City to run a bank, and made a fortune. The lodge's odd name, it turned out, was both a play on words and an acronym of his children's names. There were glamorous parties here in the 1920s, Baldwin told me, celebrity guests arriving by private train at a private rail station near the main road: George Gershwin, John Barrymore, Mary Pickford, and lots of others. He had heard Kaufman had pioneered branch banking and believed he had been involved in a famous takeover of General Motors in 1915 and then in the financing of the Empire State Building.

A millionaire from the Upper Peninsula of Michigan with Jewish and Native American ancestry, who dabbled in acronyms and bankrolled the Empire State Building? There was another story here, one that had apparently never been told. I now understood what—or more specifically who—had drawn me to the lodge with the odd name: Louis Graveraet Kaufman. With a start, I realized that Baldwin had moved on and was now chronicling Granot Loma's construction. The lodge, he was saying, had been built with unusually large pine logs, individually wrapped in burlap and brought by train all the way from Oregon. Hundreds of laborers had worked here, he told me proudly, and then a team of Finnish craftsmen, schooled in the old ways, made the Adirondack-style furniture and decorations with local roots and branches. An on-site blacksmith had turned out those serpent hinges; the stones in the foundations and chimneys had come from the lake.

I had my story, and it was time to go. As I drove the narrow, forested road that connected Granot Loma to the local highway I felt as if I was surfacing into the present, climbing out of waters as deep as the lake. I did so reluctantly, with a sense of unfinished business: I was leaving Tom Baldwin's house, but it was not he who had built the incredible lodge I would soon celebrate in the pages of *Architectural Digest*. Granot Loma was the creation of the unknown Louis Graveraet Kaufman, dead for well over half a century. I tried to imagine him bouncing along this corrugated road in a 1920s roadster (with George Gershwin riding shotgun?), but the picture wouldn't come into focus. What did he look like? How did he get from Marquette to Manhattan? How could the man who built Granot Loma have been so thoroughly forgotten? I knew the answers to none of these questions, but as I reached the highway and turned back toward Green Bay, I promised myself that someday that would change.

I

HOW IT ALL BEGAN

The Upper Peninsula of Michigan sits high above the Lower, and a world away. There is no Detroit or Grand Rapids up here, no water parks, international airports, or miles of expressway. There are many log buildings and boats. Residents celebrate these differences: they refer to themselves as "Yoopers" (UP-ers) and to their Lower Peninsula neighbors as "Trolls" because they "live under the bridge." (The Mackinac Bridge is the only in-state connection between the two land masses.) A surprising number of Trolls have never visited the land above the bridge nor have much interest in doing so. They should think again: the UP is an experience as well as a place, a chance to visit a beautiful, uncrowded world that seems to exist alongside, as well as inside, contemporary America. Its scant population (3 percent of Michiganders) stretches thinly over sixteen thousand mostly wooded square miles that extend to the edges of three giant inland seas. Lake Superior, which takes up most of this watery real estate, is larger, colder, and rougher than the other Great Lakes, and on its rocky shores time seems to slip in an elastic way. It's as though the boulders, trees, and miles of water that stretch as far as one can see have always been, and will always be, the same.

The Anishinaabe, the Native Americans who have lived near these shores for millennia, were part of this seemingly endless continuum. But in the 1840s, a generation before the birth of Louis Graveraet Kaufman, they suddenly faced great change. Iron ore, the raw material of America's burgeoning industrial age, had been discovered in the Upper Peninsula and European colonizers would soon arrive in droves to mine the ore. There were no roads in Iron Country; the lake was the only way in for miners and out for the valuable ore, and so the newcomers felt a port town was needed immediately. The miners chose a site on a calm bay on Lake Superior's southern shore, and it was here, in a raw lakeside settlement called Marquette, that two men with European backgrounds formed the family that would produce Louis Graveraet Kaufman. As it happened, neither Robert Graveraet (1820–61) nor Samuel Kaufman (1837–1900) was classically "white"—a fact that would one day haunt their common descendant. But these genealogical travails were yet to come, in an era when the Kaufman family would dominate the entire area and prosper beyond Robert and Samuel's wildest dreams.

Robert Graveraet's ancestors emigrated from Holland in the middle of the seventeenth century and settled among the Dutch in New Amsterdam, now New York City. In the 1770s, his grandfather Gerrit Graveraet, a fur merchant by trade, moved north to the Dutch town of Albany, then to Pennsylvania, and finally west to Mackinac Island in present-day Michigan where fur-bearing creatures (particularly beavers) were plentiful. His new home was more than a giant beaver dam: Mackinac Island, located in the strait where Lakes Michigan and Huron meet, between the Upper and Lower Peninsulas and just south of today's Michigan and Canadian border, was a military post of great strategic value—a "must have" for anyone jockeying for possession of North America. For centuries, control of the island ratcheted back and forth between the French, Americans, and British: the French military constructed a fort there in 1715 but their reign did not last. By the start of the American Revolution, the British were in control, but the island was in American hands by the war's end. Then came the War of 1812: the British took Mackinac Island back from the newly minted Americans and built a second fort there, only to lose the island once again when the Treaty of Ghent returned it to the United States in 1815.

Mackinac Island was of incomparable importance to the region's Anishinaabe people. Its protected location and teeming hunting grounds had made it a summer gathering place and sacred burial site for thousands of years, and by the nineteenth century it was home to Odawa (Ottawa), Ojibwe (Chippewa), and Bodéwadmi (Potawatomi) tribes of the Anishinaabe people year-round.

Since the coming of the Europeans the groups had shared the island. When Gerrit Graveraet's son, Henry Garrett Graveraet (1784–1860), married, he chose Charlotte Livingston, also known as Ada be te ge shick a qua and A-mud-wa-ge-wum-a-quaid (ca. 1785–1861). Charlotte's mother was the daughter of a French nobleman and the grand sachem or chief of the Algonquin Confederation, while her father was a Scottish officer called Livingston.[1] She was considered mixed race, or Métis, and her children and grandchildren, including Louis Graveraet Kaufman, would be too.

Henry and Charlotte prospered. Henry became a judge, and thanks to his family connections and linguistic skills, he was appointed chief interpreter for a local general. Educated Métis families like the Graveraets had become an important government resource. By the 1840s the United States was actively encroaching on Michigan's Indian territories and the Mackinac tribes were increasingly unhappy. The "Indian Department" (the Bureau of Indian Affairs, founded in 1824) began recruiting mixed-race "Indian agents," interpreters, and other bilingual staffers to improve communication, convey goodwill, and generally keep the Native population quiet. Annuities, consisting of cash (and sometimes goods) granted in return for Native lands whisked away by treaties, were part of this plan. These shameful payments were distributed by Indian agencies like the one at Mackinac Island and Henry and Charlotte's many children were beneficiaries. Identified by his or her Native American name, all appear on a contemporary list of those receiving yearly money from the government.

One of those children followed in Henry's footsteps. At fourteen, Henry's son Robert Graveraet spoke several Anishinaabe dialects as well as English, French, and Dutch, and at that tender age he was appointed interpreter to Henry Rowe Schoolcraft, the Indian Commissioner for the entire United States. Schoolcraft was "local" and was married to the Native American literary writer Jane Johnston Schoolcraft (1800–1842), of Ojibwe and Scots-Irish ancestry. Henry Rowe Schoolcraft established the headquarters at Mackinac and constructed an "Indian Dormitory" there for people who came to the island to receive their yearly cash. Interpreter to the Indian Commissioner was a plum job for Robert, if a painful front-row seat for the systematic disenfranchisement of his relations. Because in spite of his apparent sympathy for the Anishinaabe, after signing the Treaty of Washington (1836), which had provided permanent reservation rights to Michigan tribes ceding their claim to most of the Upper and Lower Peninsulas, Schoolcraft callously changed the deal and endorsed the tribe's removal from much of the state.

Was Robert ashamed of his job and angry at his two-faced employer? It's hard to say. Although a speaker of Anishinaabemowin and a willing recipient of the government's handouts, he almost certainly identified as "white" and may have considered his job more commercial than cultural. But then again, maybe not: the Graveraet family married into more than one Anishinaabe family, and a few decades later Robert's brother and nephew would serve as officers in an all–Native American regiment and die leading Native men as they fought the Rebels in the Civil War.

Whatever his feelings about broken treaties, Robert Graveraet's gig with Henry Schoolcraft changed his life: the large deposit of iron ore discovered in the UP in 1844 had thrown the country into a greedy tizzy and was attracting prospectors from hundreds of miles away. Schoolcraft was already there and in prime position to receive ore-location tips from the local Indigenous people (who knew to steer clear of such deposits because of the possibility of lightning strikes), and he was anxious to cash in. Around 1848, accompanied by his bilingual sidekick Robert, Schoolcraft undertook several ore-hunting voyages along the southern shore of Lake Superior. On one of these trips Robert himself filed a mineral claim near present-day Negaunee, about ten miles inland from Marquette. As translating for dollars was keeping him fully occupied, he returned to Mackinac Island and sent Newaquay-geezhik, nicknamed Kawbawgam, an Ojibwa of the Echo-maker–Crane totemic clan whom he had encountered at the UP town of Sault Ste. Marie, to settle on the lake in the vicinity of the claim and look out for his interests.

Then Robert had a bit of luck: a Dr. Edward Clark from Worcester, Massachusetts, arrived on the island and began asking around for anyone who knew where ore deposits might be found. Robert told Clark about his claim and produced ore samples as proof of its riches. Impressed, Clark promptly founded the Marquette Iron Corporation (named for French Canadian missionary Father Jacques Marquette, also the founder of Sault Ste. Marie) and made Robert a member. Robert tendered his notice to Schoolcraft, and in the spring of 1849 he joined Clark and his Worcester investors, and Peter White, a nineteen-year-old

Mackinac youth who also spoke an Ojibwe language, and sailed west from Sault Ste. Marie toward Robert's claim, in an open, flat-bottomed boat known as a "mackinac." It was a dangerous trip: storms were common on the huge lake; waves could rise quickly; and the water was so cold that a spring shipwreck would have meant almost certain death. This group was lucky; "after eight days of rowing, towing, poling, and sailing" they had traveled safely over one hundred miles.[2] They landed on May 18, 1849, near the mouth of the Carp River and were received at the house of Robert's advance man, Kawbawgam—happy to be on dry land and grateful for the meal of fresh venison, bread and butter, potatoes, coffee, and tea he offered. (Although it was only May, the newcomers were soon to learn that the locals buried potatoes and other root vegetables in the cold ground to help them last until more could be harvested.)

They also learned they were not the only ore hunters in the area. Members of the Jackson Mine Company, founded by Philo Marshall Everett of Jackson, Michigan, had arrived three years earlier and were still nearby, although so far the group had built only a forge and two small log houses. The Marquette party immediately set about constructing a permanent settlement, clearing land, planting crops, and building log cabins for shelter until a sawmill could be erected. It was soon clear why their competition had made so little progress: "There was no horse to be had," wrote Peter White of the Marquette Corporation's first days in Iron Country, "no matter how heavy a log might be the men pulled and hauled it about as best they could."[3]

As the settlement began to take shape the group began to think about a name for their new home. Their first idea was to call it "Worcester" in tribute to their moneymen, but they ultimately settled on "Marquette" in honor of Father Jacques Marquette and, not incidentally, their own corporation.

The backbreaking work went on: a dock had to be built

immediately—everything needed had to arrive by boat—and so, still lacking a sawmill, the settlers improvised. They felled small trees, dragged them into the water, and piled them lengthwise and crosswise until they had a structure even with the surface of the water, then poured sand and gravel over the top. The result seemed sturdy enough but three weeks later they awoke to find the bay completely empty. Superior had reared up overnight and washed away every stick of their impromptu construction. They had to start all over again, working more quickly now because time was ticking and they needed to leave their work at the lake and commence a series of twelve-mile trips inland and up into the hills to do the vital work of claiming and surveying iron-rich territory—ahead of the Jackson group and any others who might come along.

Anyone who has spent time in the UP during black fly season will cringe imagining those long, hot, humid climbs undertaken without repellent or modern equipment. Peter White never forgot the experience: "the activity of the mosquitoes and black flies was so incessant that the surveyors were forced to wear buckskin masks over their faces," he wrote near the end of this life, "as the masks speedily became grimy with dirt, the sight . . . to the uninitiated was formidable and terrifying."[4] Sweating and swatting, the settlers covered over twenty-four miles on foot before returning, exhausted and covered with itchy welts, to the scant comforts of Marquette. Fortunately, a few months later another party of settlers arrived from Mackinac bringing horses and a few women, and by 1850 the little port was coming to life: there was finally a sawmill, as well as a new forge, a cluster of dwellings, and even a few shops.

Nobody was making money yet, and there was continual sniping between the Jackson and Marquette companies over mineral claims, but hopes were high. The ore was coming out of the ground and being loaded onto boats for transport and sale.

Even better, after 1855 this valuable payload could be delivered to any Great Lakes port from Chicago to Erie. That year a set of locks opened at Sault Ste. Marie—formerly a shipping logjam between Lakes Huron and Superior requiring a lengthy portage—allowing ships free passage throughout the entire Great Lakes system. Marquette was now on the map and, attracted by its centrality to the iron industry, new settlers were arriving all the time. The livestock and horses that accompanied them had a rude introduction to their owners' new dwelling place: while "the propellers would come to anchor some times as far as two miles from the shore and the freight and passengers had to be landed in small boats," wrote another chronicler of the era, "cattle and horses were always pitched overboard and made to swim ashore."[5]

The arrival of the "propellers" (the steamships that were then supplanting sailing vessels on the Great Lakes) was always a cause for celebration. They were the settlers' only connection with the rest of the world—the only way to get mail, food, clothes, and other necessities—and when they were late, as they often were as the weather grew colder and the lake wilder, the town was anxious and sometimes hungry. "November came with its storms and snows and still no boat came," wrote Mehitable Everett (Philo's wife) about 1850. "At last it was decided to kill the horses and divide the coarse feed left among the most needy families."[6] Fortunately those measures proved unnecessary: a ship finally arrived on December 15 and "who can imagine the feelings of the crowd that greeted that boat," Mrs. Everett wrote, then added, all sniping and claim jumping forgotten: "Nothing unites a community like the sharing of each with the other in joy or sorrow."[7]

Robert Graveraet was not on Mrs. Everett's radar. She saw Marquette as her husband's town and considered Graveraet a latecomer and rival; he is barely mentioned in her memoir of those early days. But Peter White more than made up for her neglect: "Graveraet was not an ordinary man," he wrote near the end of his life; "he would be singled out as a natural leader among thousands. He was ambitious," White continued, "he had a will of iron; he had the faculty of winning men; he was generous, gentle but firm; he had great intelligence and energy; and his mother [here White is likely referencing Robert's Native American heritage] had given him a constitution that did not know the meaning of fatigue."[8]

White, a happily married man with many children, also noted Robert Graveraet's physique: "For grace of bearing and beauty of proportion," he wrote, "Graveraet challenged instant admiration; and moreover his muscles were of steel."[9] Could White's unexpectedly fulsome admiration of Robert Graveraet have been of the paternal sort? White had left his own father behind at thirteen and followed Graveraet to a wilderness settlement, so it's possible that the older man had become a father substitute. In an account of one of those weary, bug-infested uphill trips to the ore claims, White recalled an instance of quasi-paternal intervention: "Graveraet observed that one member of the party, a well-formed though slender lad [White himself] was staggering under his load," he wrote, "and as he passed he whisked it from off his shoulders and threw it upon his own, much heavier pack as if it had been a feather."[10] "Robert Graveraet is but a memory now," White concluded sadly, "but while he lived he was a force . . . (with) an imperious will and fascinating personality."[11]

While the elderly Peter White no doubt remembered Robert Graveraet fondly, his memoir glossed over his earlier, less than generous treatment of a financially vulnerable friend. For in spite of his many talents, Graveraet was not equipped with business chops of any kind. When the Marquette Iron Corporation became part of a larger mining company in the early

1850s, he was unsuccessful in retaining a profitable share and some say it ended up in Peter White's hands. As Graveraet leap-frogged from business to business, operating a forge, a sawmill, and a general store—none with notable success—he was forced to borrow money from White, who was now rising rapidly in boom-time Marquette, and instead of cutting the older man some slack, White initiated foreclosure proceedings on a piece of land Graveraet owned.

Still, the two men are said to have remained lifelong friends, and Robert Graveraet, although continually pressed for cash, found his footing in public life. He was appointed an early superintendent of the Marquette and Ontonagon Railroad and a member of the first Board of Inspectors of the Marquette school system. In 1856 he was elected the first state senator for Marquette County and environs, and later he became Receiver of the U.S. Land Office under President Buchanan. Along the way he married one of Marquette's first female settlers, Lucretia Barney (b. 1825), and though the couple had no children, the union was a short-lived but happy one: when Lucretia died at thirty of typhoid in December 1855, a heartsick Robert wrote to a friend that "her loss to me is without limit."[12]

That loss precipitated our story: in 1855, with Robert Graveraet grieving alone in Marquette and his parents, Henry and Charlotte, getting on in years, the aging couple decided to leave their home in Mackinac and set up housekeeping with their widowed son. They arrived in Marquette later that year, and not alone: one of their daughters was with them, their youngest but one, pretty, fourteen-year-old Juliet. Perhaps the family believed that Robert's new and thriving town would be a good place for his sister to find a husband, and if so, they were right: Juliet was rising seventeen and apparently ready for love when a twenty-one-year-old peddler named Samuel Kaufman came to town.

Sam Kaufman had traveled a long way to get there. He was born in 1837 in Bamberg, a Bavarian river town just north of Nuremberg, but spent only thirteen years in Germany before planning his escape. Sam was Jewish, and in the middle of the nineteenth century, most Jews in Bavaria were living limited, frustrating lives. Barred outright from most trades and professions, and with other kinds of work possible only with the possession of hard-to-obtain governmental "letters of protection," young Jews faced lifelong poverty and a sort of catch-22 of enforced bachelorhood. If a Jewish man wanted to marry, he needed to prove he was engaged in a respectable trade (impossible without that letter of protection) and to purchase a special marriage certificate costing more than most families could afford. With personal and professional advancement out of reach, boys like Sam were easily tempted by the literature describing the good life in America widely circulated by Jewish newspapers and shipping agents.

In 1850, thirteen-year-old Sam Kaufman and his younger brother Mayer began an overland journey by wagon or on foot to Hamburg, Rotterdam, or Le Havre, then endured the arduous monthlong voyage to America. It is not known if the two young boys traveled on their own or in the company of their parents, but there is no mention of those parents after the brothers reached the New World. Sam and Mayer went first to New York, then Detroit, then finally made their way to the Upper Peninsula of Michigan where Sam planned to set up as a peddler in Iron Country. The two spent some time peddling in the UP towns of Ontonagon, Escanaba, Negaunee, and Ishpeming before Sam saw which way the wind was blowing. In 1858, he moved his operation to the area's fastest-growing metropolis: Marquette.

Peddling—one of the few professions open to Jews in the Old Country—was readily transferrable to America and when

Sam immigrated, the UP was a particularly attractive peddling destination. A recent influx of miners and lumbermen, all needing overalls, shirts, boots, and other "gents furnishings," made it an excellent market for Jewish newcomers. Dozens took advantage of the opportunity: in Sam's day, almost every UP town was home base for a Yiddish-speaking traveling man and, later on, for at least one Jewish-run clothing shop. By the 1880s, S. Kaufman and Sons, Sam's shop at 207 South Front Street, was competing with already established shops run by Isaac Neuberger and Louis Getz. These emporiums were the apogee of peddler success. Their owners had all started out "on the road" walking with heavy packs on their backs or lurching down rutted trails in horse-drawn wagons, braving freezing winters and summer heat (and black flies) as they made their way to customers at distant mines and lumber camps.

There they received a warm welcome—from the workers anyway. The bosses who ran the company stores that kept miners and lumbermen in perpetual debt through pricey, enforced purchases tried to shoo peddlers away (sometimes at gunpoint). Guys like Sam were bad for business. They gave workers a square deal, offering easy credit to suit fluctuating paychecks, better quality, and lower prices. They stocked everything—work clothes, of course, but also suspenders, underclothes, shoelaces, razors, hats, handkerchiefs, and pretty things for lady friends and wives. What was not to like? Their appearance raised no alarms among the workers—they dressed nicely in ties, waistcoats, and bowler hats. They learned English quickly and behaved like any other American salesman. Although many of the Michiganders Sam encountered had never met a Jew before, in the mid-nineteenth century anti-Semitism was still rare in the UP—at least among working people. Jewish peddlers were seen as hardworking, freedom-loving young strivers—useful additions to the American melting pot. Nor was there any barrier to marriage with local, non-Jewish women. While some peddlers actively sought out Jewish mates (often traveling long distances to do so), many others married into Christian families and gradually shed their Jewish identity.

That was the route that Sam took: it is not known exactly how he and Juliet Graveraet met, only that the two young people encountered each other in Marquette, courted, and were married there by a justice of the peace on July 12, 1861. There was little family there to stand up with Juliet. Both of her parents had recently died, as had her brother Robert. He had died only the month before the wedding of a "hemorrhage from the stomach" (possibly appendicitis). The *Detroit Free Press* took notice of the passing of an ore country pioneer and public servant, calling Robert Graveraet "an illustrious statesman" and anointing him the "Father of Marquette."[13] Mayer Kaufman may have been present at his brother's nuptials—but perhaps not, as soon thereafter the two apparently parted company. Mayer was listed in the *Mining Journal* in 1865 as a dealer in dry goods and he was still alive in 1870 and living in Negaunee, but he is mentioned in no Kaufman family letters or any other family records of the 1860s and 1870s; after 1870 he seems to disappear into thin air. Perhaps the brothers quarreled, or Mayer left Michigan for some other reason. Or perhaps he fell ill and died young; either way, he does not seem to have been a part of Sam and Juliet's married life in Marquette.

By the time that married life began, Sam Kaufman was one of the most popular men in town. He was affable and easy to like, as well as nice-looking with regular features, straight dark hair, and a bushy walrus mustache. A year before his wedding the twenty-three-year-old peddler with a Yiddish accent had been appointed the town's delegate to the Democratic State Convention in Detroit, beating out his friend Peter White, now a rich man and town pillar, for the post. The press approved:

"Mr. Kaufman is one of our intelligent and thorough business men and will doubtless do honor to the party he represents," cheered the *Lake Superior Journal*.[14] He acquired a nickname—"Cheap John"—which sounds negative and frankly anti-Semitic to modern ears but was then a positive handle, signaling an easy sense of humor and good prices. Certainly, Sam liked the sobriquet as he used it himself. Marquette bought Cheap John's "gents furnishings," rode in his stagecoach (a new sideline), and rewarded his business acumen and easy people skills, attributes that would later be inherited by his son Louis Graveraet. The year after the wedding Sam was elected sheriff of Marquette County. He made a good living, and the family finances were augmented by the sale of a piece of land given to Robert Graveraet by the American government (and which he managed to hold onto in spite of Peter White's machinations), which passed to his sister Juliet after his death.

Sam's local prominence may have saved his life. The Civil War had begun, and a draft had been initiated, but Sam Kaufman was a man with political clout and instead of being sent to the front, he was appointed second lieutenant and made a recruiting officer for a local unit, the Fourth Michigan Volunteer Cavalry. Even for someone engaged in this military sideline, in the UP the war must have seemed very far away. Mail deliveries to Marquette were still unreliable in summer and almost nonexistent in winter, and news of draft riots, Union defeats, and other Civil War developments arrived late or were simply absent. The town was enjoying a growing prosperity thanks to the army's skyrocketing demand for iron ore, and the less welcome aspects of the conflict seemed somehow elsewhere. As battles raged hundreds of miles away, local doings filled the *Lake Superior Journal*, including a reference to seasonal isolation and Sam's own role in its termination: "Last week the rush to the outside world commenced," the paper rejoiced. "On Monday last Sam'l

Kaufman left (by stagecoach) with a number of passengers and about fifteen hundred pounds of fur."[15]

It would have been late the following summer, or even autumn, before news of the deaths of two soldiers—Juliet's brother Henry Graveraet and Henry's son Garrett Graveraet—reached Juliet and Sam, bringing grief and a shocked realization of the scope of the American cataclysm playing out invisibly, to the south and east.

Henry and Garrett Graveraet played a unique role in that conflict. Indigenous men had tried to enlist as soon as war was declared in 1860, but often speaking no English, they were rejected by the Union army for the first two years of the war. The Indigenous community wanted desperately to fight, having personal motives for supporting the Union cause. Aware of the treatment of enslaved Black people in the South, Indigenous people feared victory for the Rebels would mean slavery for their people as well. "If the South conquers you will be slaves, dogs," an Ojibwe chief warned his people in July 1863.[16] If the Union prevailed, Native Americans reasoned, their service might result in renegotiated treaties, more land rights, and better social standing. There was every reason to sign up, and in 1863 their turn finally came. Mounting losses forced the North to allow Indigenous men to take the field and, as blending the races still seemed a stretch, segregated units were planned, and bilingual Native American officers were needed to lead them.

Garrett Graveraet (born 1840), whose grandmother Charlotte was part Ojibwe and whose mother, Sophia, was the granddaughter of an Odawa chief,[17] spoke several Anishinaabe dialects. Understanding that his linguistic skills would be useful for troops who could not communicate with white officers or sometimes with each other, he accepted a commission as a second lieutenant in the all–Native American Company K of the First Michigan Sharpshooters. Garrett had moved from Mackinac to Little Traverse (now Harbor Springs) near the Bear River at the top of the Lower Peninsula, and when the call went out for recruits, hundreds of Ojibwe, Odawa, and Potawatomi men from the Upper and Lower Peninsulas answered, and many in the northern part of the state reported to Lieutenant Graveraet. He quickly signed up twenty new company members.

"Sharpshooter" was a class of soldier unique to the Civil War. Sharpshooters were sent ahead of major troop movements to hide behind rocks and climb trees and pick off enemy soldiers—particularly officers—knocking out the chain of command and creating useful confusion in the ranks before the battle even began. They were experts at neutralizing soldiers trying to load cannon (and at shooting the horses that pulled unwieldy gun carriages) and they were, of course, the sworn targets of sharpshooters on the other side. Not everybody qualified for this kind of work but, trained for generations as hunters with bow and arrow and more recently with rifles, making every bullet count, Company K men had nothing to fear from the draconian marksmanship test aspiring sharpshooters had to ace. Variously described as being asked to hit a five-inch target at 220 yards, or a twelve-inch target at 300 yards, the exam quickly weeded out the punters. Company K could shoot the eye out of a fly, and they did not require rifles equipped with telescopic sights like those issued to many other sharpshooters.

Garrett Graveraet and his deadeye dozen and a half headed south to Company K's mustering place at Dearborn, near Detroit. Once there, Lieutenant Graveraet realized he was going to have a problem. So many tribes were represented in his new company that the position of first sergeant, traditionally the "management guy" for the troops, was proving particularly hard to fill. What he needed was impossible to find: a man who could speak many Native dialects and encourage soldiers from historically warring tribes to pull together for the greater good. Then Garrett thought of his father: bilingual, of course, and a judge so well respected that the Indigenous people of Mackinac all wanted him to settle their disputes. He could be Garrett's solution—except for the fact that he was fifty-five years old. Garrett wrote to his father, explained why he needed him, and suggested that when asked, he should simply claim that he was forty-five. Soon First Sergeant Henry Graveraet had joined the 139 men (137 enlisted men, 2 officers) of Company K of the First Michigan Sharpshooters, which was mustered into service in January 1863.

After a stint guarding a Union prison in Chicago, Company K proceeded south in the spring of 1864. It first saw action in the Battle of the Wilderness—part of Grant's push to take Richmond—which, as the name implies, took place in nearly impenetrable Virginia woods. Used to being out in all kinds of weather and conditions, the new Company K soldiers felt perfectly at home in this difficult terrain and immediately used it to their advantage. They rolled in the dirt to make their dark blue coats and pale blue trousers less visible and further camouflaged themselves by wearing leaves in their hats and over other parts of their uniforms. Thus attired, they hid behind trees or in the brush, waiting to blow away any Confederate who unwisely raised his head. Fellow Union soldiers soon began to copy these camouflage techniques, and even Confederate fighters noticed Company K's unusual skills. One Rebel, surprised to find himself confronting a company of Indigenous men, wrote admiringly of their abilities. "The Indians fought bravely in the woods," he admitted. "When driven into the open they did not again fire on us but ran like deer. We captured not a one of them."[18] When Grant led his forces further south toward the town of Spotsylvania Courthouse, Company K picked off Confederates before the battle and returned their "Rebel Yells" with their own piercing war cries.

But even their immense skills were not always enough: twelve Company K soldiers died at Spotsylvania on May 12, 1864, including Sergeant Henry Graveraet, who was killed outright when a shell exploded on top of him. Garrett waited for a lull in the fighting, then, using metal mess plates and other makeshift tools, buried his father, carefully marking the grave so he could find it later and bring Henry back to Mackinac for final burial. (Henry's body was later found and reinterred in the Fredericksburg National Cemetery.) Then Garrett fought on alone in what must have been a maelstrom of grief—and guilt. It was he who had recruited the aging Henry, who had written the letter that had brought his father into harm's way. But his emotional suffering did not last long. For Company K was next posted to Petersburg, and soon Garrett too was gone.

Company K had been sent ahead to deal with lurking Confederate artillery before the second assault on Petersburg, and toward evening on June 17, 1864, Garrett sustained a serious rifle ball wound in his left arm. He was taken by ambulance wagon, jolting painfully over country roads, to a field hospital where his wound was assessed and his arm amputated just below the shoulder. It's terrifying to imagine the conditions under which this was accomplished. There was no anesthesia and overworked Civil War surgeons reused bandages and barely rinsed their saws in dirty water before turning to the next patient. Lieutenant Graveraet was given whisky for shock and an opium pill for pain, and his stump was coated with cerate (beeswax mixed with various other resins). He was put on a train and traveled prone on the floor of a boxcar to City Point, Virginia, then transferred to a steamer for the last leg of the trip to a hospital in Washington, D.C.

He was still alive when he reached Washington, but by then he had spent days lying in filth with a nasty wound at his shoulder. At the hospital he was given more opium but little else. On

June 22, he wrote to his mother expressing regret that he had not written to her about his father and telling her he expected to be home soon. Sophia wrote back immediately but it was too late. Garrett died of sepsis on June 30, 1864, at the age of twenty-four. His body was interred in the Congressional Burying Yard and later returned to Mackinac, where his grave now stands alongside one erected in his father's memory. The *Detroit Free Press* did not grant Garrett the respectful obituary that had marked the death of his uncle Robert. Garrett's notice did not mention his military rank nor his death in service to the Union. Having noted the nature of the company he had led, it incorrectly reported his death as that of "a Chippewa Indian of the Bear River Band,"[19] referencing a tribe long settled near the Bear River on Little Traverse Bay (Garrett had gone to that area as an adult to teach in a local school).

An English-speaking Métis, Sophia Graveraet had no trouble collecting the pensions she was due after the deaths of her husband and son. Other Indigenous widows weren't so lucky: the variable spellings of Indigenous names and the fact that many soldiers had been married in tribal services only and lacked official papers allowed the government to dither and withhold needed support. As for Anishinaabe hopes that their lands would be safer after their military service, this was not to be.

In Marquette the local iron industry was booming—by 1868 the town was shipping half a million tons annually. The white population was booming, too, and settlers were trespassing on and appropriating Indigenous lands at ever greater rates. The area's Anishinaabe population was soon relegated to the edges of the community north and south of the city. Although they attempted to continue their traditional lifestyle, they grew increasingly dependent on white citizens for whom they worked at menial jobs and to whom they sold fish, blueberries, maple sugar, and other commodities they had sourced or produced, often door-to-door.

Sources for these products were now further away: Marquette was growing fast and was now a bustling lake port at the end of the line of twelve miles of track upon which Iron Mountain Railroad locomotives (which had replaced those straining horses) hauled ever increasing payloads from the mines. In the warmer months when lake transport was safer, it was not uncommon to see twenty vessels docked in the bay—their masts and smokestacks bobbing like a parallel village on the waves. In winter, when train travel was impeded by heavy snowfall, horse-drawn stagecoaches on runners (including the one owned by Sam Kaufman) ran between Marquette and neighboring towns, transporting passengers and bringing mail and supplies.

The town was well equipped in other ways—boasting four blacksmiths, a sawmill, a livery stable, a harness maker, a carriage maker, a shipbuilder, two coopers, three doctors, four general stores, a daguerreotypist, a courthouse complete with jail cells, and five churches. Five streets were graded and graveled, giving the customers of the carriage maker and livery stable a reason to spend their money, and an icehouse was about to open, to the delight of Juliet Kaufman and other local housewives. In 1864 a group led by Peter White further greased the wheels of local commerce by founding the First National Bank of Marquette. One of Marquette's First Citizens, White was also jockeying with another familiar First Citizen—Philo Everett—for control of the local insurance business. The *Lake Superior Journal*, the predecessor of today's *Mining Journal*, was in print, spreading news from Marquette throughout the area.

Not surprisingly, given the composition of the nearby forests, nearly every one of Marquette's offices, houses, shops, churches, and stables was built of pine. The town was an urban tinder box and on a June night in 1868 disaster struck: the blaze started in the workshops of the Marquette and Ontonagon Railroad near Front Street and soon block after block was on fire, as well as three of the ore docks on the lakefront. Little could be done to stop the inferno. At this time Marquette had only a volunteer fire department and it had just one hand-pumped "engine." A bucket brigade was organized to bring water from the lake, but it was a hot windy night and despite all efforts to control it, the fire continued to spread. After four hours most of the business district was gone, along with forty private houses. Peter White saved his by covering his roof with wet blankets, and the Kaufmans may have done the same. In the morning the inhabitants of Marquette surveyed a flattened, smoking ruin. One hundred structures had been lost and damage was estimated at $1.5 million (over $32 million today). For years thereafter Marquette citizens designated everything "before or after" the fire, the most important event in their lifetime, and Peter White joined with other town fathers to raise money for water pipes and hydrants.

Marquette after the fire of 1868. Courtesy of Superior View Photography, Marquette, Michigan.

Citizens who were left homeless or who had watched their businesses burn to the ground were devastated by the conflagration, but there were others who thought the fire hadn't been an entirely bad thing. The town's wealthier element—Gilded Age aspirants who admired the "nicer" neighborhoods in Chicago and Detroit—couldn't help feeling that piney, pre-1868 Marquette had been shoddy and subpar. This group had something more cosmopolitan in mind for their UP capital, and after the fire had conveniently "cleared the decks" they made their vision a reality. Following a new town ordinance that all buildings must be made of nonflammable materials, Marquette's upwardly mobile set about constructing a new "Queen City of the North," using ruddy, easily carved Lake Superior sandstone, quarried nearby in South Marquette. The new buildings were not only fireproof but rich with towers, porticoes, and decorative flourishes that gave Marquette the charming, haute Victorian look it retains today.

Juliet Kaufman had little time to admire the town's new architecture. By 1868, she was a young mother juggling four sons under the age of six. In spite of Sam's choice to intermarry and assimilate, his Semitic antecedents informed their names: these first children were not given Graveraet family names like Robert or Henry but handles familiar to every American Jewish family. Nathan (b. 1862) was followed by Samuel (b. 1864), Bernard (b. 1866), and Daniel (1868). But the children kept coming, and for whatever reason, when a fifth son arrived in 1870 his parents chose differently, bestowing on Louis Graveraet a grander, more neutral name to go with the implacably Semitic "Kaufman." After Louis came four daughters—Sarah (b. 1871), Charlotte (b. 1873), Miriam (b. 1876), and Callie (b. 1879), and then a final son, Harry (b. 1881). Sadly, their last daughter, Maude (b. 1884), would live only until the age of six.

Juliet found her two decades of childbearing difficult as she was alone with her growing brood far more than she liked. Sam was either out driving his stagecoach (which was now transporting freight and passengers all the way to Green Bay, Wisconsin, and back), on the road selling, or establishing nebulous peddling outposts in nearby mining towns. In 1865, the *Lake Superior Journal* suggested that customers "call around and see Cheap John's Opposition Store" in Negaunee, and he later opened one in Escanaba.[20] On that occasion, he uprooted his whole family and moved everyone to the smaller UP town where, shortly thereafter, Louis Graveraet Kaufman was born. Poor Juliet: it couldn't have been much fun to move house pregnant with four small children, or to give birth in a strange town, especially as the move did nothing to slow Sam's peripatetic lifestyle. He continued to be absent for long stretches, making a living and/or shaking off the shackles of family life.

An itinerant lifestyle suited Cheap John and was part of his appeal for cronies and customers. In 1874, with his family safely back in Marquette, the local paper (now called the *Mining Journal*) found Sam in Ishpeming, spreading gossip and good cheer along with his suspenders and razor blades. "Sam is the original Cheap John who has sold 'sheeps cloding [*sic*] all wool, a yard wide' in the Lake Superior country for the last hundred years or more," the paper guffawed, then, practically poking the reader in the ribs, it continued: "He is a good boy but his extreme modesty and bashfulness have always prevented his attaining that high position as a merchant prince for which his talents so eminently fit him."[21] A couple of months later Sam moved on again and the paper printed this knee-slapper: "Sam Kaufman, we miss you. Since you left us we find it very hard to collect news. There are men in this city (Ishpeming) who probably know as much news as you did, but unlike you they are very careful to keep it to themselves."[22] A year later Sam was peddling at Calumet, a hundred miles from home.

While the *Mining Journal* was amused by Sam's wanderings Juliet Kaufman was not. In the spring of 1876, Sam had been all the way to New York City (presumably on a buying trip) as well as traveling to various UP destinations, and now wrangling eight children including a teething baby, Juliet penned an emotional letter to her husband. "I am not writing this for the purposes of complaining," she began, "but the truth is I am tired of keeping house and trying to take care of this family and house. The boys are getting large to be governed by me. Then with poor help and a cross baby I think I would rather be dead." After this desperate attempt to get her husband's attention, Juliet made the rest of her appeal in a lower key. "I would like you to write to the boys to keep out of the streets and remain at home more than they do," she wrote, returning to the practical, "they could be of more help to me if they would try."[23] It is not known if her husband ever complied, only that he was not in Marquette for the town's elaborate Fourth of July Centennial celebration, which included a parade of forty carriages, fireworks, and a failed (but not fatal) tightrope walk.

Sam's traveling days continued. He'd alight in Marquette for a few months and earn a paycheck working for Isaac Neuberger's store at 56 Front Street; then, apparently too restless to stay on, he'd take to the road again, leaving his teenaged son Nathan to tend the shop in his place. But in 1878, Nathan left home to become a traveling salesman for a Chicago firm. Soon after, the *Mining Journal* was announcing cheerily that "Cheap John, alias Sam Kaufman, the inimitable, unquenchable Teutonic orator with Disraeli-like proclivities who never leaves Marquette without gravitating back again, can once more be found at I Neuberger's clothing store."[24] Sam felt at home at Neuberger's, where common origins made for easy understanding and communication. Ike could read the letters in German that Sam sometimes received from customers at the mines, and the two men could write to each other in Yiddish, their other common language. One letter, though written in English, includes distinctive Hebrew characters as Sam wishes a mutual friend a hearty "Mazel tov!" in Yiddish.[25]

In spite of his peripatetic ways (or perhaps because of them), Sam was making a good living and the family was doing fine financially: by the 1870s, the Kaufmans lived in a substantial Victorian clapboard house on Ridge Street, one of the most fashionable in town. It was not as grand as some of its neighbors (and not nearly as grand as the house in which Louis Graveraet Kaufman would later reside), but it was commodious and sat on a corner lot on a bluff high above the lake. Juliet's children were happy there—whether Sam was home or not. Louis Graveraet would later recall that he had "lived a normal, healthy boy's life" and "knew all of the favorite swimming pools where he and his companions repaired after school was out. He played ball and 'shinny'"[26] and, like a UP Huck Finn, was known as the boy who was the first to go barefoot in the spring and the last to put his shoes on in the fall.[27] When the shoes went on, he pumped the organ during Sunday services at St. Paul's church and rolled empty barrels down Washington Street to the old lime kiln for pocket money.

His mother was the foundation of this small-town happiness: his sister Callie would later recall "the wonderful family life in the Kaufman home and of Juliet Graveraet Kaufman, the gracious mother who did so much to bring her children up as ladies and gentlemen."[28] Family solidarity was also on Juliet's syllabus: "let anyone pick on one of the boys outside of the home," Callie said, "and these lads became one in their common defense."[29] Sam was not mentioned. Louis Graveraet adored his mother and would later celebrate her (in stained glass and in other ways) as something akin to a saint. His childhood—mother-centric and quasi-fatherless—would have a major influence on his own parenting, as he left child-raising to his wife and replicated Sam's absences.

It was not until 1885 that Louis Graveraet experienced a steady two-parent household: that year Sam opened Kaufman & Sons Clothiers at 207 South Front Street and retired from the road forever. Perhaps he could finally afford his own shop, or perhaps at nearly fifty he found constant travel more difficult and his Marquette household—now peopled with more teenagers than babies—more hospitable. He also had sons enough to man the counters and lighten the load: Nathan had left town, but over the next decade Sam Jr., Bernard, Daniel, and Louis Graveraet all worked at the Front Street emporium after school, and sometimes full-time. The paterfamilias was home for dinner every night, and Cheap John funneled his "inimitable, unquenchable" personality into ad copy: "Kaufman & Sons strain every nerve to please their patrons" read one typical example.[30] The shop prospered, and the family moved to a larger Ridge Street house.

The pioneer peddler Cheap John was now a respected elder statesman. When he retired in 1894 and the shop closed its doors, the *Mining Journal* ran an entire column on the event, tweaking its coverage to make it sound as if Kaufman & Sons had graced South Front Street for many decades: "with his going out," the paper noted solemnly, "will cease as a business designation a name which has been identified with the mercantile interests of Marquette for the last thirty years."[31] His name continued to be—in a different way. Perhaps bored with retirement, Sam developed and began hawking a patent medicine called Kaufman's Rheumatic and Kidney Powder. No doubt at Sam's request, his old friend Peter White wrote an 1896 version of a five-star review of the elixir, concluding his written testimonial: "I keep it on hand now at all times in my house."[32]

White's unqualified support may have puzzled older residents of Marquette, who recalled a mythic, less friendly chapter in the Kaufman-White relationship. While the tale of their disagreement borders on preposterous, it is repeated in many books and articles about Marquette and is even framed on the wall of a guest room in Marquette's most popular hotel. Back in the 1870s, so the story goes, Peter White sold Sam Kaufman some land and gave him a "bad deed" that kept Sam from taking proper ownership. The Kaufman family believed that White had done it on purpose and, recalling his sneaky dealings with Juliet's brother Robert back in the 1850s, they may have been right. In any case, in retaliation, one of Juliet's sisters put an "Indian curse" on Peter White. His children promptly came down with diphtheria, and he went to the Kaufmans to beg them on bended knee to lift the curse, but to no avail. All of White's sons died, the tale concludes dramatically, and there was nobody left to carry on his name.

Two of White's sons and a daughter did die of diphtheria in 1878, a common disease at the time. But given the fact that White had a friendly relationship with all of the Kaufmans (including Louis Graveraet Kaufman, as we shall soon see) throughout his life, it seems unlikely White blamed the family for this terrible loss. The story is a myth of a Christian's murder perpetrated by the "other"—one in a long line of similar tales dating back to medieval times—fueled by the anti-Indigenous and anti-Semitic feelings harbored by Marquette's citizenry late in the nineteenth century.

These prejudices would have a lasting effect on the Kaufman family. In 1901, when a story in the Midwest shipping magazine *Marine Review* mentioned in passing that Robert Graveraet had been part Native American, Juliet became upset at being "outed" in such a way, and asked Robert's old friend Peter White to write to the editor and tell him that it wasn't true and how "offended" she was.[33] While Juliet (and White) knew the editor's information was correct and that there was nothing anyone could do after the fact, she was clearly frightened to have this information about her family in the public domain and eager to go on the record with a denial.

For the young Louis Graveraet Kaufman, who grew up with parents who did not speak of their origins, and who had heard the "Indian curse" story whispered behind his back, the situation was clear. If identified as Native American and Jewish rather than white, his life would be harder and less successful. His family history was an impediment not to be spoken of, and Louis Graveraet Kaufman never did—for the rest of his life.

2

THE KAUFMAN FAMILY CONQUERS MARQUETTE

As a boy Louis Graveraet Kaufman had been known in Marquette as the son of Cheap John, but by the time he graduated from high school his fellow citizens knew him best as the brother of Nathan Myron Kaufman.

His oldest brother was a Big Man in town: Nathan had gone into business early and never looked back. He dropped out of high school and worked at Ike Neuberger's store, then left Marquette and went "on the road" for a Chicago men's clothier and made enough money to open his own "gents furnishings" emporium in Negaunee. Its sale allowed him to leave overalls behind and follow the money into the local mining business. He turned out to be a natural in this lucrative sector: he acquired and developed a mine, sold it at a profit, and invested the money in other UP mines, and by 1880 he had rolled up enough ownership and expertise to attract the attention of one of the wealthiest mining magnates in the state. Edward Breitung (1831–87), aka the Iron King of the Lake Superior Region, was impressed by Nathan's business acumen and energy and invited him to become his general manager and right-hand man. Nathan jumped at the chance.

In doing so he was exchanging one German American

mentor for another. Like Nathan's father, Breitung had emigrated from Germany and settled in the Upper Peninsula in the 1850s. But while both men had started out in mercantile pursuits, Sam stuck to peddling menswear while Breitung, who was not Jewish and had attended a mining college in Germany, pivoted quickly to minerals. As the money rolled in Breitung dabbled in politics, serving as mayor of Negaunee, then as a Michigan state senator, and finally as a U.S. congressman. Along the way he acquired a wife more than twenty years his junior, had a son, Edward N. Breitung, and built a grand house on Ridge Street complete with parquet floors, mahogany columns, tapestries, and a huge, free-standing china bathtub on a raised platform. Replete with money, family, and property, Breitung turned to Nathan Kaufman to help him organize and safeguard all he had accumulated. This help Nathan would give in full measure.

Like Sam Kaufman, Breitung was away a lot. Nathan soon found himself handling many of the magnate's local affairs—even traveling with Mary, his twenty-something wife, to Chicago and other cities as his employer's amanuensis. After years of such responsibilities the aging Breitung appointed Nathan agent for his estate, and when he died in 1887, a year short of Louis Graveraet Kaufman's high school graduation, the twenty-five-year-old Nathan was left in charge. It was a golden door to a bigger life and, cloaked in his new dignity, Nathan made his move on Gilded Age Marquette. In 1890 he founded and assumed the presidency of the Marquette County Savings Bank, commissioned a decorative, turreted building of Marquette sandstone to house it, and, heeding Juliet's lessons in family solidarity, installed several of his brothers on its board. He purchased a significant interest in the *Mining Journal* and with several partners founded a trolley car line, the Marquette Street Railway. All the while he continued to run the Breitung properties for Edward's widow and son, working closely with the family whose wealth still dwarfed his own. This propinquity soon produced useful results: in 1892 Edward N. Breitung, now one of the richest young men in the UP, married Nathan's sister Charlotte. Edward presented his bride with a $10,000 necklace and took her on a honeymoon to the East Coast in a private railcar.

A year later the inevitable happened: Nathan Kaufman and Mary Breitung too were married. She was thirty-eight, he was thirty-one. The Bishop of Marquette himself performed the ceremony and a local newspaper put a good face on what could otherwise have been seen as a sordid union between a rich older woman and a younger man: "Mrs. Breitung, who was much younger than her former husband now bestows her hand upon a trusted and tried friend whose long and intimate identification with the family teaches her his worth," the *Marquette Times* assured its readers. Then, after announcing the newlyweds' departure for a three-month European tour, the paper threw its support behind a possible run for mayor by the groom. "Mr. Kaufman is not of the political faith of the *Times*," the editor allowed, "but if he should consent to run for an office we would certainly have to make an exception in his favor for we need about a dozen men of his caliber in our public affairs."[1]

Not everyone agreed. While Sam Kaufman had encountered little anti-Semitism among the miners and loggers of the UP in the 1850s and 1860s, by the 1890s his children faced a different reality. During what became known as the Progressive Era (1896–1917), immigration, urbanization, and industrialization were rapidly transforming America's formerly rural society. Many Americans were not happy about these changes and suddenly Jews were on their minds—and not in a good way. Thanks to a recent influx of Jewish immigrants from Russia and eastern Europe there were so many more of these poor, Yiddish-speaking newcomers, and as most were traders, merchants, and moneylenders—not farmers—they were seen not just as beneficiaries of the new order but as its agents as well. The Panic of 1893 and ensuing economic depression only exacerbated the feeling in gentile America that there was not enough to go around and fed resentment of Jews who were getting "too big" a share. Unlike African Americans, Asian Americans, and Indigenous people (who, in 1887, had been effectively removed from society by the Dawes Act, which codified the reservation system), who experienced much worse discrimination during this period, Jews were not people of color and could assimilate more easily into a white and racist society. Still, they were viewed as a separate race with unpleasant characteristics and dangerous politics and were less and less welcome among gentiles.

So, in the increasingly stratified Marquette of the 1890s, Nathan Kaufman did not seem a slam dunk for public office. There was the Jewish father and the mother from the "Indian curse"-hurling family, not to mention the persistent rumor that Mary and Nathan had slept together long before their wedding day. Plus, Nathan's sister had snagged the Breitung heir, and Nathan himself was now the husband of Mary Breitung and master of the grand house with the tapestries and the china tub. And, having assumed the presidency of a number of profitable Breitung companies and mines, he was—annoyingly—as rich as many in the town's Protestant elite. When it came to the vote, however, none of this seemed to matter: perhaps Marquette's largely Catholic population was more sympathetic to a non-Protestant, or many of its citizens no longer recognized him as compromisingly Jewish nor Métis. Perhaps older citizens who did were nonetheless glad to see Cheap John's son succeed. In any case, when Nathan ran for mayor on the Republican ticket in 1893, he was elected.

To lend gravitas to his new office, he immediately set about building Marquette's first proper city hall. The elegant sandstone and brick Romanesque Revival building that he dedicated in early 1895 (which still stands today) boasts an arched entryway flanked by columns, tall arched windows, and a fancy roofline. Having come into office on the eve of the biggest world's fair the country had ever seen, Nathan began his term with a mayoral boondoggle of major proportions. He rented a train car and took the entire City Council of Marquette as his guests to the opening of the World's Columbian Exposition in Chicago. "The city council of Marquette took their departure for Chicago Sunday to attend the opening exercises of the World's Fair," reported the *Sault Ste. Marie Evening News.* "They went in a special palace car which was elaborately decorated with banners, flags and bunting as the invited guests of Mayor Kaufman."[2] In Chicago the openhanded mayor housed his councilmen at a posh hotel favored by Euro stars Sarah Bernhardt and Lily Langtry and was introduced to his "colleague" Chicago mayor Carter Harrison at the opening of the fair. A good time was had by all.

Nathan continued to have a good time. He and Mary spent much of the 1890s spending the Breitung fortune in Chicago and the cities of the East, flaunting their financial and social bona fides and making well-to-do friends. When they were at home in Michigan a steady stream of posh people visited their Marquette manse, filling the guest rooms and dining parlor on Ridge Street and mixing with the extended Kaufman clan. There was method in this entertaining madness: most of Nathan's brothers and sisters were unmarried and while he and his sister Charlotte had found appropriate local mates, Marquette—a small town with an unfriendly establishment—was not an easy place for the others to find marital gold. That establishment groused as Nathan introduced his siblings to rich, socially prominent people from Chicago and elsewhere, and wedding bells rang. In 1896 Samuel R. Kaufman married Una Libby, the only child of a wealthy, deceased Chicago corned beef canning magnate, in the Libbys' turreted mansion on Michigan Avenue. Among the many newspapers documenting the event was the *American Israelite*, a national Jewish newspaper published in Cincinnati. In future years the paper would continue to report frequently on the doings of the (presumably Jewish) Kaufmans—a family who considered themselves to be no such thing.

The late Mr. Libby was a minnow compared to Nathan's next catch. Otto Young (1844–1906), the future father-in-law of Louis Graveraet Kaufman, was one of the three richest men in turn-of-the-century Chicago. Like Sam Kaufman and Edward Breitung, Otto Young had also immigrated to America in the 1850s, but his backstory was different and his trajectory even steeper. Born in Prussia, Otto lost his father at an early age and was abandoned by his mother, who moved to America with a man who wasn't keen on small boys. Undeterred, Otto moved alone to England at age fourteen and worked on the docks until he had enough money for a passage to New York. There he found work as a traveling salesman for a jewelry firm and by 1867 he was doing well enough to marry Ann Elizabeth Murphy of Virginia. Four years later, hearing that the Great Chicago Fire had destroyed over seventeen thousand of that city's buildings, Otto scented opportunity in its ruined streets. He and his wife left New York and set off for the Midwest.

Nineteenth-century conflagrations, it turns out, could be surprisingly helpful in many ways. The Great Chicago Fire of 1871 was the making of Otto Young. In Chicago he opened a wholesale silver, jewelry, and watch company and with his earnings proceeded to buy up vast tracts of the city's undervalued, fire-ravaged real estate at bargain prices. Soon Young, now known as the Titan of State Street, owned many blocks of that famous thoroughfare and of Michigan Avenue as well. His holdings included the land under the Carson Pirie Scott Building and Louis Sullivan's Auditorium Building, as well as many buildings in the "Loop." Otto then turned back to merchandizing and in 1886 purchased a half interest in the Fair Store, a local discount department store. By 1904, under his management, the Fair Store employed three thousand people, and Otto was listed among the top taxpayers in the country, higher on the list than Pennsylvania-born coal and steel magnate Henry Clay Frick. Otto and his wife built an elegant town house on Calumet Avenue near the home of fellow tycoon Marshall Field in which to raise their four pampered Chicago princesses, Cecile, Marie, Catherine, and Laura. The only thing clouding their joy was the death of their only son, John, who succumbed to tuberculosis in 1896 at the age of twenty-four.

By 1899 Otto had recovered sufficiently from his grief to think about building a summer "cottage" in the "Newport of the Midwest" on the southeastern shore of Wisconsin's Lake Geneva. Only eighty miles northwest of the Loop, this bucolic spot had been a popular destination for well-heeled Chicagoans for twenty years. Luxurious mansions already dotted the lakeshore, but Otto's dream palace would outshine them all. He recruited architect Henry Lord Gay, instructed him to copy the over-the-top Renaissance grandeur of the Breakers, the Vanderbilt cottage at Newport, and warned him not to stint on luxury or amenities. One million dollars later, Otto was the owner of Younglands, a fifty-thousand-square-foot Classical pile embellished with frescoes, inlaid floors, chandeliers, gold-plated fixtures, and marble fireplaces. Flattering goddess-like portraits of his daughters were carved into the house's exterior stonework. There was a bowling alley in the basement, a garden on the roof, a dining room that could accommodate one hundred guests, and a steam-powered seventy-two-foot yacht at the end of his dock—perfect for lavish parties on the lake. Thirty servants catered to the family's every need, on land and water.

Younglands was very grand indeed and life there became a

crucible of entitlement for several generations of the Kaufman family. When asked to describe the personality of Otto's favorite daughter, Marie, the future Mrs. Louis Graveraet Kaufman, Marie's granddaughter responded with one line, which she felt said it all: "My grandmother," she responded, "was brought up in a palace on Lake Geneva."[3] Although Younglands was not finished until Marie was in her twenties, it greatly influenced her worldview and expectations. The extravagant lakeside mansion and the life her family lived there shaped a persona of grandeur and privilege. All of her life Marie would expect to live amid beauty and space and to have whatever she wanted as soon as she wanted it, and she would pass along these expectations to her children. Granot Loma also has its roots on the shores of Lake Geneva: Louis Graveraet Kaufman loved and admired his father-in-law and identified strongly with his drive to create a personal architectural masterpiece. Two decades later he would channel Otto when he built his own private kingdom in the UP.

Sadly, Otto Young enjoyed Younglands for only a few years. It was finished in 1902 and Otto died there in 1906 of diabetes and tuberculosis, leaving behind his Lake Geneva palace and an estate worth \$20 million. Both would have an unusually long afterlife: five decades later Otto's heirs were still squabbling over the convoluted trusts he'd set in place, and more than a century later Younglands is still a landmark on the Lake Geneva shoreline.[4]

The Princess of Lake Geneva met Louis Graveraet Kaufman just before the turn of the twentieth century. Their introduction likely occurred in Marie's native city and, like his brother Sam's, it was almost certainly a Nathan Kaufman production. Otto Young served as the secretary/treasurer of the 1893 World's Fair (he raised the \$5 million that secured the fair for Chicago) and so he may well have been on hand when Mayor Kaufman arrived—conspicuous in his decorated railcar—to attend the opening ceremonies. Nathan may have chatted up Otto on the spot, or later finagled an introduction through Peter White, who was a commissioner of the fair. Even if the two men didn't meet in 1893, Nathan and Mary spent so much post-mayoral time cultivating the wealthy of Chicago that it wouldn't have been long before the couples crossed paths and Nathan discovered the Youngs had a daughter of marriageable age. Then he had only to push Louis toward said daughter (genteelly, of course, with a chaperone present) and let hormones do the rest. His younger brother was an attractive young man—5′10″, trim and well-built, with a high forehead, medium complexion, dark hair, and strong regular features. And by 1899 the timing was fortuitous: in August of that year Marie, known to all as Daisy, was engaged to an actor and singer called Walter Newton Jones, who jilted her the following month in favor of one Beatrice Elizabeth Champlin, daughter of another rich Chicagoan. Autumn 1899 was likely the first of many times Louis Graveraet Kaufman would survey the territory and turn circumstances to his own advantage: he may have known Marie for some time, had perhaps even proposed before, unsuccessfully. Now, realizing that she was heartbroken and humiliated and that his surname and provincial background might seem less objectionable to Otto Young (he was no show business sharpie, after all), he took his shot: family legend has it that on the day, Marie told him she would marry him if he could hit a coin in a tree with a bow and arrow, but this story is likely cross-pollinated with tales of Civil War sharpshooters from Louis Graveraet Kaufman's maternal side and is almost certainly apocryphal. In any event, Louis proposed and Marie said yes.

It is not known if, in spite of circumstances, Otto and his wife raised objections about their daughter's unusual, socially dodgy choice. Louis had only recently begun his ascension in Marquette's banking world, but the canny, entrepreneurial Otto may have

Marie Young Kaufman, ca. 1900, and Louis Graveraet Kaufman, ca. 1905. Collection of Peter Kaufman.

recognized a kindred spirit in the young man with dark eyes that missed nothing—and decided to overlook LG's provincial origins and dicey surname. (For brevity's sake, Louis Graveraet Kaufman, who was known as LG in life, will be referred to by those initials frequently throughout this narrative.) Still, a big church wedding was out of the question. The Youngs (and possibly Marie herself) did not want all of Chicago society to witness a union to a man (however promising) of Semitic parentage with a passel of oddly named relations. Marie and Louis were married in the parlor of the Young family's Calumet Avenue house on the evening of January 8, 1900, in front of just forty family members and friends. Numerous members of the groom's family—including Nathan and several other brothers and sisters—did not attend. Juliet was present (luckily the

Youngs did not read the *Marine Review*) but Cheap John was not. The society pages gamely accentuated the positive, mentioning selected WASP attendees and describing the groom as the brother-in-law of heiress Una Libby. Flower girl Juliet Breitung and best man Harry Livingston Kaufman—the Kaufman brother with the posh East Coast middle name, who would later collect pricey antique furniture and marry a debutante cousin of financier George Gould—were paraded front and center.

Although the wedding was small, the nuptial trappings were those of a society event many times its size: Marie and Louis were married under a canopy of asparagus fern and lily of the valley (no doubt procured at great expense during the coldest month of the year), the parlor was awash in palms, ferns, lilies, and white roses, and the tables for the supper were decorated with roses and lilacs. The wedding party was nearly as large as the congregation: the bride, swathed in duchesse lace, was preceded down the aisle by a flower girl, a maid of honor, and four bridesmaids—none were Louis's sisters—elegant in white tucked crepe de chine and white mousseline de soie. Otto Young gave the bride away, no doubt hoping the entire thing was a good idea. The young couple took a wedding trip to the South and returned to Marquette in March 1900.

The metropolis to which LG brought his bride had grown exponentially since his childhood: now boasting a population of nearly ten thousand, Marquette's distinctive skyline—bristling with sandstone towers, steeples, and ore docks—was visible a mile out in the lake. Down below these edifices, a grid of houses, offices, workshops, and Front Street shops with jaunty striped awnings was spreading fast. New technologies developed to serve the iron industry were everywhere: train cars full of ore from nearby mines now rumbled to the top of tall "pocket docks," positioned themselves next to their individual slots or "pockets," and let gravity do the rest. The ore slid down handy chutes that angled away from the docks and into the holds of the waiting steamships now crowding the city's harbor. Shipments had recently reached twenty-two million tons annually and the city was battening on the profits.

The city streets were illuminated by an electric light plant and crisscrossed by streetcars (some from the street railroad owned by Nathan Kaufman). Other railroads now connected the city to the world: passengers could board an evening train in the Windy City, sleep in a comfortable Pullman car, and arrive rested in Marquette at 9:30 the following morning. Upon arrival visitors had several elegant hotels from which to choose, including the giant, turreted Hotel Superior which opened in 1892, the same year as the impressive Marquette Opera House. The town even had its own sport—Cornish wrestling—brought to the UP by Cornishmen who came to work the mines, and tournaments dotted Marquette's summer calendar, attracting bleachers full of cheering fans. For the uninitiated, the rules took some getting used to: participants wore special collarless

Ore docks stretching into Lake Superior, Marquette, ca. 1900. Courtesy of Superior View Photography, Marquette, Michigan.

canvas jackets with loose sleeves upon which all "holds" had to be secured. A wrestler might put his hands up his opponent's sleeves, for example, and pull hard, trying to lay him out flat. LG would later tell his family that he had participated in this sport in his youth, and it is not impossible that he did so, although he was a bit vague about the details.

As an older man, LG enjoyed sharing picture-perfect stories of his Marquette youth and young manhood, although he would invariably skip over some of its less photogenic details: for while Nathan Kaufman had quickly parlayed a traveling sales job into shop and mine ownership, LG's professional career got off to a slow start. Once out of high school he jumped from one job to another with no clear plan and little apparent ambition. He took a job as timekeeper at the Iron Bay Manufacturing Company and was promoted to the post of bookkeeper, then left to clerk in a grocery store. By the early 1890s, he'd moved on again and was working for his father at his Front Street clothing emporium. Even when Nathan's 1893 marriage to Mary Breitung opened up new employment possibilities, LG's ineffective commercial hopscotch continued. Nathan employed his brother in one formerly Breitung mine after another and LG was promoted in each job, but then lost interest and moved on, finally leaving the mining field altogether to spend two years managing a local insurance agency. He seemed to be sleepwalking through his professional life. Anyone observing him during these years would have concluded that he wasn't a patch on his older brother, and never would be.

That is, unless that observer was a member of Marquette's Masonic Lodge No. 101 F&AM (Free and Accepted Masons). Freemasonry—which traces its roots to the stonemasons' guilds of thirteenth-century Europe—was a Kaufman family tradition: Cheap John was a lifelong Mason (the lodge would later organize his funeral), and most of his sons followed Sam into

Masonic life. (Although Masonry was officially a gentile organization during this period, it admitted those who did not identify publicly as Jews.) The Masonic Lodge was Marquette's version of a big-city men's club—a place where middle- and upper-class businessmen came to gossip, mingle, and network. It was an education in itself—a training ground for getting along, managing people, and advancing in an organization. LG joined the Masons in the early 1890s and made the most of it. Personable and easygoing like his father, he added his own innate smarts and climbed swiftly through the ranks of the brotherhood, learning as he went and racking up an impressive constellation of titles: in 1893 he ascended to membership in the Marquette Chapter of the Royal Arch Masons, the Lake Superior Commandery

Front Street, Marquette, ca. 1900. The Marquette County Savings Bank is on the right. Courtesy of Superior View Photography, Marquette, Michigan.

Knights Templar and Ahmed Temple, York Rite, then continued his climb, becoming a Noble of the Mystic Shrine or "Shriner"—one of Masonry's highest designations.

It all came in handy in 1899 when at the age of twenty-nine LG was tapped by Nathan to join the staff of the Marquette County Savings Bank. The discovery of the banking world was a revelation for the younger man, and it unleashed a flood of interest, energy, and talent that no one, perhaps not even he himself, had known existed. Nathan installed his unpromising brother in the bank's most menial slot—messenger boy—then watched in surprise as LG climbed the rungs of the banking ladder with unexpected speed and skill. LG would later explain that he had spent his evenings studying the principles and history of banking in the United States and Europe and that this nighttime cramming was responsible for his ascent. Perhaps—but all of the information in the world would have been useless in less talented hands. From the start LG seemed to know exactly what he was doing—grasping financial and managerial concepts and utilizing them with energy, charm, and finesse. Just one year later, the year of LG's marriage, Nathan elevated him to the rank of vice president of the Kaufman family's flagship concern.

It would be the last time Nathan would call the shots. Later that year when the Kaufman brothers made the play that catapulted them to real financial power in Marquette, it was LG who took the lead. He had surveyed the economic landscape and, displaying the discernment, insider knowledge, and utilization of connections that would characterize the rest of his career, decided to take control of the First National Bank of Marquette, a pillar of the city's business community since 1864. The bank's founder Peter White (a fellow Mason) was a Kaufman family friend, he was aging, and he owned a majority of the bank's stock. Sensing that the time was right, LG suggested that he buy White out, and the old man agreed. When the deal was announced in January 1901 two things were clear: the Kaufman family now controlled Marquette's premier financial institution and the pecking order in that family had changed. Three Kaufman brothers (LG, Nathan, and Samuel) had been added to the bank's board of trustees but only LG had been designated a vice president, and of the 754 shares of the First National Bank (out of a total of 1,500) now owned by the Kaufman family, 600 belonged to Louis Graveraet Kaufman.

Something else was clear as well: the rise of Louis Graveraet Kaufman did not sit well with the WASP establishment that had been in charge of the bank, and much else in town. This element had grumbled when Nathan Kaufman married Mary Breitung and became Marquette's mayor, but LG's unexpected banking coup brought out the verbal pitchforks: although LG was Protestant (his mother was not Jewish) and he and Marie were pillars of Marquette's St. Paul's Episcopal Church and attended regularly, his father had been a Jewish peddler and he had a Jewish surname, and there was the pesky Indigenous connection as well. In short, to Marquette's upper crust LG Kaufman was not the right stuff and should not be running their bank: "In the early days in anti-Semitic circles, the Kaufmans were always referred to as being Jewish," wrote UP historian Fred Rydholm.[5] The bank takeover, he did not have to say, was seen as an instance of "Jewish" behavior. "Many people objected to doing business with the Kaufmans," wrote bank board member John Longyear in his history of these years.[6] There would be no cooperation—no sharing of town institutions: "When the Kaufman brothers purchased the controlling stock in Peter White's First National," wrote Rydholm, "to many this was the beginning of a struggle for [Jewish] financial control of Marquette."[7]

Peter White, who remained president of the bank and on friendly terms with the Kaufmans, suffered for being on the wrong side of the fracas. "His friends thought that his sale of the bank was due to failing mental powers, attributable to old age," wrote Longyear.[8] Still, the elderly man would have to be punished: soon after White sold out to the Kaufmans he suddenly "resigned" from the exclusive Huron Mountain Club, a private fishing and hunting club founded by himself, Longyear, and other wealthy men from Marquette and Detroit.

Other First National Bank directors were as appalled as Longyear at the Kaufman coup: one Edgar H. Towar resigned his vice presidency, explaining that "it was so unpleasant for me that I couldn't stand it."[9] Towar then joined with other local businessmen and founded the Marquette National Bank, a new institution unsullied by Kaufman participation. Annoyed by the new competition and the repudiation of his family, LG decided to have a little fun: he bought shares in the new bank as well, causing Longyear to write: "The Kaufmans . . . have seemed to feel much bitterness toward me on account of the new bank. . . . They have purchased from weak stock holders nearly one quarter of the stock in the Marquette National Bank, paying more for it than it is worth."[10]

Twenty years later nothing had changed: when the charter of the Marquette National Bank ran out, its officers transferred its assets to yet a third bank, specifically to cancel out its Kaufman ownership. LG brought suit for compensation, making the bank's machinations public and causing one publication to marvel: "The case is quite out of the ordinary in the records of bank suits . . . this was done openly and legally to get rid of an objectionable stockholder, LG Kaufman."[11] The objectionable shareholder won the suit, but a bank spokesman piously mouthed the party line, skirting the prejudice that had caused the kerfuffle in the first place: "The result is cheap, even at the price. The city which we all love is not now and will not be I hope, at any time under the financial control of one man."[12]

Once again, the general citizenry of Marquette seemed unperturbed by the fact that a Kaufman now controlled many of the town's financial and business institutions: deposits at the First National Bank nearly tripled after LG was elevated to first vice president in 1903 and continued to grow after 1908 when Peter White had a heart attack and died on a street corner in Detroit (LG was an honorary pallbearer at the funeral) and LG became the bank's president. He was also the treasurer of Nathan's Marquette City and Presque Isle Street Railway and a director of several local railroads—the Manistique, Marquette and Northern, and the Traverse City and Leeland, among others—and of several local mining companies as well. Otto Young had been right to bet on the untried young man from Marquette. The money was rolling in. Marie and LG now lived in one of the grandest houses in town—a large, elegant Victorian at 453 East Michigan Street with a garden that stretched for several blocks, originally built for another founder of the Huron Mountain Club, the wealthy, New York–born Horatio Seymour.

Horatio Seymour did not wish to associate with the sons of Jewish peddlers, and in ordinary circumstances LG wouldn't have gotten anywhere near 453 East Michigan. But when the house came on the market Mr. Seymour's circumstances were anything but ordinary. Determined that his offspring not associate with inappropriate local children, Seymour had been careful to send his brood east to boarding school and in summer to the WASP-y Huron Mountain Club, to avoid unfavorable associations. But all of his precautions were in vain: like many wealthy families with homes in wilderness areas, the Seymours employed an Indigenous "guide" as a professional hunter, fisherman, and servant to help them enjoy the outdoors. In addition to scouting out likely trout streams and cleaning guns, such guides hauled provisions, cooked outdoors, and watched the family's children.

Henry St. Arnold (called Santinaw), a man of Indigenous and French heritage, had served Mr. Seymour in these capacities for many years when in 1901, the fifty-year-old Santinaw eloped with Seymour's beloved twenty-year-old daughter Mary. Horrified, the Seymours disowned their daughter and decamped so precipitously to New York that they sold their house to the first qualified applicant, who just so happened to be Louis Graveraet Kaufman.

The Kaufmans were happy to have the Seymour house, but as the decade wore on, they were often not in it. News of LG's achievements had percolated south to Chicago, and he was soon known as "one of the famous northern Michigan Kaufmans who has been named . . . as desirable presidential timber for Chicago institutions"; he was spending quite a lot of time in the Windy City.[13] His banking prowess was also well known, and he was called upon in several bank mergers and other reorganizations of big banks in Chicago. His social life expanded along with his reputation: he and Marie became members of Chicago's Grace Episcopal Church (once again, they attended regularly) and the South Shore Country Club, LG joined the Midday Club, a lunchtime lair for successful businessmen, and his attendance at a performance by Isadora Duncan at Orchestra Hall was noted in the Chicago newspapers.[14]

Marie had her own reasons to be in Chicago: she was pregnant for much of the first decade of the twentieth century, and she headed south before every confinement for the best natal care and to recover amid the luxuries of Calumet Avenue and Younglands. Her first five children, Graveraet Young (b. 1901), Ann Elizabeth (b. 1902), Otto Young (b. 1904), Louis Graveraet Jr. (b. 1906), and Marie Joan (b. 1907), were all Chicago born. Marie's fecundity may have been a testament to the strength of the Kaufman ménage (or just inevitable in the days before birth control), but there may have been another reason why Marie spent so many years in maternity clothes (and on trains). According to Kaufman family lore, Otto Young was so eager for grandchildren that he gave Marie $1 million (over $35 million in today's money) for every child she brought into the world during his lifetime. According to the legend, he did not make the same pledge to his other three daughters, who were said "not to mind." Such windfalls would have made Marie one of the wealthiest young women in the Midwest, and as early twentieth-century wives rarely owned separate property would have added considerably to LG's growing stash—if the money was actually given. The gifts were recorded nowhere in the Chicago press during the years of Otto's purported largesse, nor were they mentioned anywhere else for the next three decades, only to pop up suddenly decades later in an interesting and possibly clarifying way. (More about this later.)

While Marie was having babies (million-dollar or otherwise) her husband was making money and climbing the ladder in the organized banking world, and the same year (1908) he assumed the presidency of the First National Bank he was elected president of the Michigan Bankers Association—one of the youngest men ever to receive that honor. His new office was a handy megaphone through which to broadcast his talents statewide, and the association's annual meeting was the perfect place to start. Channeling Nathan and that bunting-festooned railcar, LG decided to make his annual meeting an affair to remember. In July 1908 the Great Lakes steamer *City of St. Ignace*, newly renovated and decorated, left Detroit with flags flying and an onboard band playing jauntily. On its bow a large banner identified its destination—"Michigan Bankers Association at Marquette 1908"—and onboard were three hundred happy bankers and their wives, the largest turnout ever recorded for such a meeting.

In addition to a trip on a luxurious steamer (instead of

lectures in a hot room in a Detroit hotel), LG had given the bankers another compelling reason to attend: he had written to William Howard Taft, then secretary of war and presidential candidate in waiting, asking him to address the Michigan bankers on the boat ride up to Marquette and to be his guest in the UP. He must have known Taft's acceptance was a long shot, but that didn't matter: tipped off by LG, the *Detroit Free Press* tantalized its readers with Taft's possible appearance on the *City of St. Ignace*, emphasizing LG's clout and political connections and stirring up interest in the trip.[15] In the end, of course, Taft couldn't make it, but by that time nobody cared. The bankers were wined and dined in the fresh breezes off Lake Huron, LG's onboard address was well received, and a good time was had by all. At Sault Ste. Marie the group was transferred to a private train to Marquette where the bankers were given a look at the local mining industry and, not incidentally, at the hefty slice of UP business dominated by Louis Graveraet Kaufman. As LG had known it would, the speech (and the junket) attracted the attention of the national banking world, and the following year LG was invited to join the executive committee of the American Bankers Association.

Although he didn't make it to Marquette in 1908, Taft actually answered LG's letter: something about the confident, young Michigan man elicited this collegial response: "If I can come I shall be glad to do so," Taft wrote, "but the trouble is that if I am nominated I shall be in the hands of a committee and they may limit my peregrinations. I have never been up in northern Michigan and should be delighted to go."[16]

Had Taft visited the UP that summer, he would have found his accommodations up to presidential standards. The Kaufmans were among Marquette's wealthiest citizens and were living a seriously luxurious life. The grounds of the sprawling house on East Michigan Street were equipped with tennis courts, formal gardens, and an expansive terrace overlooking Lake Superior. In the barn, organized to accommodate both carriages and motor cars, silver mounted harnesses hung above chests of fur robes, to be used on days when the snow was too deep for a motor. A photo from these years shows a red fox lap robe enveloping a family group sitting in a cutter, with a bearskin, for extra warmth, slung over the back. A few years later the cutter would be pulled by a pair of elegant prancing horses said to have been presented to the family by a new business associate, circus impresario John Ringling. Trained as performers, they were said to dance whenever they heard music. LG was seen casually lighting his cigars with $10 bills. The family had a full roster of servants, including tutors and governesses, and the children enjoyed the companionship of five championship St. Bernard dogs.

But their lakeside idyll did not last. In 1910, on the day when his eldest son was to take the train east to boarding school, LG must have watched with mixed emotions as the nine-year-old Graveraet took desperate measures to avoid the journey and slipped away to the only place no one could follow: a wooden rowboat on the rough lake. "He rowed back and forth along the shore while they all stood on the beach calling to him," an observer wrote, and after being coaxed back to shore had to be lifted "into the carriage as he would not of his own accord go away from that beloved place."[17] As he watched the unhappy boy, LG would have known what his son did not—that Graveraet's absence from Marquette would stretch far beyond his school term. The servants would soon be packing up Marie's favorite glassware and china, the family would follow Graveraet east, and the beloved place on the lake would become an occasional summer destination. LG had been tapped to be the president of the Chatham National Bank in New York City.

3

LOUIS GRAVERAET KAUFMAN CONQUERS NEW YORK

The man who did the tapping was Elbert Gary (1846–1927), the president of U.S. Steel and one of the most powerful men in the country. Gary was a director of the Phenix National Bank, a venerable New York City financial institution established in 1817. The Phenix had once handled important estates like those of the Astor and Goelet families, but forty years on it

*Louis Graveraet Kaufman, ca. 1916.
Collection of Peter Kaufman.*

was flagging. Unhappy with its lackluster performance, Elbert Gary and others on its board of directors had formulated a plan. They would merge their burdensome bank with the Chatham, another underperforming National Bank, and create a new institution stronger than the sum of its parts. All they needed was a man to take charge, manage the merger, and take the future Chatham Phenix National Bank to glory.

Elbert Gary "discovered" Louis Graveraet Kaufman at meetings of the Michigan Bankers Association and its national counterpart, the American Bankers Association. These institutions were obvious places to troll for talent, and there LG's financial smarts, appealing personality, and ability to organize a good junket had been showcased to advantage. And once LG caught Gary's attention the younger man's positive thinking and way with words added to his interest: during the bank panic of 1907, for example, LG employed a flood of persuasive rhetoric to assure the readers of the *Detroit Free Press* that the banks of the UP were in "splendid shape and the people prosperous," ending with a poke at his interlocutor: "We would never know a disturbance in the money market had occurred," he concluded slyly, "did we not read about it in the papers."[1]

Checking out LG's bona fides, Gary would have learned of his successful Chicago bank consultancies, his precipitous rise to the presidency of his local bank, and, more personally, the many similarities between himself and the man from Marquette. Like LG and his brothers, Gary had been born in the Midwest (Wheaton, Illinois), established a bank in his hometown, and become that bank's president. Like Nathan Kaufman, he had also become the town's mayor. Both Gary and LG had grown up hunting and fishing and were still avid practitioners of woodland sports. Finally, LG's elevation to the presidency of the Chatham National Bank would be an echo of Gary's own past, when his rise to the presidency of U.S. Steel had been affected by another kingmaker—banker

J. P. Morgan. As Gary's biographer wrote of him in 1925: "He was a figure the more watched because he was new and from another city . . .[and] because Morgan had chosen him."[2]

Now, in 1910, the young banker from the UP was the chosen one, and all eyes were on him. Gary's choice was a virtual unknown on Wall Street, one of the youngest bank presidents in the country, and the only one running two different national banks, in two different states, at the same time. With typical self-confidence, LG had made it a condition of his move to New York City that he remain the president of the First National Bank of Marquette, and he was allowed to do so by special dispensation of Lawrence O. Murray, the Comptroller of the Currency. It is not clear why this unusual arrangement was permitted, but Murray and Elbert Gary were both close to President Theodore Roosevelt at the time and it is likely Gary was able to call in a few favors to secure his man. In December 1910 the Chatham National Bank paid $1.88 million to absorb the assets of the Phenix National Bank, creating a new institution with resources of $20 million with LG at the helm.

Initial reactions to the newcomer were cool: "Generally when a big Wall Street bank changes presidents the new man is someone who has had his training south of Chambers Street," sniffed the *New York Times*; then, referencing LG's children, it added: "One was born in New York. The other five are Westerners."[3] But local condescension didn't last long as it was soon clear that the man from Michigan had been a brilliant pick. "Although it is less than a year since the merger . . . business . . . has increased beyond the greatest expectations of its officers and board members," wrote *Bankers Magazine* of the new and improved Chatham Phenix. "Mr. Kaufman has shown himself to be a natural born leader and now, barely in his fortieth year has made for himself a position in the financial life of the city of New York which few men achieve in a lifetime."[4]

Actually, the new wunderkind of Wall Street was well into his forty-second year. LG's press-savvy was second only to his financial chops and, having predicted the public interest in his rustic backstory, he had shaved years off his age and the time frame of his rise from messenger boy to New York bank president, making it cleaner, faster, and therefore more impressive. He'd also pushed his arrival at Nathan's bank back to 1891. Dozens of newspapers printed these doctored stats. One, *Clover-Land*, a boosterish UP rag straight out of Sinclair Lewis, obliged by skipping all the dead-end jobs that had come before and moving LG's appearance at Nathan's bank back an entire decade.[5] Later, when youth became a less important calling card and LG's family background was in the spotlight, a new set of alternative facts was deployed: the Yiddish-speaking Cheap John was presented as the John Jacob Astor of the UP and LG as Waldorf Astor. "The members of my father's family," LG told a reporter with a straight face, "were originally well to do pioneers from Switzerland and became, after a stay in Pennsylvania, one of the leading families of Northern Michigan. My mother was a Graveraet," he continued, "related to the noted Livingston family of New York . . . like my father and my brother I became a banker."[6]

As the banker began his New York career the Kaufman family was settling into their new East Coast home. Short Hills, the wealthy enclave they chose, was twenty-five miles west of Wall Street, just across the Hudson River in the township of Milburn, New Jersey. The town had begun as a planned community and was laid out in the 1870s by Stewart Hartshorn, the inventor of the self-acting shade roller. Having made a pile on this snappy apparatus, Hartshorn set out to create a harmonious community "where people of congenial tastes could dwell together."[7] He began with just thirteen acres but ultimately expanded his holdings to more than fifteen hundred and, over protests from many neighboring towns, kept the less than graceful name given centuries earlier by the local Lenape tribe. Hartshorn took pains with Short Hills, laying out graceful, curving roads that hugged its gentle slopes and paving them with crushed rock from his own quarry. To ensure an easy commute into the city, he built a train station and then convinced a local railroad to have trains stop there twice a day. The community center he commissioned was designed by society architect Stanford White. (It still stands today.)

Short Hills caught on nicely. By the time the Kaufmans arrived many other wealthy people had built large houses there, each surrounded by several acres of land. It was not unusual for these householders to employ a dozen servants, inside and out, and one particularly juicy Short Hills estate was known to employ forty. Few Short Hills families spent the entire year in residence. Some New Yorkers "summered" there while other residents moved out in the spring, migrating to houses in Maine or on Nantucket or Long Island. (LG and Marie would later do the same, moving between Short Hills, Granot Loma, Manhattan, and Palm Beach.) It was all a far cry from the UP and one could almost hear Marie Kaufman's sigh of relief. She had left a provincial Michigan town where, in spite of her exalted Chicago connections, she remained outside of "good society" and had relocated to one of the grandest suburbs of the social capital of the land. As her children grew older, they would meet and marry people of the "right" sort and elevate the Kaufmans into the Social Register and beyond. LG wasn't the only one who had a job to do: as soon as she arrived Marie began to build a life that would make that happen.

Her new house was equal to the task: designed by architect John A. Gurd, it was suitably grand, if a bit unusual. Commissioned in 1908 by a couple who had lost their previous Short Hills manse in a devastating fire (the family had barely managed to escape alive), it was built entirely of fireproof concrete. It was not as bad as it sounds: tinted pale gray, under blue-green tiles covering an attractive array of rooflines, and with multiple facades enlivened with shuttered and mullioned windows, the four-story house looked little different from other large English and American houses of the period. In fact, it bore a resemblance to the Arts and Crafts–style country houses built around that time by the famous English architect Sir Edwin Lutyens. (One feels Gurd knew and admired Lutyens's work but feared too "Lutyensesque" a design would have been a bridge too far for his sad, singed clients.) The house was larger than it appeared from the front as a side wing extended out from the back and down a hillside. There was also a charming brick terrace and loggia, and in front, a gravel driveway and a covered entranceway. The presence of five chimneys attested to the large number of fireplaces, one of which was located in a second loggia on a rooftop terrace. There was a detached two-story garage with quarters for a chauffeur, tennis courts, a bowling alley in the basement, a ballroom, and more than enough bedrooms for the whole family, including his and hers master suites located at opposite ends of the upstairs hall. The solid gold fixtures in Marie's dressing room would not have been out of place at Younglands.

As at Younglands, the rest of their Short Hills interior was standard issue for the wealthy of the period and featured the tasteful French, Italian, and English furniture obtainable from auction rooms and society decorators. One more unusual piece of decorative kit was designed for the house but never installed. Soon after moving in, Marie went to the forward-looking Tiffany Studios and asked them to design a tiled surround for one of her house's many fireplaces. Noting the house's nod to the Arts and Crafts Movement, Tiffany produced a rather clean, rectilinear composition of midnight blue and multicolored iridescent glass tiles above a black marble hearth that would have suited a Lutyens house, or an early work by the forward-thinking Frank

Lloyd Wright. A watercolor of the design created by Tiffany Studios is itself a work of art and is now in the collection of the Metropolitan Museum in New York. LG and Marie were clearly attracted by Tiffany's work—this would not be their last interaction with the Studios—but on this occasion they apparently decided to pass.

It was certainly not a question of resources: the Chatham Phenix Bank was growing exponentially. Deposits multiplied by five in the first five years of LG's tenure, and the series of takeovers of smaller local banks that would swell its assets and power had begun. The rise of LG's bank was so precipitous that it almost looked like sleight of hand and produced the same sort of fascination. This magician could do no wrong: "Whatever Mr. Kaufman has to announce," gushed the *Brooklyn Daily Eagle* in 1916, "Wall Street is sure it will not be merely interesting but positively thrilling."[8] Louis Graveraet Kaufman was now a household name, mentioned almost daily in press coverage ("the financial Lochinvar who recently came 'out of the West'") that recapped his provenance and accomplishments and praised his astounding business chops.[9] This coverage only accelerated when in 1915 LG pulled off a coup that not only astounded Wall Street but catapulted him into banking history: he found a way to make the Chatham Phenix the only national bank *with branches* in the city of New York.

Why was a hydra-headed bank—something we now take for granted—such a big deal? Picture the New York City of the early twentieth century: in that era similar businesses tended to cluster in one area of the metropolis, so every meat-processing plant, clothing factory, and furniture wholesaler did business with whichever bank happened to be located in its neighborhood, regardless of its capacity or level of service. If that bank didn't suit for some reason, at a time when horses were still on the streets, a working person would have to spend much of his day traveling to reach a better one. True, some state banks had branches, but they were no one's first choice as they were not backed by the Federal Reserve and could not issue nationally backed notes. The no National branch mandate was a huge inconvenience, but in 1915 it appeared to be carved in stone.

Here's why: in the early twentieth century, most American banks were not in big cities but out in the heartland, in small towns and at country crossroads where each enjoyed a monopoly over its surrounding area. These institutions (known as "unit" banks) had long constituted a powerful lobby determined to help each member protect its own turf and, in particular, to make sure urban banks could not open branches in the unit banks' territories. When the secretary of the treasury had recommended branching rights for national banks in the 1890s, the pro-unit group had made such a fuss that the bill was defeated. Since then, in spite of constant discussion in Congress and in the banking community—branch banking was a hot topic in early twentieth-century America—branches were strictly verboten.

LG alone found a way around the impasse. The germ of the idea had come to him years before: in 1908, when he was boning up on banking law for his speech on that trip up Lake Huron on the *City of St. Ignace*, he had come across a forgotten statute from 1865. Years later, he spoke of his discovery with Clarence W. Barron, the owner and publisher of the *Wall Street Journal*. "When I was president of the Michigan Bankers' Association and studying to make an annual address," LG told Barron in the late 1920s, "I discovered that under the law you could have branches for national banks with permission of the Comptroller of the Currency. That," he continued, "was too valuable to put into my address."[10]

Permission from John Skelton Williams, the Comptroller of the Currency in 1915, was only part of LG's savvy plan. To make sure Williams could give it without having every national bank in New York City beating down his door to do the same, and inciting the wrath of the "unit" bank lobby, LG made the Chatham Phenix unique: he had recently annexed the Century Bank, a state bank with a number of New York City branches and, as its chairman, he applied for a National Charter. When the charter had been granted, the Century (the smaller institution) took over the assets of the Chatham Phenix, effectively liquidating it. Then, when all of the stock transfers had been completed, the Century Bank simply changed its name to the Chatham Phenix. That final move made the "new" Chatham Phenix something that had never existed before—a national bank with ten legal branches in New York City—a reality that was then blessed with "permission" from John Skelton Williams. It was a brilliant plan that not only created a huge advantage for the Chatham Phenix but made it difficult for other banks to do the same.

In his conversation with Clarence Barron, LG enlarged on his process, taking the opportunity to drop a few names: "I went to Mr. Wilson [President Woodrow Wilson] and John Skelton Williams . . . and finally received permission . . . to merge these banks as branch banks . . . through one of my directors, Bolling [Richard Wilmer Bolling, 1879–1951], who was a brother in law of Wilson and could talk to him in his bedroom."[11] LG was proud of his association with Bolling (and by extension Woodrow Wilson, whose portrait, autographed to himself, he kept until the end of his life) and mentioned these connections on all possible occasions, but while name-dropping, was he admitting to Barron that he had achieved his coup through "pull"? Not really: while some back-channel discussions may have taken place, LG had brainstormed that clever Century/Chatham Phenix switch-up, and Williams had his own reasons for allowing it to work. Tenacious of power, he was anxious to keep as many banks as possible in the National system and under his control. It was early in the life of the Federal Reserve System (founded in 1913), and he did not want to lose a major New York member. Still, LG added yet another layer of security by penning a flattering letter to Williams in September 1915 suggesting the entire scheme had been the Comptroller's brilliant idea. "Under your able guidance," he wrote, "the consolidation of the Chatham and Phenix with the Century Bank . . . is progressing in a manner prescribed by you."[12]

The branch banking scheme illustrates LG's lifelong modus operandi: the consummate deal maker, he would see an opportunity, muster his connections, and, acting covertly behind the scenes, take the (often lengthy) series of steps that got him where he wanted to go. He had used the same tactics back in Marquette when he had chosen his moment, quietly leveraged his friendship with Peter White, and taken control of the First National Bank. While stealth is common on such occasions, this method seemed to particularly suit LG, a man who had created his personal and financial persona out of thin air and, even after years of success, may have felt the spotlight should not be upon him until his object was achieved. Only then did he feel free to step out of the shadows.

The reaction was cataclysmic: "There is no precedent in national bank history for the step which has been decided upon," marveled the *New York Times* when the scheme was revealed, while the *Brooklyn Daily Eagle* cheered: "Marquette . . . until within the past few years . . . was content to be great in name only. Now it boasts that it is the birthplace of Louis Graveraet Kaufman."[13] At the 1915 American Bankers Association meeting in Seattle the subject was front and center and the *Seattle Daily Times* wrote of "the colossal merger . . . of the Chatham and Phenix with the Century" and specifically of "Louis G. Kaufman a native son of Michigan whose phenomenal career . . . has been the talk of the financiers of the country."[14]

And as LG had predicted, the Chatham Phenix remained the only national New York bank with this huge advantage: Congress would continue to stall and it would be 1927 before more national banks were allowed branches and later still before they were commonplace. (N.B.: LG has sometimes been referred to as the "father of branch banking" but as his bank was the only one to benefit from his machinations, that accolade is a bit of a misnomer.)

But with twelve convenient locations from the Bowery to Harlem, his bank was raking it in: the Chatham Phenix had been admitted to the New York Stock Exchange in October 1915 and by December it was number three in the country for profits earned on capital stock (stockholders were earning 37.3 percent). Deposits soared and by the end of 1916 LG's bank was one of the largest in New York and the sixteenth largest in the country. It was now a local brand—its neighborhood signage as familiar to New Yorkers as ads for Arrow Collars or Pear's Soap. And as for the Chatham Phenix's main office, it needed no signage at all to get the public's attention: this Wall Street temple of banking was so impressive and reassuring that clients immediately felt they were in the right financial hands.

This architectural security blanket was another Louis G. Kaufman production: back in 1913 when a fire at the Chatham Phenix's longtime headquarters at Broadway and John Street mandated a move, LG had made the decision to relocate to the Singer Building at the corner of Liberty and Broadway. The Singer Building was a city landmark—familiar to all New Yorkers—a destination in itself. A forty-story fairy tale of a building topped with a soaring Baroque/Beaux Arts turret, it was designed in 1908 by architect Ernest Flagg for the Singer Sewing Machine Company and briefly reigned as the tallest building in New York and (save the Eiffel Tower) the tallest structure in the world. In 1913, when the Chatham Phenix moved, excited visitors were still paying a fee of fifty cents to enjoy the view of the city from its observation deck on the fortieth floor, after goggling at its elegant lobby where squads of marble columns embellished with bronze medallions bearing the Singer name and its emblem, a stylized needle and thread, supported a canopy of delicate plaster domes.

It was the perfect gateway for LG's Palace of Financial Invincibility. Encompassing twenty-six thousand square feet and created at a cost of $500,000, the new Chatham Phenix offices welcomed customers through a grand entrance then wowed them with blue and gray marble columns rising to ceilings striped in gold. In the main banking room thirty-eight tellers' cages of decorative bronze catered to every banking need and bronze Chatham Phenix insignia decorated every pillar. In an adjoining room one hundred fifty adding machines stood at the ready, a state-of-the-art pneumatic tube system allowed bank documents to circulate quickly, and employees enjoyed the use of three private dining rooms on an upper floor. The private offices were appropriately luxe, from the giant Oriental rug in the boardroom to the massive Italian walnut furniture in LG's own corner sanctum, looking out over Broadway. It was from this office that he had planned his branch banking coup, organized the stock transfers, telephoned Richard Bolling, written to John Skelton Williams and perhaps Woodrow Wilson as well, and watched the money roll in.

When LG closed the door at the end of the day, he often made his way uptown to the Manhattan apartment he had taken for the nights he could not/did not make it back to Short Hills. His home away from home was the Carlton House, a wing of the city's grandest hotel, the Ritz-Carlton. Brand-new in 1910, the Ritz's Adam-style building designed by society architects Warren and Wetmore took up the entire west side of Madison Avenue between 46th and 47th Streets and featured public rooms that were the most fashionable in the city. While most Ritz clients rented by the day or week, by 1912 the hotel also catered to more permanent lodgers who paid an annual rent in its Carlton House wing behind a separate entrance at 22 East 47th Street. Sixty of these ritzy flats were quickly snapped up by a socially prominent clientele that included architect Whitney Warren himself. LG's apartment suited him down to the ground: it came with Ritz food and service, making it easy for him to entertain business colleagues, and it allowed him to mention casually to one and all that he "lived at the Ritz."

In 1918 when his older children began to attend debutante balls and other events in New York and Marie wished to be on hand to oversee their entry into society, LG gave up the Carlton House and the family took a large apartment in a new building just across Madison Avenue at 270 Park Avenue. Another Warren and Wetmore creation, the neo-Renaissance apartment house stretched from Madison to Park Avenue and boasted an enclosed Italian garden and covered colonnade where limos could discharge passengers on rainy days, as well as a restaurant and café run by the Ritz. The family's twenty-room flat was larger than most suburban houses and included a foyer seventeen feet square, a living room over thirty-three feet long, and a servants hall. Rent was about $15,000 annually (about $300,000 today), which was a bit dear, but there was Ritz food on tap and the location was convenient to the many debutante balls held in the hotel just across the street.

Marie Kaufman approved of 270 Park, then an epicenter of society money and power: their neighbors included financier, diplomat, and Chatham Phenix director August Belmont, Standard Oil bigwig Harry Harkness, Harold S. Vanderbilt, and Millicent Rogers, a photogenic young heiress whose deb party took place at the Ritz in 1919. Another neighbor, banker James Stillman, made headlines when his wife, Anne, cuckolded him with yet another "Indian guide." (This event ended more happily than the one that had devastated the Horatio Seymours. After a trip across the pond to consult Carl Jung, the couple patched it up and returned together to 270 Park.) LG too was at home in this rarified company. "The Kaufman mansion at 270 Park Avenue is one of the most distinguished New York salons and the Kaufmans are of the socially elect," crowed an article syndicated to dozens of newspapers, adding an unusual personal tribute to New York's favorite banker: "Mr. Kaufman is massive, vigorous and dominant."[15]

Mr. Kaufman was also very busy: in 1915, the same year he finagled the first national bank with branches in New York City, LG played a central role in the takeover and restructuring of an iconic American corporation. There have been dozens of books written about this landmark event in business history but LG's role in it has been underestimated in all of them, until now.

The story began in a carriage works in Flint, Michigan, in 1900. The company, founded by William Crapo Durant (1861–1947), was the largest carriage maker in the country and like everyone in his line of work Durant was not happy about the coming of newfangled vehicles powered by gasoline engines. But Durant was flexible and ambitious. When it became clear automobiles were there to stay, he purchased the struggling Buick Motor Company and in 1908 founded a holding company for it and future auto-related acquisitions. He called his new company General Motors. Thus equipped, Durant proceeded to go on an automotive spending spree, adding the Cadillac and Oldsmobile cars to his roster, along with a dozen manufacturers of auto parts and accessories (spark plugs, headlights, etc.) and automobile paints. It proved to be too much too fast: by 1910 General Motors was in such financial trouble that Durant was forced to cede control of his company to a cabal of bankers who brought in $15 million to keep it afloat.

For a while Durant watched impotently from the sidelines as the bankers closed plants and refused to pay dividends to stockholders, and as Ford Motor Company powered up, General Motors made fewer of the nation's cars. But by 1911 he had had enough. He decided to compete with his overseers by building and selling his own motor car, a new model designed by race car driver Louis Chevrolet. Money was raised for a new plant—not in Flint or Detroit but on 11th Avenue and 57th Street in New York City. There, Durant believed, Wall Street bankers would visit the factory floor, get excited about the possibilities of the American auto business, and provide financing on demand. The factory was in a rough neighborhood and Durant had to pay Tammany Hall for protection from petty criminals who tried to shake down his workers, but he barely noticed the inconvenience, and soon enough he no longer cared if Wall Street came sniffing around 11th Avenue or not. He had met Louis Graveraet Kaufman.

In the years to come Durant and Kaufman would often be described as two Michigan men who had known each other out in the heartland and gotten together to retake control of GM. It was an appealing tale of Midwest solidarity, but it wasn't true. Durant was born in Boston, Flint and Marquette were hundreds of miles apart, and the two men did not meet until 1914 in LG's apartment at the Carlton House in New York City. The meeting, described by Durant's biographer Bernard A. Weisberger as "of far-reaching reverberations," was arranged by a wealthy New Yorker called Nathan Hofheimer with whom Durant had shared his need for capital to build more Chevrolets.[16] Hofheimer, a tall German immigrant with a thick accent, had invested in a small way in Durant's other companies and he knew whom to call when small investors weren't enough. He picked up the phone and arranged a meeting between Durant and Louis Graveraet Kaufman. (It is not known how Hofheimer and LG knew one another but the connection would have been strictly business. Hofheimer identified as Jewish and Marie Kaufman would not have been eager to mix socially with the Hofheimers.)

Durant and a GM colleague enjoyed an elegant lunch (provided by the Ritz) in LG's plush quarters, then got down to business. LG asked Durant how much money he needed and was told: "Eventually we can use many times the capital and surplus of your bank, but for the present five million will do."[17] LG didn't bat an eye. Casually, he informed his visitor that the brokerage house Hornblower and Weeks owed him a favor and that he might be able to work something out. Soon Hornblower and Weeks had underwritten fifty thousand shares of Chevrolet stock with a par value of $100. The deal, signed in July 1915 and witnessed by the ever-helpful Mr. Hofheimer, provided Durant with his financing and LG with $1.9 million of stock in Chevrolet and $475,000 in commissions.

It was, as they say, the beginning of a beautiful friendship. Each man recognized a fellow deal maker, the make-it-happen chutzpah, in the other. As GM historian Richard Langworth wrote: "If these two had a talent it was an uncanny ability to pull off sensational deals without their seeming in any way unusual."[18] Complementary skills helped: Durant was a charming, persuasive front man, unafraid to take bold action at all times. LG was a financial wiz with useful connections among money men of all kinds, willing to stay in the background as the two strategized and implemented the details of Durant's grand plan—to take GM out of the hands of the bankers and run it again himself.

The first step was taken that summer when the partners merged Durant's three existing automobile companies into a single Delaware corporation capitalized at $20 million, thanks to LG, who became the chairman of the finance committee of the new Chevrolet Motor Car Company. Chevrolet put out a car called the 490 that sold for a strategic $490 (a Model T Ford then sold for $495) and quickly racked up orders for eighty-two thousand cars—more than for any other model, at any price, in motoring history. This new, rocketing company would be a major building block in their grand plan.

The bankers' oversight arrangement at GM officially ended in September 1915 but the group had no intention of stepping down. They still controlled the board and they planned to attend the September board meeting and simply vote themselves into power for another five years. LG and Durant were not going to let that happen: if they could line up enough GM stock and proxies to unseat the current regime, they could announce *their* majority at the September meeting and take back control of the company. It would not be easy: strategy sessions lasted late into the night and spilled over into weekends. In the late summer of 1915 Durant attended a house party at LG's Short Hills manse and the two men huddled for hours, honing their plan of attack. Another guest, the gossip columnist and radio personality Elsa Maxwell, overheard some of the conversation and wrote about the day forty years later, when she admitted her Short Hills eavesdropping (and lack of understanding of what she'd heard) to LG. She had missed a great opportunity, he told her, and if she had rushed out and bought GM stock in 1915, she could have made herself a fortune. "Anyone," he added, with the benefit of hindsight, "would have given his right arm to have heard those conversations."[19]

The summer of 1915 was a season of conversations: LG and Durant spoke to every GM stockholder they knew personally, convincing them that prices and dividends would skyrocket when Durant was back in charge and lining up their support. Durant chatted up his Flint cronies and the heads of the companies he'd acquired in his ill-fated buying spree, and LG talked to wealthy, influential clients of the Chatham Phenix National

Bank, including a particularly important threesome: Pierre S. du Pont, president of DuPont de Nemours, the giant Delaware-based gunpowder, dynamite, and chemical company; his brother Irénée du Pont; and DuPont's financial guru John J. Raskob. LG knew this group well: Pierre was a director of the Chatham Phenix, and the DuPont Company did much of their business through the bank. He was aware that the trio owned thousands of shares of GM stock (it was the kind of thing LG knew); he hastened to advise them of the takeover plan and of the financial benefits they would soon reap. Meanwhile, Durant bought every share of GM he could afford, often using the Chevrolet Motor Car Company as his piggy bank.

Chevrolet came into play in another way: its stock became bait for a switcheroo that echoed LG's plan to obtain legal branches for the Chatham Phenix. In that case he had exchanged the assets of one bank for another. In this deal, consummated the same year, he and Durant offered to exchange shares of stock—five shares of Chevrolet for every share of GM an owner was willing to trade. When enough shares had been exchanged, the Chevrolet Motor Car Company would in effect take over GM (as the Century Bank had "taken over" the Chatham Phenix) and Durant and LG would be back in charge. The conservative bankers who had run GM since 1910 had continued to balk at raising the stock's dividend and Durant and LG expected a stream of eager traders, but what followed was more like the opening of a spigot. Soon suitcases of GM stock certificates were being brought to the Chevrolet offices on West 57th Street where their contents were piled high in bushel baskets. On the night before the September 15 board meeting Durant and his team sat up all night passing them from hand to hand, calling out and inscribing names and numbers. That evening Durant wrote to his son-in-law of his positive expectations for the next day, adding a shout-out to the man who had masterminded the scheme that was about to return him to power: "Kaufman," he wrote in his Midwest shorthand, "say, he's a beaut."[20]

The GM board meeting was scheduled for 2:00 p.m. the following day but when the directors entered Room 282 of New York's Belmont Hotel at the appointed hour they found the action delayed. Earlier that morning one of their number, banker James Jackson Storrow, had been bidden to a meeting with Durant and LG where the duo informed him that they had amassed enough shares of GM to take back control. Crucially, Pierre du Pont and John J. Raskob were also at the meeting before the meeting. They had come at LG's suggestion to be "in at the kill" and the first to hear that GM would soon be in friendlier, more generous hands. But when all were assembled the men from Wilmington discovered that LG had exaggerated the position. While he and Durant *likely* controlled a majority of GM's stock, the numbers were too close to call. An official count or serious negotiations would be needed to get to a final resolution.

As neither side wanted to risk the public failure of a count-off, negotiations commenced. But after each "team" had repeatedly named six candidates for the eleven-member GM board and each slate had been rejected by the other faction, the two sides remained deadlocked. Hours passed. Then James Storrow suddenly approached Pierre du Pont as he and LG stood chatting, awaiting developments. Storrow suggested a new plan: that the GM board be expanded to seventeen, with fourteen members chosen by the two original factions and the final three chosen by a "neutral party"—in fact Pierre du Pont himself. The gunpowder magnate agreed. The new plan would break the deadlock and put his financial guru (John J. Raskob) inside the company. As LG knew, du Pont and Raskob had come to believe that, even with war in sight, automobiles would soon be more profitable than gunpowder and dynamite. GM stock now made up half of du Pont's investment portfolio. Du Pont named his brother-in-law Lammot Belin, longtime DuPont executive J. Amory Haskell, and John J. Raskob as the three "neutral" GM trustees, and everyone repaired to the Belmont Hotel to inform the current board of the new state of play.

History hangs on confluences, coincidences, and decisions that might have gone the other way. If Durant had agreed to a count-off, thanks to LG's help he would have been proved the majority GM stockholder and he would have become the unchallenged head of his former company, without DuPont participation. (He was later shown to have been in control of 450,000 of GM's 825,589 shares of common stock.) And if LG had not invited Pierre du Pont and Raskob to attend the meeting before the meeting with Storrow, the banker might not have suggested that the DuPont faction join the GM board—a suggestion that would change the company's trajectory for decades to come. In the end, however, there was no count-off and the du Ponts joined the GM board.

Why did James Jackson Storrow choose the gunpowder magnates to break the deadlock? He was surely aware of their relationship with LG and knew that by bringing them into the mix he was, in effect, handing over control to Durant. A note Storrow wrote to Pierre du Pont the next day may explain his thinking: "May I congratulate you and Mr. Raskob upon the success of your day's work in New York?" Storrow wrote, then added, "It seems pretty clear that the stockholders are much better off than otherwise would have been the case."[21] Storrow may have realized that the bankers' days were numbered and believed that DuPont participation was the best way forward. The presence of the du Ponts and their rigorous financial henchman Raskob on the board would curb Durant's financial incontinence and keep the company on a solid footing. Was this what Storrow was thinking when he wrote the note? We may never know. We know only that on September 15, 1915, the du Ponts were in Storrow's line of sight because LG put them there and that (partly on LG's advice) they were already heavily invested in General Motors. All of America knows that John J. Raskob ran General Motors for more than a decade and that the du Ponts would own much of the company well into the 1960s.

But in 1915 the du Pont era was yet to come. In September of that year William Crapo Durant was back in control and he and Louis Graveraet Kaufman (now out of the shadows and identified with the deal) were the talk of the town: everyone in Michigan had rooted for GM's comeback kid, and Wall Street was fascinated by his heretofore unknown alliance with the president of the Chatham Phenix. "The entrance of Louis G. Kaufman into the affairs of General Motors is a story in itself," wrote the *Flint Daily Journal*.[22] Outside of Flint, LG's role in those affairs *was* the story. "A new stock has taken the place of Bethlehem Steel as the center of interest in Wall Street," crowed the *New York Sun*. "General Motors . . . has become the wonder of the financial district . . . new directors were elected to the board . . . LG Kaufman . . . and others whose mere connection with a company lends confidence in its future."[23]

Durant and LG moved quickly to control that future. From his perch at the head of the finance committees of both GM and Chevrolet, LG organized another stock-trading scheme. He and Durant traded another $13.2 million worth of Chevrolet stock for GM stock, reserving $6.8 million worth of shares to support the continued manufacture of Chevrolet cars. Chevrolets sold like hotcakes, share prices continued to rise, and all went smoothly. Ninety days later the duo initiated step two and "recapitalized" Chevrolet at $80 million. With a new $60 million tranche to play with, they offered another trade opportunity: four shares of Chevrolet stock for every share of GM (not five this time as Chevrolet had become too valuable). LG even found a way to protect the trading scheme and make extra money on the side. He organized the Chevrolet Motor Company Underwriting Syndicate (members included Durant, LG, Elbert Gary, and Nathan Hofheimer): if, during the Chevrolet trade offer, Chevrolet shares had dropped below a certain level, the money contributed by the syndicate would have been used to prop them up until the danger passed. This being an LG Kaufman production, the market for Chevrolet stock stayed strong, the syndicate never had to ante up, and each of its members made a profit of just over $100,000.

James Jackson Storrow was not happy about any of it. Only a few months into their new reign, Durant and his financial Svengali had already rejiggered the company with airy "capitalizations and stock manipulations," and the DuPont faction had just stood by and watched. Concerned, in early 1916 Storrow and the banking faction made one last stand to protect the company. They wrote to GM stockholders apprising them of the danger ahead, asking them to stop trading their shares for Chevrolet stock and to support another three years of conservative banker control. Few responded. Durant had declared a juicy dividend for stockholders, everyone who had jumped on the Durant/Kaufman bandwagon was making money, and nobody wanted to get off. Defeated, Storrow gave up and resigned from the GM board.

Durant and LG pressed on: Durant bought up companies that manufactured radiators, horns, and other automotive accoutrements, added them to GM's existing roster of makers, and stashed them all in United Motors, a new holding company founded for the purpose. The new purchases—acquired to assure their cars a steady stream of parts and accessories—were financed in the usual ways, with capital supplied by LG and a stock-for-stock share exchange, this time using 1.2 million shares of GM. LG became finance committee chairman of

United Motors (the third Durant company in which he held this position) and much richer: for his help with financing he was said to have received a block of United Motors stock worth $9 million (over $200 million today). In August 1916 Durant wrote jokingly to LG: "Your latest baby—a weak, struggling infant which I adopted and which has cost me to date somewhere between $4,000,000 and $5,000,000 cash, with careful nursing begins to show signs of strength and will in time, I believe, become a very healthy child that you will be proud of."[24] (Their "youngest" would present no "custody issues": LG had made sure that only five thousand shares of United Motors came with voting rights.)

United Motors' stock soared from 62 to 94, everyone was happy, and LG was suddenly a national spokesman for the motor industry as well: "The automobile, according to Louis G. Kaufman," wrote the *New York Sun*, "is no longer only a pleasure vehicle but even more largely a commercial vehicle while the business itself . . . has become a transportation business. One thing that impresses Mr. Kaufman is its growing use by women who are thus enabled to 'get out the house a bit.' It is making mothers healthier and more self-reliant."[25] Already celebrated as a banking whiz, LG was now looked to as an industry prognosticator and, of course, deal maker extraordinaire: "When William C. Durant returned to power . . . he was assisted by Mr. Kaufman," one magazine reported, "who with characteristic foresight, realized the enormous demand the war would create for automobiles. He backed Durant, but even better, he backed his own judgement—and he was right."[26]

Durant and Kaufman were buddies as well as colleagues and would be as long as the good times rolled: in 1916, having realized that Durant and Marie Kaufman shared the same birthday, LG wrote to his friend to tell him that his gift to his wife that year would be one hundred shares of Chevrolet stock. "I want her to own in her own name some stock in the Chevrolet Company," LG wrote, adding jocularly: "It is your birthday also and I regret that I cannot give you Chevrolet stock as I understand your strong box is not big enough to hold any more."[27] (One wonders how Marie Kaufman felt about receiving a modest roll of stock certificates on her big day. Perhaps they were tied with a diamond bracelet.) Gifts are a recurring theme in letters between the partners: that same year Durant and LG discussed and jointly purchased a $1,000 wedding present (a whopping $25,000 today) for the daughter of a du Pont executive. In other letters LG invited Durant to "camp" with him in the UP and when his partner was in Michigan Durant tried to lure him down to Detroit, volunteering to call a special meeting of the GM board to make his trip worthwhile.[28]

But the Durant-LG show would soon be canceled: six months later the United States entered World War I, setting off a series of events that changed the balance of power at GM. Widespread speculation that the company would not be selected to provide vehicles for the war effort walloped its stock price and it dropped like a stone. Domestic car sales slowed, and the stock dropped further. Ever impetuous and optimistic, William Durant began to buy up large tranches on margin, eager to protect his own holdings and, more generously, the holdings of friends and colleagues who had bought GM stock on his advice. The stock did not rebound, and Durant became more and more overextended, but he kept buying, putting GM itself in danger. Finally, in 1920 the du Ponts lost patience, turned to J. P. Morgan to save the company, and took steps against its improvident founder. The bankers pressured Durant to admit his level of debt—a moving target estimated to be as high as $38 million—then insisted that in return for a bailout, he relinquish all power at General Motors. Durant had lost his company—again—as well as a personal fortune of more than

$100 million. The du Ponts then proceeded to invest $50 million in GM (the largest outside corporate investment ever recorded up until that time) and took control of the company. Pierre du Pont became the president, and, under Raskob's leadership, General Motors became the largest company in the world. The du Ponts would remain at the helm of GM until the 1950s when the Clayton Antitrust Act forced them to sell their stake.

Back in the 1910s, LG didn't wait around to see Durant self-destruct. He saw the writing on the wall and resigned from the finance committee of GM in 1918. By the time Durant got the boot he was long gone from the halls of automotive power (although he retained a seat on the GM board for twenty-two years). Business was business and while it had been exhilarating and profitable to organize and juggle motor car companies, Durant's stock manipulations had foiled LG's ability to continue in that industry and adversely affected his own bottom line. Specifically, LG, who had owned a major chunk of United Motors, blamed Durant for accepting only $44 million for the company when Morgan and the du Ponts took over. The two men parted coolly, and later LG was short and rather offhand when, in an interview with Clarence Barron, he recalled his years with his former colleague: "After I set him up in General Motors he was at one time worth $100,000,000," LG sighed, tsk-tsking over Durant's financial downfall and speaking of his own exit from the car business as business as usual. "I got the DuPonts in and they took in Morgan," LG continued casually. "As I am in the banking business I then left P S DuPont locked in with Motors and returned to my banking."[29]

What he did not say, of course, was that with Morgan aboard and the wealthy du Ponts in the mix GM no longer needed his financing help, and that his association with Durant likely did him no favors with the new regime. Publicly LG also escaped without a scratch: having been lauded daily in the press for

GM's successes during the Durant era, he suffered no discredit when his partner's star shone less brightly. The press merely noted that LG had resigned from GM's Finance Committee, adding respectfully that "he had been a big factor in the organization and direction of the General Motors Corporation, the Chevrolet Motor Car Company and the United Motors Company."[30]

And by 1918 LG was in the press for other reasons: World War I was raging, and with it had come many opportunities for a savvy moneyman in the mayoralty of wartime New York. LG's war work began modestly in 1917 when he joined Mayor John Mitchell's Committee on Films (moving pictures in support of America's entry into the war) but quickly ratcheted up when John Francis Hylan became mayor the following year. Motivated by patriotism, an understanding of the uses of civic power, or perhaps some combination of the two, LG became Hylan's go-to money guy, expertly wringing money out of fellow millionaires for a never-ending list of war-related committees and projects. As one of Hylan's minions wrote in a letter asking for fundraising help: "I have heard it said in Wall Street that when any institution is in financial difficulty and it needs assistance, that the one surgeon who can successfully relieve and resuscitate the dying patient is Louis G Kaufman."[31]

And LG was soon providing more than fundraising assistance: red-haired "Red Mike" Hylan, who was not known for his brains or speaking ability, apparently found Cheap John's personable, well-spoken son a valuable addition to his party and LG found himself attending many social and ceremonial occasions where His Honor was present: in 1918, for example, LG was in attendance when the mayor attended a dinner on an Argentinian battleship in New York harbor and at a luncheon in honor of Prince Axel of Denmark, and he was part of a reception committee to honor the Golden Jubilee of the well-known

Catholic prelate Cardinal James Gibbons. In December 1918 LG joined Hylan and other grandees on a police boat in New York harbor where, under a sky bristling with dirigibles and biplanes, the mayoral party welcomed American seamen home. The same month LG was the mayor's guest on a reviewing stand in front of the New York Public Library on Fifth Avenue where, along with thousands of New Yorkers, he watched a homecoming parade for returning troops.

Nor was LG's "war work" confined to fundraising and supportive attendance at mayoral events: after America entered the war, he quickly earned a name for himself as an advocate for the sale of Liberty Loans. The Liberty Loan program allowed private citizens to help finance World War I (World War II was financed by war bonds) by buying government bonds, issued five times between 1917 and 1919, providing a competitive rate of interest. While LG cajoled his fellow millionaires into making hefty investments (and sent personal letters to Chatham Phenix stockholders and branch managers with subscription forms attached), he also put his own money where his mouth was. In the run-up to the war LG bought $1 million worth of Liberty Loans (over $22 million today) and he later invested another half million, personally loaning the government more than many banks and corporations of the day. To tap the buying power of New York's rank and file, in 1918 the Chatham Phenix took a full-page ad in the *New York Times* announcing the coming of Liberty Loan Week at the Chatham Phenix—days when the bank would make all facilities and personnel available to explain the advantages of Liberty Bonds to the bond-buying public and help them invest. Other Chatham Phenix ads pointed out that the bank's many branches made the purchase of Liberty Loans wonderfully convenient and urged all citizens to take advantage of this fact. They did so—in droves. Thanks to LG the Chatham Phenix set the U.S. record during the second and third bond drives, underwriting the largest number of subscriptions in the entire country.

While his bank was his chief subscription-seeking tool, LG also made eloquent personal appeals for investment, in person and in print. He gave public speeches on the topic and, speaking through the powerful megaphone of his own financial success, assured the readers of the *New York Sun* that "the Liberty Loan is the best possible investment an individual can make," using memorable rhetoric to remind them what was at stake: "so if you are optimistic back your optimism with your dollars, if you are pessimistic do the same. It is your only chance to hang onto your freedom and your privileges."[32] Determined to do both, LG was also a major donor to the Red Cross, the high bidder at $500 (nearly $10,000 today) when an Iron Cross taken from a dead German was auctioned for the war effort, and a member of the board of managers of the Morris Plains State Hospital (a psychiatric institution in New Jersey) that treated returning veterans suffering from what we would now recognize as PTSD.

After the war ended, perhaps habituated to the ownership of civic clout, LG continued to work with/for Mayor Hylan. He joined (and raised money for) useful extensions of Red Mike's political machine, including the mayor's Committee for Public Welfare, formed to control the sale and use of explosive chemicals and habit-forming drugs, and another to erect a memorial to the city's heroes. As a banker with branches that might be robbed at gunpoint, he was even asked by the mayor to influence the press to discontinue articles that "encourage crooks, criminals and hold up men to come to this city."[33] In 1923 he joined Hylan's Committee of Celebration of the 25th Anniversary of Greater New York, was tapped for the Broadway Association's "thought campaign" to clean and improve Broadway, and was asked to be on the board of directors of a new police club that, while organized to strengthen relations among members of the force, no doubt had many other uses. With civic connections now piled upon major financial chops, the newspapers noted that "Louis G. Kaufman . . . has made his presence felt in so many ways that the bankers of the city are now prepared to recognize him as one of the great influences in the fields of finance and national economics."[34]

Everyone wanted to know the "great influencer," and invitations poured in. LG attended exclusive dinners like one given for the president of the Chamber of Commerce at the tony Metropolitan Club (with Averell Harriman, Otto Kahn, and F. W. Woolworth also in attendance) and gatherings at the more intellectual Lotos Club (he joined in 1912), where well-known politicians, writers, and intellectuals delivered erudite after-dinner addresses over brandy and cigars. In April 1918 he hosted a dinner there in honor of helpful police adjunct and friend Dr. John A. Harris (who, incidentally, invented the traffic light). LG was also bidden to more entertaining entertainments: at a fancy dress party that went on 'til 7 in the morning, *Town Topics* found LG "disguised as himself and shaking a very wicked hoof with all the dolled up girls, young and old."[35] He was also to be found, along with artists James Montgomery Flagg and Howard Chandler Christy, at the "annual racket and blowout of the Chu Chin Chow Association" (named for a long-running Broadway musical based on the story of Ali Baba) held at the famous New York studio building, the Hotel des Artistes.[36]

Marie was present at few of these evening affairs. LG often stayed over alone in New York and, having grown up in a household in which his father was away more than he was at home, he would have seen nothing wrong with doing so. Like his mother before her, his wife was left at home with many children (ages one to nineteen), although ensconced in a mansion in beautifully landscaped ground, with two Rolls Royces in the garage and a full complement of servants, Marie had less need to write (or call) LG with desperate complaints. The Kaufman family's life in Short Hills was plush and seamless: the younger children roller-skated happily on a large wooden platform erected for that purpose near the tennis court, chatted in French or German with whichever foreign governess was in residence, and played with their wire-haired terrier Bubbles. Nannies, butlers, and cooks leapt to Marie's command.

Apparently, LG did not recall the loneliness of his mother during his own childhood and come home to Marie and the children more often. His easier, less autocratic personality made him the more natural parent ("Marie scared her grandchildren, LG didn't," as one descendant later noted), so it seems a shame that making time for child-rearing was not higher on his agenda.[37] His children were clearly on LG's mind as he publicly expressed love for, and interest in, them on many occasions. In an article showcasing his Short Hills manse he flagged them as the "Kaufman treasures" and called them the house's most precious contents. He told the writer of a "banker at home" piece that his children were his "number one hobby," ranking above more predictable favorites like hiking, motoring, and golf.[38] Still, he did not often put that "hobby" into practice. While his mother's parenting remained a clear and cherished memory, having grown up with Cheap John, the role of father was likely less clear to him as he repeated the pattern that had characterized his own childhood. Like his father he went about his business and left his wife single-handedly in charge of their brood. It was a decision he had cause to ponder as the treasures grew up and began to make their way in the wild world of the Roaring Twenties.

For LG that decade began with a bang. On September 6, 1920, just before noon he was leaving a meeting at J. P. Morgan's bank at 23 Wall Street when he noticed a horse-drawn wagon stopping in front of the Treasury Assay offices directly across the street. As he watched, the driver jumped down from the wagon and moved quickly away. LG began walking toward his next meeting and was less than two blocks away when the earth shook under his feet, windows above him shattered, and plumes of smoke rose from the spot he had so recently occupied. The horse and wagon had been a bomb on the hoof. Minutes after LG left the scene, one hundred pounds of dynamite had exploded, propelling a cargo of iron window sash weights as shrapnel in every direction. The explosion and flying metal killed 38 people who happened to be nearby and seriously wounded another 143. The horse was unrecognizable, and parts of the wagon were found on a window ledge on the twenty-fourth floor of a nearby building. Windows were blown out in every direction, motor cars were upended by the blast, and stone facades were pitted by rocketing iron.

It was a frightening near miss. Had LG left 23 Wall Street a few minutes later he would likely have been one of the higher-profile victims of the incident. That reality was clearly on his mind as he retreated to the safety of the UP (not usually a September destination), where he recovered his equilibrium amid the pines and, making the most of being a witness to history, favored the *Mining Journal* with "the gruesome details and terrifying incidents that happened in the Wall Street district after the death dealing bomb did its work."[39] No one was ever charged for the Wall Street bombing, but it is widely assumed to have been the work of anarchists (then active in New York City) who had chosen a site between a government building and a capitalist cathedral to demonstrate their feelings about both. Defiantly, J. P. Morgan ordered the broken, pitted facade of his bank to remain unrepaired and the damage remains visible to this day.

4

GRANOT LOMA RISING

I t was 1917 and Louis Graveraet Kaufman was riding high. He was the president of one of the biggest banks in the country—the only national bank in New York City with branches—and the head of the finance committee of a booming General Motors. He was rich, well-connected, and comfortably ensconced in the upscale precincts of Short Hills and Park Avenue. Yet something was missing: like his mentor Elbert Gary, LG longed for the north woods, for happy days hunting and fishing with companions of the "right" sort. The solution seemed at hand: he would join the gentry of the Midwest—many of whom he could now buy and sell several times over—at the Huron Mountain Club, that WASPs-only UP bastion of wilderness sports less than fifty miles from his house in Marquette. If a voice in his ear whispered that he was half Jewish and part Native American and that his background would be an impediment to inclusion in this particular club, he did not heed its warning.

LG was still in high school when John Longyear, Horatio Seymour, Peter White, and other prominent citizens of Detroit and Marquette organized the Huron Mountain Club. A "back to nature" movement was then sweeping the country and elaborate family compounds constructed of logs, twigs, and stones were rising on Adirondack lakes, commissioned by Rockefellers,

Vanderbilts, and others who wished to enjoy the outdoors conveniently and privately, with cocktails. Midwesterners followed suit—with a twist. The Huron Mountain Club (HMC) would provide privacy and access to nature to a *group* of wealthy, socially appropriate families. Each family would have its own "cabin," but members would eat communally and share access to the club's forests and lakes. In the Adirondacks and Michigan's north woods, "camps expressed a complex blend of assertiveness over the natural environment and submission to it," wrote the *Social Register Observer* in 2007. They were luxurious and comfortable, yet they blended seamlessly into the wilderness their builders wished to experience. They also presented an array of social challenges and were so ubiquitous in the 1910s and 1920s that Emily Post devoted an entire chapter of the 1928 edition of *Etiquette* to the proper behavior of guests in a camp setting. (Hint: One must disguise one's hatred of red ants.)[1]

To create their "camp" the HMC's founders purchased a tract of UP acreage encompassing several inland lakes and a chunk of Lake Superior shoreline. They arrived in 1887 via the big lake, chose a site at the mouth of a river in the general vicinity of Big Bay (later famous as the town in Otto Preminger's 1959 thriller *Anatomy of a Murder*), and began the labor-intensive business of wilderness construction. The UP still had few roads, club land was accessible only by water, and building a dock that would withstand Superior's fury had gotten no easier since Robert Graveraet and Peter White's attempt in 1849. The resourceful John Longyear designed a special ferry called the *What's Wanted* to carry visitors, workmen, and building supplies from steamer to shore, and construction began.

By 1893 a rustic wood and stone clubhouse stood ready, and members were beginning to construct Adirondack-style "cabins" on a dramatic spit of land where a local river meets the Lake Superior shoreline. Membership was sluggish at first, but in 1896 Carter Harrison II, the mayor of Chicago during the World's Columbian Exposition, visited the club in the company of another former Chicago mayor, Hempstead Washburne. After a nude swim and a bracing wrangle with some lumberjacks over a case of champagne, the two Hizzoners pronounced themselves enchanted with the HMC, commissioned their own cabins, and so efficiently spread tales of the club's glories that its planned membership of fifty filled up quickly.

It's still full today. The Huron Mountain Club remains a pinnacle of Midwest society, a lodestar for a cluster of families from Detroit, Chicago, and further afield—and entirely off the radar for everyone else. Its membership cultivates a purposeful privacy rare in this instant-information age. Descriptions of the club are never mentioned in the press—not even *Town & Country*—never tweeted about or identified in images on social media. If you have not been invited to visit by a club member you will never find it. When invited, you will need careful directions to locate a small wooden gatehouse in the middle of nowhere, and after you've been admitted by the gatekeeper, a few minutes to make your way through the forest to the lakeshore. This all adds to the secret, untouched quality of the place when it finally appears quite suddenly, as if out of nowhere—a midwestern Brigadoon on the shore of an endless inland sea.

It could be any year in this charming waterside village connected by wooden bridges and plank walkways. Dwellings are multiroomed masterpieces of the Adirondack style incorporating stone chimneys, graying log or shingle walls inlaid with twig patterns, branch railings, and balustrades, finished with rustic screened porches. The long, open veranda of the clubhouse, a charming, slightly scruffy time capsule bristling with deer heads where members dressed for dinner well into the 1990s, faces the rolling breakers of the lake. (As dining has always been communal many of the older HMC cabins were built without kitchens.) Members' cabins line the river and the lakefront, while outbuildings and dormitories for the help are tucked discreetly out of sight among the trees. The club's staff has always been capacious—generations of UP working-class teens started their careers there—but the babysitting, maintenance help, and boxed lunches it now supplies are a pale version of the service enjoyed by HMC families of earlier days. At the time LG was seeking entry butlers, chauffeurs, and chambermaids were provided to members who came up to Marquette by private railcar from points south.

Those members were carefully chosen using criteria that excluded many applicants, including several well-known American millionaires. Harvey Firestone (the Ohio tire king) and inventor Thomas Edison were rejected by the HMC, as was auto magnate Henry Ford. The club likely had no wish to find newspaper reporters camped outside the gate, nor could they be sure possessors of new wealth would adhere to the unspoken codes of behavior of the WASP establishment. When Henry Ford finally gained admittance to the HMC in 1929 after using his influence to prevent a state highway from being built on club land, he built a too large, too fancy cabin designed by famed Detroit architect Albert Kahn that is still considered tacky by old-timers. But in 1917, around the time LG applied for membership, the wealthiest man in the Midwest was still on the outside looking in.

While LG may not have known the fate of Ford's first application, he should have suspected that his own would not be met with cheers. His wealth was barely a decade old and his mixed parentage and Semitic surname and its meaning ("merchant" or "businessman" in German) were hardly advantageous. Nor would he have forgotten the local vitriol that had greeted his family's purchase of First National Bank of Marquette stock, as well as Peter White's ensuing "resignation" from the very club he was now attempting to join. But having experienced an almost miraculous rise in his fortunes in a city where money talked, newspapers sang his praises, du Ponts mixed with Kaufmans, and no one questioned his sanitized version of his family history, LG may have come to believe that anything was possible. He applied for membership in the Huron Mountain Club and looked forward to a favorable reply.

What happened next has become the stuff of UP legend. When the inevitable rejection letter arrived, LG turned to architectural one-upmanship on a titanic scale. His exclusion from the Huron Mountain Club was the catalyst for the creation of the largest, most elaborate Adirondack-style lodge in the country. Stung by the club's high-handedness and sitting on $150 million in assets (close to $4 billion today), LG vowed to build himself a UP palace for hunting, fishing, and entertaining that would eclipse the genteel cabins and creaky boathouses of the HMC by a country mile and show its members what real money looked like. His wilderness lodge would blow the Huron Mountain Club, and everything it stood for, out of the water.

He already had the land—ten thousand wooded acres encompassing several miles of Lake Superior shoreline and a small offshore island—in the township of Birch, Michigan, fifteen miles northwest of Marquette. LG had purchased this tract back in 1905, when he still assumed Marquette would be his year-round home, and in the process may have piled another log on the fire of John Longyear's smoldering dislike. The land had been Longyear's (at one time he owned 3 percent of the entire state of Michigan) and, knowing that a Longyear would never sell anything to a Kaufman, LG reportedly arranged for someone else to "buy" the land and then "sell" it immediately to himself. The new owner of the ten thousand acres would be revealed to Longyear only when it was too late.

This financial sleight of hand would have been communicated

to Longyear by post as he and his family were no longer full-time UP residents. After the 1900 drowning death of their son in Lake Superior the Longyears turned their backs on Marquette, but not on their sixty-four-room turreted Marquette sandstone mansion sitting on grounds designed by landscape architect Frederick Law Olmsted (of Central Park fame). The massive house was taken apart in 1903, packed in 190 railcars, and moved to Brookline, Massachusetts, where it was reassembled, further enlarged, and sited in another Olmsted landscape. (It still stands and now serves as a museum dedicated to the life of Mrs. Longyear's personal heroine, Christian Science founder Mary Baker Eddy.) But even with his house and family in Brookline, John Longyear's connection to the HMC remained strong. He was an influential member there until his death in 1922 and so was on hand to vote against LG's bid for membership and to help pen his uncompromising rejection letter, which reportedly included the word "never."

The letter was a blow not just to LG but also to Marie, who had her own score to settle: LG's lakeside acreage had come with a rustic, mouse-infested hunting and fishing camp and for years LG and his brother Sam had repaired to this woodland snuggery for sporting adventures. But in 1917 Sam (the brother who had married meatpacking heiress Una Libby) upped the ante: he bought his own thousand-acre tract adjoining LG's land and built an elaborate hunting and fishing lodge on Lake Superior at the mouth of the Big Garlic River. His three-story, five-thousand-square-foot log manse had its own power plant, fifteen bedrooms, five bathrooms, a large kitchen and a butler's pantry with a panel of call buttons that brought servants running, and a walk-in fridge cooled with ice harvested from the lake. The woods lit up when guests arrived by train and boat for festive weekends of hunting, fishing, and partying in luxury. Everyone liked Una—the Chicago swells who filled her fifteen bedrooms, and the UP locals, who appreciated her friendliness and lack of pretension. All of Marquette mourned when her beloved matched pair of Belgian horses strayed out onto the imperfectly frozen lake one winter and drowned.

Una's new establishment was said to have made Marie Kaufman furious.[2] The Princess of Lake Geneva was used to being the girl with the biggest house in any community and she no doubt disliked being upstaged by another Chicago heiress—especially one who associated with townies and had a nobody for a husband. It was embarrassing having nowhere except the Marquette house and a backwoods camp to invite New York friends for sporting weekends. A cabin at the exclusive HMC would have fixed the problem and bested Una, but that apparently was not to be. As competitive as her husband (or likely more so), Marie wanted to make sure everyone in Marquette, Chicago, and New York knew the man *she'd* married was the true king of the UP. When LG began to plan his rustic Versailles, Marie was right beside him.

The couple decided to build on the site of LG's lakeside camp—a dramatic rocky peninsula of sandstone and granite stretching out into the lake toward picturesque Saux Head Island. True, the island's history was anything but picturesque: it was said to have been named by Chippewas who had avenged a murder there perpetrated by the Sauks, a tribe from the Green Bay area, by displaying the Sauks' bloodied heads on the island's many pine trees. But its presence would afford some protection from Superior's relentless wave action, and the point's unique geography would provide sweeping water views on three sides. It was so obvious a place to build that LG would later make it part of his press-ready UP life story. Skipping neatly over the debacle of the HMC, he would tell reporters that he had long dreamed that "someday he might have a little cabin among the pines and near the shore of Lake Superior and he had the location pictured—a granite point that thrust its rugged hand into the lake."[3] Sometimes he added that the place had been a favorite boyhood picnic spot—a charming detail, but likely apocryphal. In the 1880s the point was three-plus hours from Marquette by horse and buggy and was part of someone else's hunting and fishing camp.

Now it was his, and he needed an architect who could make the most of it. There was no one appropriate working in the UP and the distance from Manhattan to Michigan made the services of the eastern architects inconvenient. A Chicago architect was the obvious solution and once LG turned his attention to the Windy City, Benjamin Marshall (1874–1944) of the firm Marshall and Fox quickly floated to the top of the list. Chicago was dotted with country clubs, theaters, North Shore estates, and hotels (including the famous Drake) designed by Marshall for wealthy clients like LG and Marie, and his elegant revival style would have been well-known to the couple—along with Marshall himself: boyishly handsome and stylishly dressed, he was a member of all the right Chicago clubs and a fixture at all of the best parties, and he had likely crossed paths with the Kaufmans many times.

They might have seen him arriving in one of his snazzy Packard automobiles (after the publication of Fitzgerald's novel he ordered one in Gatsby Yellow stripped down in "hotrod" style) and were likely bidden to his lavish studio parties. Marshall entertained constantly—in his role as rainmaker for Marshall and Fox and from personal inclination—and thanks to his many theatrical commissions, he could produce celebs like Fred Astaire, Irene Castle, and Ethel Barrymore to ramp up the glamour of his gatherings. Even Edward, Prince of Wales (later the Duke of Windsor), made his way to Marshall's studio, a pink stucco extravaganza overlooking a private yacht harbor in Lake Michigan near Chicago. In this aerie an Egyptian porch, an

East Indian lounging room, an Algerian-tiled swimming pool, and a tropical garden awaited. The building also boasted a full-size stage for visiting performers and all of the latest gadgets: at the touch of a button, a table would rise up through the floor from the kitchen below, heaped with food, hot and ready to serve. Rivers of bootleg booze were also on tap, but the host was always quietly sober. Marshall did not drink and was known to tip the contents of his glass into the nearest potted plant when no one was looking.

Marshall's glamour and connections likely appealed to LG, as did his personal bona fides: the architect was a midwesterner of about the same vintage, he too had not gone to college, and he had made much of his money in business by owning, as well as designing, a number of grand apartment buildings on Lake Shore Drive. (These buildings were so well-known that among Chicago's wealthy they were referred to simply as "209," "1550," etc.) Finally, having seen his work, LG would have been confident that Marshall could combine the best aspects of the Adirondack style and produce a grand, elegant example of the genre, replete with modern conveniences. As for the technical challenges of erecting a giant log house on a rocky site, which—in spite of its island windbreak—was constantly buffeted by wind and water, Marshall and Fox came equipped: Charles Fox was a graduate of the engineering school at MIT and a specialist in the art of construction, with many helpful ideas about concrete foundations and steel armatures.

Marshall's design did not disappoint. It was classic Adirondack—but bigger and grander: many eastern great camps are clusters of single-story structures connected by covered walkways, but for this site, and this client, Marshall envisioned a large single building—a sort of Newport cottage of logs and stone. The plans he presented showed a twenty-six-thousand-square-foot, two-story, L-shaped lodge of fifty-plus rooms. Soaring log walls, crenelated with bays, were elevated on a tall foundation of lake stones and capped with a slate roof dotted with chimneys in the same rustic stone. The design was vintage Marshall, but the architect had also borrowed from the best—that is, a much-admired camp designed by Davis, McGrath and Shepard for William A. Read in 1906 and featured in *House and Garden* in 1907. The Read camp's two-story plan, great room, owners' bedrooms at the corners closest to the lake, and octagonal room all enhanced his plan. The rustic exterior read as an architectural outgrowth of its site and the forest at its back. A cluster of outbuildings housing its water system, laundry, heat and power plant, and extra lodging for servants blended into the trees. LG's lodge would showcase its owner's wealth and his ability to provide a luxurious, elegant experience for family and guests in the middle of nowhere. Log walls and lake-stone chimneys would radiate rusticity and simplicity, while occupants enjoyed modern bathrooms and a servant ratio of three to one.

What LG's new build would never be was a "camp." From the beginning, he referred to his wilderness manse as a "lodge" and in years to come he would correct anyone who used the wrong nomenclature. (This may have been a personal preference or perhaps he felt the designation was more appropriate for a single-building configuration.) When Marshall and Fox didn't get the memo, someone hastily set them straight: in the firm's contract ledger, on a drawing of Marshall's design dated December 14, 1920, and labeled "LG Kaufman Camp Birch, Michigan," the word "camp" is crossed out and "lodge" added. In the same ledger is a letter stating the firm's terms of engagement: Marshall and Fox was to be paid 10 percent of the cost of the project (budgeted at $2–5 million). In return, the architectural firm would provide all required drawings and a man to supervise construction on-site.[4]

Supervision was key as hundreds of men would soon be at

work in the woods at the edge of the Big Lake. After the site was cleared and leveled in 1919, the first team to arrive was under the command of a local, Swedish-born concrete specialist named Gus Anderson (known as "Cement Gus"), who was tasked with the job of laying the lodge's massive foundation. Per engineer Charles Fox's instructions, the concrete he laid was more like that in a Detroit factory than in any private home. Anderson poured it six feet thick on the lake sides and four and a half feet elsewhere, then poured extra concrete between each floor. Into these acres of cement were embedded steel beams that ran from the floor of the basement to the top of the lodge's roof, carefully reinforced at every juncture and branching out as they rose so that steel snaked through every wall and supported every foot of the new structure.

None of these underpinnings was visible. They were hidden within walls of perfectly matched logs—the largest and best on the market. As architects of other great camps had done before

Octagonal room of Granot Loma under construction in 1920. Collection of Peter Kaufman.

them, Marshall and Fox had specified logs of Idaho pine, also known as Western white pine, a particularly long-lived tree that produced logs of exceptional size. They grew thousands of miles away, but thanks to LG's seat on the board of the Chicago and Erie Railroad this was no problem. The giant logs were sourced in Oregon, individually wrapped in burlap, loaded onto railcars, and transported with care and dispatch across the country to Marquette. Soon a forest's worth of Idaho pine was arriving by truck and horse-drawn wagon to the building site. There, each log was examined for imperfections, then handed over to a waiting team of Finnish "log butchers."

Fortunately for LG, there were many of these talented craftsmen in the UP at this time. Local mining jobs had attracted Finnish immigrants to the area since the late nineteenth century,

Second story of Granot Loma under construction in 1920.
Collection of Peter Kaufman.

and by 1920 Finns represented its largest foreign-born group. They brought with them the traditional Finnish skills of "scribing" and "hewing" a log so that it fit snugly against its neighbor (avoiding the uneven, drafty log construction familiar to any reader of *Little House on the Prairie*). Using an ax, a mallet, and a "gouge" (a chisel with a rounded blade) and employing age-old techniques learned from parents and grandparents, log butchers from Finnish communities in nearby Negaunee and Ishpeming fashioned LG's Oregonian imports into artfully tight, beautifully fitted log walls.

Finnish-born Nestor Kallioinen was the leader of this Scandinavian crew. He could make logs "melt" together and could place the most intricate log work in the lodge's most prominent locations. Fascinated by his technique, LG sat on his lodge's construction site for hours, watching him work. (LG might have been less riveted had he known that "his" Nestor was working on cabins at the Huron Mountain Club at the same time.) It was Nestor who followed the architects' deceptively simple instructions that "all ends of logs around windows and door openings and at corners of building to be cut uneven and all valleys to be curved and ridges to form an uneven line."[5] These details added greatly to the lodge's rustic, handmade charm, but the right look wasn't easy to achieve. Too perfect and the lodge would read modern and sterile, too uneven and the look would be sloppy. Thanks to Nestor the level of imperfection was perfect.

Stone masons—many of them Irish—were an equally important crew. The log walls nearest the water were erected atop massive foundations of lake stones—sometimes flush with the logs above, sometimes jutting out to form narrow terraces. Composed of thousands of similarly sized, gently rounded stones in grays and whites, they echoed the lake bed, carefully chosen to meld with the lodge's rocky site and form a pleasing contrast with the color of the logs. Inside, the masons topped many of the lodge's thirty fireplaces with visible chimney stacks of the same stones, including a massive fireplace in the great room—big enough to camp in and boasting a built-in stone fireside seat. Similar lake stones formed the lodge's multiple outside chimneys and the rustic signage that proclaimed its unusual name. Embedded in a chimney above the main entrance (visible to those arriving by carriage or motor car) and in a foundation wall on the lake side (visible to those arriving by boat) were stone panels bearing the name of the new lodge: Granot Loma.

That name, which would rivet my attention so many decades later, had little in common with the Knollwoods and Kamp Kill Kares of the Adirondacks—it does not even sound American. But it is distinctive and, once understood, clever and rather endearing. Having noted that his lodge was built on a flat-topped hill or loma, partially made of granite, LG put his "treasures" front and center and used the first letters of the names of his first five children to create a more personal spelling of "Granite Hill." The GR is from Graveraet, the AN is from Ann, the OT is from Otto Young, the LO is from Louis, and the MA is from Marie Joan. (By the time construction of the lodge was underway Marie had given birth to three more daughters, but LG's elegant wordplay was set in stone, and the names Juliet, Marie Louise, and Jane were not incorporated into the signage.)

During construction Marie was often at the work site and she took a particular interest in the selection of stones for the lodge's interior chimneys. Commandeering a team of men, she would have herself rowed out into the lake, peer down into the clear, cold water, and point imperiously at her choices. The chosen stones would be hauled into the boat and the process would begin all over again. An oft-told tale of the raising of the "keystone" for the great room fireplace may be apocryphal but then again maybe not. It certainly aligns with Marie's personality and imperious worldview: after demanding to be rowed into deeper water than usual Marie spotted a very large stone and signaled her approval. The men protested—it was too large, the water was too deep, they couldn't possibly raise it—but Marie was adamant. Every day she sent a team out to fetch the giant stone and every day they returned empty-handed. After a while the standoff was no longer about stones and the men decided that two could play Marie's game. A stone was procured (some say the men found it in shallow water down the beach) and it was presented to Marie as her deep-water prize. If she recognized the substitution she gave no sign, and "her" keystone was installed with a flourish above the largest fireplace in the lodge.[6]

Stone selection was equally important to LG, but he took a different approach: when he noticed a large stone crisscrossed with distinctive quartz veins on the lake bottom, he did not ask everyone to stop what they were doing and attempt to drag it in. He ordered up a steam dredge and retrieved it, then placed the rock near the lodge's entrance, where with the addition of a jet of water gushing from its top it became a favorite frolicking place for his children and grandchildren. Another of his projects—finishing the lodge's many chimney tops with whimsical stone "ducks"—caused no angst. The search for multiple pairs of rounded stones, sized and shaped so that one sat ducklike atop the other, was remembered fondly by those who took part.

Otherwise, the mood on Granot Loma's construction site seems to have fluctuated. The sequential firing of four contractors (reportedly the work of Marie, who did not think anybody was working fast enough) likely made life difficult, but there is also the testimony of Wilfred Fleury, who was employed as an on-site timekeeper during the summers of 1922 and 1923. Fleury earned $60 a month clocking in and out the 250 workers building Granot Loma, plus bed and board in the workers' barracks. He had nothing but positive memories of his experience

("Food was good and the coffee pot was always on") and he basked in the lodge's reflected glory: "All of the materials they used on the project were the best, there was no expense spared," he proudly told a reporter many decades later, adding that as he worked, he knew he was helping to build "something of lasting significance."[7]

And so it was: the National Register of Historic Places would later call Granot Loma "the ultimate expression of the American wilderness camp" but LG's lodge was even more than that.[8] Completed in 1923 (finishing and decorating went on until 1927), it was a rustic work of art with quality, imagination, and unusual details, inside and out. Log walls—laid in imaginative patterns, chinked in red or hand hammered to the texture of repoussé silver—rose above floors of hand-pegged, highly polished oak. The stairway risers were also logs—flat on top, stripped of their bark, and polished until they shone. In one of its rooms, what appears to be an over-mantel "painting" of the lake is actually a glass-paned window cut into a chimney, while smoke is routed to either side. Wrought-iron hinges (said to be designed by LG himself in the shapes of arrows and serpents), grates, latches, and torchieres, made by hand by an on-site blacksmith, finish walls, lamps, and doors. The mantels of the great room and library fireplaces are deck timbers from the *Independence*, a historic ship that was hauled over the portage near Sault Ste. Marie before the locks were installed and became the first steamship on Lake Superior. After her boiler exploded in 1853, the wreck attracted many history-minded salvagers and pieces of the ship are preserved all over Michigan.

Rustic furniture and decorations, also made on-site, echoed the acres of forest outside: in the hands of Nestor Kallioinen and his men, logs, twigs, bark, branches, and roots became one-of-a-kind balustrades, balconies, light fixtures, mantels, wall coverings, beds, and chairs. As their fathers and grandfathers had taught them, they selected beautifully shaped pine roots and branches, placed them in gently smoldering bonfires until the resin dripped out, removed the ashes and char from the surfaces, and polished the wood to a mellow finish. Then they let their imagination go wild: electric bulbs were mounted in polished tree knots, tree trunks were hollowed out and became newel posts, electrified so that they glowed from within. Balconies and balustrades were ornamented with friezes of writhing tree limbs, bed frames—including LG's four-poster extravaganza—bristled with swirling patterns of pine and birch branches; a huge pine root was enlivened with carved animals, electrified and hung as the great room chandelier. Every guest room featured a different pattern of logs—vertical, horizontal, birch, cedar, or pine. No two of the house's thirty mantelpieces were the same. In LG's bathroom birchbark walls and a bathtub sunk into an artful "pond" of lake stones created a fanciful "Indian" camp at the edge of a forest stream.

The lodge also featured an "Indian Room" lined with logs in a teepee-like pattern, a center totem pole, and a teepee fireplace of steel and stucco so artfully fashioned that it seemed to be made of folded hides. Portraits said to be of well-known but unidentified tribal chiefs were everywhere—on stones set into chimneys, on doorknobs, on the slate floor, and on canvases hung in corridors and featured prominently near the main staircase.

Many were the work of Orry-Kelly, a flamboyant Australian who trained as a painter before turning to stage and costume design. After meeting LG (perhaps through Benjamin Marshall or the other showbiz connections that, as we shall soon see, the Kaufman sons were making), Kelly took a break from his work on Broadway (and a love affair with the young Cary Grant) and became Granot Loma's artist-in-residence, as well as a family friend. One of his paintings, a picture of a handsome Native American man, is said to be a portrait of his patron and the face

A carved, rustic bedstead made from tree roots and branches by Nestor Kallioinen and his team for Granot Loma. Collection of Peter Kaufman.

A close-up of another rustic bedstead carved with animals, fish, and faces. Granot Loma, ca. 1925. With the permission of Jack Deo, Superior View Photography, Marquette, Michigan.

does look familiar. As Kelly sketched and painted in the halls of Granot Loma, the family could not have known that they were housing a future Oscar winner. A decade after his UP gig, Orry-Kelly went to Hollywood and became one of the great movie costume designers of the 1930s, 1940s, and 1950s. He worked on dozens of films, including *Casablanca* and *Jezebel*, and took home Oscars for *An American in Paris*, *Les Girls*, and *Some Like It Hot*.

Orry-Kelly's chiefs looked down on a small museum's worth of Indigenous objects, rugs, and textiles. Acquired by LG (often direct from their makers) on trips to the Southwest, war blankets, headdresses, tomahawks, bows and arrows, and examples of Indigenous beadwork enlivened nearly every room in the house. Bedcovers were buckskin with intricate beaded patterns, rugs—flat woven, with geometric, symmetrical

The octagonal "Indian Room" at Granot Loma, ca. 1925. Note the wigwam fireplace and handmade iron light fixtures. Collection of Peter Kaufman.

patterns—dotted every floor, and the soaring great room took its color cues from a Chippewa war blanket in orange, green, yellow, red, and black draped over its largest sofa. The curtains and upholstery—nearly everything in the room—reprised the blanket's traditional shapes and colors. In fact, this five-color combination was clearly a favorite of LG's, as the pattern on the heavy Czechoslovakian china designed for use at the lodge was glazed in the same hues.

Although many Adirondack-style camps contained the occasional Indigenous object, this steep tilt toward Native American culture and design was not typical. When reporters or guests queried LG about it, he would invariably reference his UP childhood and the glimpses of "Indian" life he remembered from boyhood tramps through the country near Marquette. He would explain that the carved chandelier in the great room was made from the root of a giant tree beneath which he had picnicked as a boy (picnicking was a favorite trope) and that the pointed steel and stucco teepee fireplace in what he called the "Indian Room" had been made to resemble those he'd seen many years ago, on the site where Granot Loma now stood. In fact, the Anishinaabe of the UP had favored domed wigwams, and it is known that when LG was young the land upon which Granot Loma was built belonged to a white man. LG likely turned to this sheaf of invented memories to obscure the true reason for his interest in these art objects and artifacts—the fact that his own mother was of Indigenous descent. "Native Americans were part of his heritage and he was proud of his past," one of his granddaughters remembers, "but it was not spoken of in those days."[9] Perhaps LG had found a way to honor his beloved mother without showing his genealogical hand.

While Granot Loma was a paean to LG's past and a rustic wonderland, it was also a modern country house of nearly fifty rooms, equipped for entertaining at scale. There was a his and hers master suite with two bedrooms and bathrooms off a private sitting room, a children's wing decorated with images from Mother Goose, so many guest bedrooms that they had to be numbered for easy reference, and fifteen bathrooms. In the great room and dining room giant lakeside windows were constructed to "disappear" into pockets in the walls, opening up those spaces to breezes on hot summer days. There was a billiard room with a custom billiard table inlaid with silver and mother-of-pearl, a library, a card room, a kitchen with capacious iceboxes and stainless steel sinks, and an adjacent butler's pantry convenient to the servants' wing.

The basement was a world of its own: it was fitted out with white tiled massage rooms, "water therapy" rooms (where guests were therapeutically assaulted with jets of water), and a sauna, and of course the most up-to-date weight-loss appliances—a belt massager and a steam box. As Prohibition was looming during construction, Benjamin Marshall provided side-by-side walk-in liquor closets sealed with webs of interlocking steel gizmos usually reserved for bank vaults. Labeled "LG Kaufman" and "Mrs. LG Kaufman," they were large enough to receive the entire contents of a New York City liquor store that LG purchased, shipped to Michigan by train, and, presumably, divided into two equal caches as soon as the house was finished. There was also a plant that created electricity for the house and a large boathouse equipped with a nifty system of rails that allowed boats to be winched up under the lodge and out again on command, launched into the calm waters inside Granot Loma's concrete breakwater.

The underpinnings of this luxury were housed separately. Granot Loma's village of outbuildings was constructed of local pine logs—not fancy Oregonian imports—but they too displayed full scribe Scandinavian log work, slate roofs, and chimneys made of lake stones. A pump house containing a

The garage at Granot Loma, ca. 1925. Courtesy of Superior View Photography, Marquette, Michigan.

seventy-thousand-gallon holding tank filled with lake water provided a constant supply to bathrooms, kitchens, and the lodge's freestanding laundry, with hot water on demand thanks to a coal-fired electrical and heating plant that consumed a ton of fuel every day. A garage had spaces for twenty-four cars with sleeping quarters for twenty-four male servants above.

A guesthouse offering eight bedrooms—each with its own fireplace—and four bathrooms handled visitor overflow. A charming playhouse was headquarters for the younger Kaufman children. Adults had to stoop to get inside, where they would find a fireplace and a child-size spiral staircase to an upper floor. There was plenty of acreage for everything: LG inherited Sam and Una Libby Kaufman's camp in 1922 and later purchased a large tract of contiguous land. By 1928 he owned more than twelve thousand acres, including the site of a once-thriving logging village—which provided endless room for hunting and fishing and LG's latest interest: a gentleman's farm.

In the early twentieth century no American millionaire's spread was complete without one of these agricultural playlands. *Home and Field*, a sort of *House Beautiful* for affluent agronomists, was then chockablock with photos of architecturally significant barns, tidy managers' cottages, and herds of prize cows. Having made millions in urban and industrial settings, American railroad tycoons, bankers, and manufacturers were eager to get "back to the land." The resulting farms were showcases for agricultural design and pleasurable exercises in scientific dabbling and one-upmanship. Fruit and veg for the table were nice, but the meat and potatoes of such places were the study of scientific breeding and the effects of feed and living conditions on animal weight and egg and milk production. The right mixtures would produce record-breaking layers, richer milk, and sweeter butter and, importantly, trounce the entries of other millionaires at local state fairs. Colonel Robert Montgomery, the owner of Ardrossan, a large estate near Philadelphia with an elegant gentleman's farm, summed up the creed: "My personal pride prompts me to sell a better product if I can than anybody else's," he wrote of his prize dairy herd, "as I never like to have to do with anything unless it is the best."[10]

Farmer Kaufman too was obsessed with the best, especially as for him, Loma Farms was an avenue of inclusion. In some company the man from Michigan was still an outsider, and this elaborate piece of kit was another way "in." Thus equipped, he could chat about winter feed and milk production with Samuel du Pont, responding as an equal when du Pont talked of barn hygiene and crop rotation at his Delaware estate. "For new money, those who couldn't get into the right clubs, a gentleman's farm was a way of competing," says Winterthur historian Jeff

Groff. "It was a way to rub elbows with the right sort."[11] Just preparing to be a farmer could start that ball rolling, and in the mid-1920s LG and Marie sailed off to Europe, where they spent weeks studying pedigreed breeds at farms owned by pedigreed people. The Kaufmans bought Percheron horses in France and chickens in Holland, then came home and embarked on a similar tour of "model farms" of East Coast aristocrats.

The look of a farm was important, and thanks to his recent road trip, LG was aware of all appropriate options. He'd seen farms designed in the style of the house to which they were attached, and others, like the one at Sagamore, the Vanderbilts' Adirondack camp, that were architecturally distinct. LG chose plan B (log and stone barns would be impractical and expensive) and in 1925, having sited Loma Farms on gently sloping, newly cleared land a mile from the lodge, he hired the Architectural Department of the Loudon Machinery Company of Fairfield, Iowa (they'd done tractor magnate John Deere proud on his Illinois farm), to design his new complex. The Bartlett Construction Company of Eau Claire, Wisconsin, was given the building contract and promised a sizable bonus if the work was finished ahead of schedule. The entire farm was built between April and October 1927.

Its fourteen buildings were in the Dutch Colonial Revival style, topped with gambrel roofs crowned with cupolas. The vibe was quaint and traditional, but Loudon had clearly consulted the Gentleman's Farm Bible, *Modern Farm Buildings* by Alfred Hopkins, and there was method in his design: built of red-brown hollow tile of vitrified clay (drier, warmer, and fireproof), the farm's structures could be grouped conveniently close together without fear of mass conflagration. (A serious fire, apparently ignited by the sun's rays on a bottle of alcohol on a windowsill, destroyed the horse barn in 1935. No neighboring structures went up in flames.) All facades faced south to make

The main barn, Loma Farms, 1927. Courtesy of Superior View Photography, Marquette, Michigan.

use of passive solar heating, and the barns, like many LG and Marie had seen on the farms of the rich and famous, were lined with white fireproof tile. The stall floors in the dairy barn were made of flexible, comfortable cork—a luxury even in this rarified world.

Other luxuries abounded: LG's one hundred purebred Guernsey cows were milked by machine and skim milk was piped directly from the creamery to the piggery, the spotless home to LG's two hundred Yorkshire pigs. "No we didn't think a piggery could be conducted in such a . . . state of cleanliness, but this one is," marveled the *Mining Journal*.[12] Even its manure pits were a sight to behold. Milk destined for sale was poured over tubes through which cold water (piped from Lake Superior) ran continuously, before being bottled and capped. The five hundred quarts of rich, unpasteurized milk that Loma Farms produced every day were trucked daily to Marquette, Big Bay, and (rather ironically) the Huron Mountain Club, but in spite of a butterfat content so high you could skim off the top of the bottle and whip it like cream, Loma Farms milk never came close to paying for itself. Aware that what he sold for a nickel a quart was costing him nearly a dollar to produce, LG made good-natured fun of his agricultural cash suck, advising guests who requested milk with a meal to "ask for champagne . . . it's cheaper!!"[13]

Much of LG's money went toward manpower: at its operational peak 250 men worked at Loma Farms, manning the slaughterhouse, the icehouse, the maple sugaring house, the garage, and the tool house. Others, dressed in special white suits, were tasked with shining up the hooves and horns of the cattle with emery boards. Still others worked in the poultry house, tending to Loma Farms' six hundred birds, and in the horse barn, taking care of the sleek saddle horses and the sturdy Percherons kept for farm work. The farm boasted an office for its full-time vet, a house for its British manager, W. W. Blake Arckoll (British managers had extra cachet), and a boardinghouse for workers where meals were served on another custom set of dishes—white ironware this time, with dark red and green edging and the name "Loma Farms" in dark red lettering. High above this bustling agricultural village, an electric Tiffany clock kept everyone on schedule and custom weathervanes signaled which animal— cows, chickens, pigs, and so on—were being raised in the barns below.

All of these creatures were subject to ongoing experiments in housing, breeding, and feeding and the results were tabulated on various charts. In addition to besting fellow millionaires at Midwest fairs, LG was determined to demonstrate that, in spite of its poor soil and short growing season, Michigan's Upper Peninsula was the right place to achieve agricultural greatness. "Since my boyhood days in this country," he told the *Mining Journal*, "I have believed that our soil and climate were as good as any in the land and that they could be made to produce good crops and fine cattle."[14] Putting his money where their mouths were, he fed his pigs oats and barley—specialties of the UP climate—added UP alfalfa to the menu in the barns the following season, and carefully tabulated the results in weight and meat quality.

Above all LG was eager to see Loma Farms become "a testing laboratory for the dairymen and farmers of the Upper Peninsula where they can come and see the latest scientific discoveries in the care of livestock and poultry put into practical use."[15] It was a nice thought, but impractical. Most of those "discoveries" worked best with purebred animals—a type of farming too pricey for most local farmers to practice. For farmers like LG, pigs and cattle with the proper pedigree reflected their own superior attributes and their families' superior standing in the social hierarchy, and they never raised anything else. Few others could do the same: like the duchess at the flower show whose staff of gardeners allow her to win "Best Rose" every year, LG never acknowledged the financial requirements involved when he crowed over the dozens of blue ribbons his purebred specimens won at state fairs all over the Midwest. He continued to insist that changes in daily practice—not massive buying power and 250 staff—were the keys to farming success. As usual the *Mining Journal* fell into line: "Loma Farms," it crowed, "are an agricultural experiment station de lux proving that stock raising from purebred cattle is a practical and not a visionary idea."[16]

In August 1930 the experiment station de lux threw open its doors and welcomed two thousand UP farmers to the first (and very likely the last) Loma Farms Field Day. The event was organized to educate attendees, showcase the farming prowess of the UP (and, of course, of Loma Farms itself), and keep pace with Samuel du Pont, who had hosted a similar open house at his farm at Winterthur. Every county in the Upper Peninsula was represented on the day—an impressive turnout, even if many had come to see the famous LG Kaufman in person and/ or enjoy the free lunch. The *Detroit Free Press* sent a reporter, who dubbed LG's agricultural spread "Michigan's greatest farm" and opined that it "ranks with the best of agricultural and dairying and stock raising projects in the United States."[17] A proud LG addressed the crowd in the cadences of an agricultural college dean: "Our hope is . . . that what you see here will help you in solving the problems on your farms" and that "Loma Farms would demonstrate to you the value of purebred breeding stock for cattle, hogs and poultry . . . and convince you that the upper peninsula lacks nothing to qualify as a good place to breed first class stock."[18] Finally, the *Mining Journal*, that cheerleader for anything Kaufman, sounded a mild note of skepticism: "Mr. Kaufman has insisted that despite the fine buildings that make up Loma Farms, the feeding and breeding of livestock shall be carried on in a way which any farmer can emulate without feeling that the resources at the command of Loma Farms make it impossible for him to successfully copy."[19]

Still, the average farmers were glad they had come: they ate their free lunch to the rousing strains of "Over There," "The Stars and Stripes Forever," and the University of Michigan's fight song, courtesy of Marquette's high school band, and enjoyed a parade of Loma Farms' prize-winning Guernsey and Holstein cows (including the one for which LG had paid $8,100—double the price of most houses in Marquette at the time). Milling crowds ogled the private fire trucks standing at the ready, the creamery sparkling with tile and polished metal, the overhead trolleys that carried in hay and removed manure, the "battery brooders" (a cutting-edge cage system for hens), and the scientifically designed ventilation and lighting systems. Junior Farmers, age twelve to sixteen, received prizes for the best cow and pig from Marie Kaufman's own hands and their fathers clustered around farm manager Blake Arckoll, receiving instruction and advice.

As LG likely knew, Mr. Arckoll's honesty was not always exemplary (he had been fired from several East Coast farms for skimming money off the top of cattle sales), but he had other qualities. Not only did he serve as a judge at many fairs where Loma Farms animals were in competition, he was a happy reminder of the defeat of John Longyear, whose perennially struggling dairy farm near Big Bay Arckoll had managed until its demise in 1915. Longyear had been dead for over a decade, but the memory of LG's rejection from the Huron Mountain Club was not. It must have been satisfying to succeed so spectacularly—with the same manager—in the space where Longyear had failed. Gleaming, bustling, lavishly staffed—Loma Farms was indeed spectacular, but then how could it have been anything else? It was the agricultural extension of Granot Loma, where life itself was spectacular—and then some.

5

WEST EGG IN THE UPPER PENINSULA

Loma Farms had been only a gleam in LG's eye when the Kaufmans first arrived at their brand-new wilderness lodge and sank into a world of luxury. Granot Loma might be miles from civilization, but it was run like any mansion in Newport or Oyster Bay. Those upstairs could ring for service any time night or day and someone downstairs, ever attentive to the call-board in the butler's pantry, would snap to it. Phalanxes of housemaids made beds, dusted the rustic furniture, and, under the direction of the housekeeper, packed and unpacked for female family members and guests; a team of valets, working under a butler and his assistant, fetched and carried all over the house and unpacked for male residents. One servant did nothing but tend the fires in the lodge's thirty-one fireplaces. Laundresses washed household linens in the purpose-built laundry with the help of a giant mangle; governesses presided over the children's wing and its meals, which were taken separately from the rest of the family; a full-time bookkeeper kept track of everyone's wages.

Outside servants shoveled coal into the lodge's massive boiler, chopped logs for the fireplaces, and cut blocks of ice from nearby Saux Head Lake for the kitchen iceboxes. A chauffeur tended the family's fleet of seven cars, including a grand 1914 Rolls Royce touring car with an open front seat and right-hand controls, and drove the family (except the oldest son, Graveraet,

The completed twenty-six-thousand-square-foot Granot Loma from the air. Courtesy of Superior View Photography, Marquette, Michigan.

who had his own chauffeur) back and forth to town. Marie sometimes drove herself, but LG preferred to be driven. In New York and Short Hills, he took his place in the back seat like any other grandee, but in the UP he sat in the passenger seat, shotgun cocked, scanning the woods for gamebirds that could be added to a future menu.

Meals at Granot Loma were local, lavish, and labor-intensive: gardeners raised and picked fruits and vegetables, while other men shot and hung game and caught whitefish, trolling behind LG's beloved green inboard motorboat. Teams of chefs, cooks, and assistants produced multicourse "farm to table" menus, ending with pies made with local berries (LG's personal favorite) and homemade ice cream. Waitresses, trim in black uniforms and white aprons, carried the food to the dining room then stood at the ready in case a diner dropped a fork or required a second helping; teams of dish-washers dispatched mountains of plates and bowls emblazoned with Granot Loma's colorful logo.

Personal service was the order of the day. When, one winter morning, daughter Joan and her young husband thought it would be a lark to travel by horse-drawn sleigh and stay overnight at the old Bass Lake fishing camp, servants made the fantasy real. A sleigh was produced, a horse was hitched up, fur robes were piled on, and away they went. The driver remained on-site, of course, invisible until wanted for two days, building and tending fires and cutting holes in the ice so the young people could try their hand at fishing. Back at the lodge, whenever Marie was in the mood for a picnic on Saux Head Island (now styled "Daisy Island" after her Gatsbyesque nickname), servants lugged quantities of paraphernalia related to food preparation and outdoor dining down to the beach and in and out of boats. These servants would often have to reverse the whole process on the double when the family ran for the boats to escape an unexpected swarm of black flies. Safely indoors again, the family settled comfortably in a darkened room to watch a first-run movie, fetched from a theater in Marquette and threaded into a "motion picture machine" by a technically proficient member of staff.

Few servants complained about picnic duty or jingling call bells: food at Granot Loma was plentiful, the wages were fair, the staff could watch those first-run movies before returning them to Marquette, and the master treated everyone with kindness and respect. True, the mistress was another matter: Marie Kaufman was famously exacting, and she seemed to be everywhere at once as she checked for dust (with white-gloved hands) and otherwise monitored the performance of staff in the lodge and outbuildings. Dressed "like a female General Patton," as one of her grandchildren described it, she mustered her domestic troops in a long cashmere sweater over jodhpurs and boots, accessorized with a huge ring of keys to the many inconveniently locked cupboards and storage rooms to which only she controlled access.[1]

Having inspected and corrected all indoor work, Marie would proceed to her favorite outdoor activity: seated high on a tractor seat or astride a horse, she presided over an endless succession of labor-intensive building projects. Marie particularly liked building roads (or rather directing road crews), but other projects also commanded her attention. The summer Young Kaufman invited the members of his collegiate polo team to Granot Loma, tractor drivers and stump pullers were assembled, a field was cleared and mowed, and a regulation polo ground created for the occasion. In 1926, apparently bored with smaller efforts, Marie announced that she planned to create a new system of locks and canals running inland from Lake Superior. These new waterways, Marie informed her work crew, would allow Chicago friends with large yachts to steam up the Great Lakes directly to Granot Loma's private rail station by way of Saux Head Lake and the Garlic River and be met with the rest of arriving guests. (It would have been easier for visiting yachts to dock out in the lake and have passengers ferried in smaller boats directly to the lodge, but that plan wouldn't have required any building crews.)

Marie styled this project a "birthday surprise" for LG and planned to kick off the work on his fifty-sixth birthday (November 13, 1926) with a festive explosion. Having taken possession of a trainload of dynamite thoughtfully provided by Pierre du Pont, Marie positioned her husband at the top of a nearby hill and motioned to her crew to "let fly." The earth shook, but it is unclear whether LG was amused by the event. It was said only that he was "surprised" by the scope of his wife's construction plans.[2] Two new sets of locks would be required just to get the yachts from Lake Superior to Saux Head Lake, and the Garlic River would have to be massively dredged and equipped with two or three more locks to finish the job. Still, LG apparently expressed support for the scheme as Cement Gus was recalled to Granot Loma and dredging and building proceeded—for a while. Marie had failed to present her plans to the proper state authorities and in 1928 the Michigan Department of Conservation, citing the environmental damage that would be caused by the alteration of so many natural waterways, closed the project down.

The yacht channel was not Marie's first venture into waterway engineering. After LG's brother Samuel died in 1922, and she and LG inherited his UP lodge and acreage, his widow, Una Libby Kaufman, continued to use it. Perhaps Marie could not forgive Una for owning a luxurious lakefront lodge before she did, or perhaps she simply didn't like her sister-in-law. In any case, she is said to have found a unique way to disoblige her: knowing that Una enjoyed drifting in a little boat on a tributary of the Garlic River, Marie ordered the river dammed, ostensibly to create a trout pond, reducing Una's stream to a trickle and putting an end to her pleasurable drifting. If the men tasked with the damming understood what was happening, they didn't dare speak up. Many had been present when Marie happened upon a team of men with heavy machinery on a project she had not commissioned. The story goes that when the men explained that they were under orders from LG, Marie is reported to have shouted: "You can tell Mr. Kaufman to mind his own business. I give the orders here."[3]

Orders regarding her children's lives at Granot Loma were apparently given less often. Marie's interest in her children's daily routines was comparatively moderate and she was content to let the help do the heavy lifting. Nannies and governesses were responsible for meals and bedtime, and valets and maids who sometimes found small Kaufman children left on their own were happy to help out. The children didn't mind: secure in their safety net of servants, they enjoyed the freedom of the North Woods. They rode, fished, and splashed in LG's rock fountain, swam to Daisy Island and back, ran the large model steamboat purchased for their pleasure, and explored nearby lakes and rivers in LG's boats—gasoline powered and otherwise. When it rained, they watched movies or were driven to Marquette to plunder Donckers, the local candy store (still in business at this writing). That establishment made an appearance in jaunty lyrics penned by the young Louis Kaufman Jr., illustrating both his love for Granot Loma and the extreme privilege of his young life. "Granot Loma, here we come," Louis wrote to the tune of "California, Here I Come," "right back where we started from.

The Kaufman family at Granot Loma, ca. 1922. From the left: Marie holding Jane, Marie Louise, Juliet, Joan, Young, Louis Jr., Ann, Graveraet, LG. Collection of Peter Kaufman.

Where kids race and cars chase to Donckers in town. Each morning, at dawning, trays go up and trays come down. So, New York, Short Hills and Palm Beach too, in the summers will not do, so we're coming back to you. Granot Loma, here we come."[4]

Chauffeurs and breakfast trays may have been available on call, but there was one privilege residents at Granot Loma had to do without: LG refused to have a telephone installed at the lodge. The lack did not inconvenience him—he could make calls from his office at the bank in Marquette—but anyone else who wished to communicate with the outside world had to walk a mile along a dirt road to the phone at the lodge's private railway depot. The depot phone was an old wall model that required extensive cranking and was connected to an insecure party line, but it was the only game in town, and everyone from the lodge—no matter how grand—flocked to use it. "I remember the Kaufman girls driving their car to the depot to use the phone," a local resident recalled, then, noting the distance between the Kaufmans and everyone else, she added: "it was the only time I saw them."[5] Other locals cackled over a famous "misunderstanding" caused by the phone line's fuzzy sound quality: Marie had used the depot phone to order a boxcar full of tar paper she needed to cover the roofs at Loma Farms. The supplier had protested that this couldn't be what she wanted, whereupon Marie had become indignant and imperiously repeated her request. When the boxcar arrived, it was full to the brim with thousands of rolls of toilet paper.

In Granot Loma's early days toilet paper—and tar paper—would have been shipped by train to Marquette—the last stop for all lodge-bound goods and people. After the long overnight trip from New York, the Kaufmans disembarked in town (in front of gawking locals who invariably gathered to see what they were wearing and who was with them) and traveled the last fifteen miles to the lodge by road in a bumpy caravan of motors, wagons, and carriages. Marie soon protested this inconvenience: her daughter Jane recalled that her mother so deplored the rough muddy roads guests had to endure "that my father went to the right people and got what she wanted."[6] Soon all Kaufman lodge–bound passengers and boxcars arriving at Marquette were coupled to a locomotive of the Lake Superior and Ishpeming Railroad, a branch line that ran north from Marquette to Big Bay, and were uncoupled at Birch, a new stop a few minutes down the line.

The stop took its name from the defunct town of Birch, Michigan. Once a thriving logging center complete with sawmill, schoolhouse, and post office, Birch had dwindled in the 1920s along with the local supply of trees. When the mill closed most people moved away, the site was purchased by LG, and many of the buildings were razed or burned. It was near the old town site, a scant mile away from the lodge, that he arranged for trains to stop on the branch line and ordered the construction of an elegant, multiroomed depot in the same rustic style. The Granot Loma experience began as soon as passengers got off the train. Ladies were served tea in front of a welcoming fireplace in one room, while their male companions enjoyed brandy and cigars in another. Soon, the clip-clop of horses' hooves would signal the arrival of carriages (sleighs in winter) drawn by gray Percheron horses, coming to carry family and guests through the forest to the lodge. During this interlude their baggage was whisked away so efficiently that by the time people arrived at their rooms, a maid or valet would already be unpacking for them. Back at the depot men unloaded supplies, cattle, and empty milk cans at its working sidings and organized the storage of the private railroad cars of the Kaufmans and their guests.

On summer weekends in the mid- and late 1920s, those sidings were chockablock: the private railroad car (also known as a "business car," a "special car," or, more appealingly, "private varnish") was ubiquitous in the circles in which the Kaufmans traveled. It was the private jet of its day. An apartment on rails bearing a jaunty name like "Adios" or "Wanderer," it was both a status symbol (everyone who was anyone traveled privately) and a true convenience, allowing its passengers a good night's sleep and separation from the hoi polloi. So common was its use by America's rich and famous that society editors soon found themselves fussing about how to report on the owners of private varnish: was Mr. Vanderbilt "aboard" or "onboard" his private car? ("in board" was the decision at the *New York Herald Tribune*).[7] Circus impresario and Chatham Phenix director John Ringling was often onboard, or inboard, his private car. So was GM's John J. Raskob, whose "Skipaway" featured a parlor, a dining room, three bedrooms and bathrooms, and a private observation deck.

Sadly, no one alive can recall the name or serial number of the private car owned and operated by LG, so we have no details about its size or appointments. But there is no doubt that it existed. Two of his granddaughters remember their grandfather's private railcar, and a generation closer to the source, daughter Jane Kaufman recalled when her family and "more than 100 guests at once would pile into Kaufman's private railway cars in New York and travel to Granot Loma."[8] We do know that LG's ability to bring his private varnish to Granot Loma, and anywhere else he wanted to go, came courtesy of his directorship of the Chicago and Erie Railroad (a subsidiary of the Erie Railroad). Frederick Douglas Underwood, the president of the Erie Railroad, was one of LG's bank directors and likely arranged for LG to have this vital board position. At this time, anyone with an official association with a railroad was the beneficiary of a "gentleman's agreement" that allowed directors of any railroad to hitch their cars to the trains of any other railroad and travel gratis anywhere they wished. Nor did the freebies end there: railroads like the Chicago and Erie commissioned fleets of private cars and made them available to their directors, executives, and important stockholders, so when one car wasn't enough to house the hundreds of New York guests Jane Kaufman remembered converging on Granot Loma, LG was courteously supplied with others.

There were more than one thousand railroads operating in the United States in 1920, so many thousands of wealthy Americans were able to benefit from these corporate perks and reciprocal arrangements. Others unaffiliated with any railroad also ran private cars but were forced to pay steep connection and other fees when they traveled. Still others rented: the Pullman Company offered an extensive line of private cars, including "an entire seven car train with baggage, dining, lounge, barber shop and library car, sleepers and an observation salon car of almost imperial dimensions."[9]

The cozy arrangement that facilitated private travel was camouflaged as professional necessity: directors were assumed to be conducting official "railway business" in their "business cars," hence that particular moniker. For years the Interstate Commerce Commission (ICC) turned a blind eye as owners hitched cars to trains to Newport in summer and Palm Beach in winter, but by the late 1920s railroad manifests were so heavy with freeloaders that the ICC took action: "Railroad officials who go joy riding in private cars have been taken to task by the Interstate Commerce Commission," announced the newspapers in 1928. "Commissioner McManamy . . . asks that steps be taken to stop railways from hauling private cars owned by other lines unless the regular charges are made for hauling them."[10] Soon each person aboard a private car was paying a first-class fare and some railroads stopped allowing directors of other lines to hitch up for free. A year later the stock market crashed, and the freeloading issue became moot. While LG and other lucky wealthy people continued to run their cars into the 1930s, the golden age of private railroading was over.

But in its heyday, private cars brought the world to Granot Loma. Carriages met train after train, cars piled up on the sidings at Birch, and the lodge filled with friends from Chicago and the East—fifty or more at a time. Marie didn't hunt or fish; she liked to entertain, and she was eager to show off her lodge and its dramatic setting. Many of her eastern friends had visited the great camps of the Adirondacks but few had been to the Upper Peninsula of Michigan, and the sight of Superior—a body of fresh water as big as an ocean with breakers rolling in and huge ships on the horizon—was a revelation to her New York chums, as unexpected as the extravagant log palace perched at its edge.

Local legend would later posit that these people came to Granot Loma in the 1920s to escape Prohibition and drink without fear in the lawless wilds of the Upper Peninsula, but there is little truth in it. The Kaufmans' crowd had no need for a woodland speakeasy. It was not illegal to drink in the privacy of one's home and most wealthy people had stocked up before the ax fell. Its liquor safes were useful, but Granot Loma itself was the main attraction. Guests galloped through the woods, played doubles on elegant grass courts, and fished in well-stocked lakes and streams. For hunters there were ten thousand acres teeming with partridge, deer, and bear, or LG would order pigeons from Loma Farms released to flutter fatally skyward as guests raised their guns. Indoors there was billiards, cards, sauna, massage, and, after an excellent dinner, first-class entertainment. Private cars sent by LG arrived at Birch and disgorged entire dance bands from Chicago and New York, along with Broadway stars who belted out the popular songs of the day. Famous opera singers trilled arias from Granot Loma's balconies.

There were famous people on the dance floor as well: "There were so many celebrities I can't remember them all,"

Jane Kaufman told the *Detroit News* in 1984, before reeling off the names of Lionel Barrymore, Mary Pickford, Fred Astaire, and world heavyweight title boxers Max Schmeling and Gene Tunney.[11] Tennis champion "Big Bill" Tilden laid out the lodge's two courts and gave lessons to the Kaufman children. While it's not known exactly how the Kaufmans knew these A-listers, there are many possibilities: Broadway designer Orry-Kelly (who dressed Ethel Barrymore on Broadway) may have made introductions, a theatrical producer friend, Charles Dillingham, may have done the same, and the couple likely met many celebs at Benjamin Marshall studio parties. Dancer Irene Castle and actress Ethel Barrymore were regulars at Marshall's shindigs, and both later made their way to Granot Loma. LG and Marie were very fond of music (witness Marie's short-lived engagement to singer Walter Newton Jones) and gravitated toward those who wrote or performed it. Artúr Halmi, the artist they hired to paint their daughter Joan, may have been chosen because he was famous for painting opera singers. Marie's frequent companion, Mrs. William Hyde, was the former Grace Marie Blakely, a singer who was cast in a Follies production of *Ming Toy*, and Broadway composer Vincent Youmans was another good friend. All added to the star power at gatherings at Granot Loma in the 1920s.

Another musical visitor, composer George Gershwin, left a more lasting mark on the lodge. Asked by the family to pick out an appropriate piano for the use of family, guests, and visiting performers, he chose an elegant 1926 Steinway grand model D in an ebony finish. Joan Kaufman would later recall Gershwin playing "his" piano during a visit to Granot Loma, as she played along on another, less impressive instrument. Marie had such strong feelings about the "Gershwin Piano" that she wrote a special trust indenture as part of her will. After specifying the trustee who was to receive the piano after her death, Marie praised its sound and identified its glamorous provenance: "I consider that said piano is an exceptionally fine instrument," she wrote, "having been selected by the late George Gershwin for both its quality of tone and fineness of action."[12] (It is not clear whether this piano was the one sold with the lodge in the 1980s or the one given to Graveraet High School and now in use in the Kaufman Auditorium.)

Louis G. Kaufman Jr. was more interested in Gershwin himself. The composer was only a few years his senior and he and LG Jr., who played the piano quite well, are said to have been friends. LG Jr. also played around: he and his brother Graveraet spent so much of their time backstage in pursuit of chorus girls and ingenues that they were known in the press as LG's "stage winged sons."[13] Gershwin (and perhaps the artist Orry-Kelly) may have been introduced to the Kaufman brothers in the wings of a musical production, or perhaps it was Gershwin who introduced them to the pleasures of the stage in the first place. In any case, those pleasures would have lasting consequences. The Kaufmans' theatrical quarry was also in pursuit and the wealthy heirs were soon caught: by 1928 each had married a performing paramour.

Miss Mae Daw appeared in the Ziegfeld Follies of 1922, 1923, and 1924 (sharing the stage with the likes of Fannie Brice and Will Rogers) and was known for organizing stunts, like learning the saxophone and challenging another actress to a cow-milking contest, to keep herself in the public eye. But when she landed Graveraet in 1924 her milking days were over: one evening she failed to appear on stage to lead the March of the Toys at the Follies, announced her marriage to the newspapers, and got on the train for Granot Loma. LG Jr.'s wife, actor/ dancer Dorothy Dilley, arrived at the lodge a few years later. Born in Venice, California, she got her start when a touring *Music Box Revue* lost a featured dancer and asked the local dancing school for a replacement. Dorothy was a minor sensation in the revue, was cast in several Broadway shows, including *Kitty's Kisses* (1926) and *Take the Air* (1927), and became a pal of Woolworth heir Jimmy Donahue, later famous for his "affair" with the Duchess of Windsor. Dorothy herself was already famous for a striking 1923 photograph in *Vanity Fair* that depicted her en pointe, bending impossibly far backward as she performed something called "The Butterfly Dance." In 1928 the butterfly became Mrs. LG Jr. and joined the throng at the lodge. Either one of these ladies could have been the "Broadway star" who gave Granot Loma butler William Peterson an eyeful one evening. Having been asked to deliver something on a tray, he knocked on the door of the room, heard someone trill "come in," and entered to find the occupant lolling nude in the bathtub. Peterson recalls blushing violently, dropping the tray on the nearest table, and running.[14]

Celebrities (naked and half naked) were the froth on a rich brew of moguls, minor aristocrats, socialites, and debutantes sloshing around Granot Loma on any given weekend. Catholic Boston was represented by bootlegger/Hollywood studio owner Joe Kennedy and his wife, Rose, and the WASP quotient swelled after 1926 when the Kaufmans became allied with one of the country's Social Register families. The wedding of Joan Kaufman and George Drexel Biddle at the fashionable St. Thomas Church on Fifth Avenue (with a reception for nearly two thousand guests to follow at 270 Park Avenue) was picture-perfect. LG wore a glossy top hat, Joan was resplendent in dull ivory satin, and her twelve bridesmaids carried orchids descending from tulle muffs. Soon Drexels and Biddles joined the crowd on the dance floor at Granot Loma, bringing other old money families with them. LG's new money provided them all a good time. "It was an F. Scott Fitzgerald existence," says granddaughter Deborah Bishop of life at Granot Loma in the 1920s. "It was one long party up there."[15]

In true Gatsby style, some of those parties did not end with the sunrise, and guests were not always present by invitation. On some weekends Granot Loma hosted friends of friends and total strangers, who dressed up and jumped aboard the private trains LG ran day and night, from Marquette to Birch and back again. "I was there with a doctor's daughter I had known for some time," Marquette restauranteur Louis Vierling remembered a half century later. "We were still there at sunrise and the girl who lived next door stayed three days. It was 'dry days,'" Vierling continued, "and they had liquor. The trains were there and you could just hop on and go. The damn party lasted for three or four days and you could come and go anytime you wanted."[16] Some guests arrived at Birch already in the party spirit, thanks to the dance bands LG had hired to play on his private trains on the way up north, but unlike at parties in Paris and New York, the talented African American jazz musicians who made up these ensembles were not allowed to mingle with LG and Marie's guests. It was the segregation era in America (1900–1939), including in the UP, and when the musicians' shifts were over they would have been escorted to Granot Loma's servants' quarters (and even there they may not have been entirely welcome) or sent back to Marquette by train.

Hundreds of revelers—invited and otherwise—attended the grand housewarming LG and Marie held in the summer of 1927 and the costume ball they gave on New Year's Eve 1928. While the details of these entertainments are lost to time it is not hard to imagine the lodge on that summer eve a century ago—the lights blazing in log rooms crowded with dancers in dinner jackets and fringed dresses, the ragtime and jazz wafting out through giant open windows, a few brave couples dancing on the breakwater just above the lake. Six months later the revelers were back at Granot Loma, now ice-crusted like a palace in a fairy tale, glittering under a cold, starry sky. Their Renaissance

Granot Loma in winter. Courtesy of Superior View Photography, Marquette, Michigan.

robes and Harlequin suits in increasing disarray, one hundred guests danced all night to a rota of imported orchestras and floated away on a sea of champagne.

Marquette was only fifteen miles from Granot Loma but for most of the lodge's occupants and guests it could have been on the moon. The UP town was a place to find beds for Black musicians, for servants to buy supplies—a railyard where one waited, shades down, for one's private car to be coupled to the train to Birch. Only for LG was it home. In Marquette every street corner held memories of his childhood, of his mother, and he, the bank president and wealthiest citizen, was greeted with reverence everywhere he went. Marquette was his town, and as his wealth grew he did not forget it. Even before Granot Loma began to rise, he left his mark on its landscape.

His first gifts were financial: he paid off the debts of St. Paul's, his family church, commissioned a stained-glass window there in honor of his mother, and gave the Marquette school board $26,000 to buy the land upon which a new high school would later sit. Then he began to build: his first project was a grand family mausoleum in bucolic Park Cemetery, finished in 1917 and not a minute too soon. Soon after its completion Nathan Kaufman died, and as he'd been posthumously divorced by Mary Breitung Kaufman for keeping a mistress on the tenth floor of a Chicago hotel and was therefore unwelcome in the Breitung mausoleum, he was the first to be interred there. Next came LG's mother, Juliet (d. 1915), and his father, Sam (d. 1900), who were reinterred in the new build. There was certainly plenty of space: the mausoleum was equipped with sixteen burial slots and was as big as a house. Even today it looks more like a chapel serving the entire cemetery than a single-family tomb.

Built of Barre granite, a smooth, pale gray stone mined in Vermont, it is a personal Parthenon with an open front portico and rows of tall, fluted columns. Construction was long and expensive, coming in at approximately $3 million ($70 million today). The burial chamber is lined with marble and to achieve this, huge slabs of the costly stone were lashed to rollers and pulled to the cemetery by multiple teams of horses. At the back of the chamber three floor-to-ceiling stained-glass windows designed by Tiffany Studios in New York were installed between fluted marble columns. The windows depicted the actual view—gently rolling terrain with a pond and trees—that would have been visible from the back of the mausoleum. Unfortunately, they are no longer in place. In the 1980s, when enthusiasm for all things Tiffany was at its height, thieves realized that windows in unattended mausoleums were easy pickings and many were stolen. The Kaufman windows were among those taken and they have never been recovered.

The window LG provided for St. Paul's Cathedral, where, four decades earlier, he had pumped the organ during Sunday service, is still in place, and it looks nothing like the stolen threesome. In 1922 he went to Charles J. Connick, a traditional Boston maker known for jewel tone ecclesiastical compositions, and ordered a two-panel window depicting Christ blessing young children representing LG and his siblings. He called the new composition (rather redundantly) "The Christian Family Window" and dedicated it to the memory of his mother, Juliet Graveraet Kaufman. It was his second such tribute to his beloved mother: six years earlier he had commissioned New York maker J & R Lamb, another traditional shop, to create "Transfiguration," an elaborate five-light window depicting Jesus and his disciples, dedicated it to Juliet's memory, and gave it to Christ Church, the tony Episcopal congregation in Short Hills to which the family then belonged.

It was between these two commissions that LG and Marie went to Tiffany Studios and ordered a cutting-edge, naturalistic landscape in glass for their final resting place. The decision is a window onto their personal taste and private concerns: a church is a public space in which one's choice of design will be scrutinized by a host of eagle-eyed, potentially censorious parishioners. The Kaufmans were likely eager to emphasize their fervent Episcopal faith and connection and so went full-on ecclesiastical with their church picks. In the private recesses of their mausoleum, however, they were free to follow their own aesthetic impulses and, bypassing images of Christ, plumped for Tiffany's modern, opalescent glass and secular composition.

LG's biggest project—a new building for the First National Bank and Trust Company of Marquette—was as classical as his mausoleum and almost as personal: the bank was the scene of his first financial triumph, its success had helped send him to New York, and as long as he remained its president, he felt responsible for its future. By 1924 he believed that future required a change of venue. The bank was still housed in an undistinguished sandstone structure built in the early 1870s (on a site donated by Peter White) that had grown shabby and worn.

Newer, grander premises would be good for Marquette, good for business, and very good for Louis Graveraet Kaufman, with whom they would forever be associated. It was time to build.

LG owned a large lot at the corner of Front and Washington Streets, and to get the ball rolling he offered to sell it to the bank at cost. When his offer was met with polite resistance, he quickly followed Peter White's example and donated the lot and (having also agreed to pay for some portion of the build) secured the go-ahead to plan an extravagant new "temple to banking." Although other bank directors remained nominally involved in the project, the building would be an LG Kaufman production. He began by selecting the architects: Mowbray and Uffinger, a New York firm known for their elegant bank designs, including one they had produced for one of the larger branches of the Chatham and Phenix in New York. Justin Uffinger Sr. had studied under famed Beaux Arts architect Richard Morris Hunt and the classic beauty of the Beaux Arts style was exactly what LG had in mind. Realizing that an unsightly neighbor would kill the classical vibe, he commissioned a Beaux Arts office building to stand next door. The Bartlett Construction Company of Eau Claire, Wisconsin, which was already building Loma Farms, was tapped for LG's new palace of commerce. (Two years later LG would again plump for a contracting firm already in his employ when he helped choose the builder for a far larger, more famous edifice.)

Mowbray and Uffinger did not disappoint: their design, Beaux Arts from sidewalk to cornice, was a perfectly balanced medley of Corinthian columns, arched doors and windows, and symmetrical courses of pilasters in pale Indiana buff limestone, all scaled to tower majestically above the surrounding sea of brick and sandstone. For the entrance, LG commissioned a set of tall, extravagantly decorated bronze doors, flanked by elegant bronze lanterns, from well-known metal worker John Polacheck of

Long Island City, New York. Among their embossed images of classical urns, ancient coins, and rosettes is the Latin phrase "post tenebras lux" (after darkness, light). Was its inclusion a poke at the snobby bankers of Marquette who had preceded (and excluded) LG, or just a comment on the bank's new architecture? I think I know, and I applaud LG's sly wit.

The interior of the bank was—and remains—as grand as the exterior, displaying an array of elegant materials and patterns. The soaring walls and floor of the main banking room are covered in creamy travertine—the same stone used to build the Vatican—quarried along the old road from Rome to Rivoli. An elaborately coined and patterned ceiling, enriched with gold leaf and Tiffany blue enamel, supports six chandeliers fashioned as

The main banking room of the First National Bank built by Louis Graveraet Kaufman in 1927. Courtesy of Superior View Photography, Marquette, Michigan.

giant candelabras. Down below, interior doors, tellers' cages, and radiator grills in intricately patterned bronze alternate with counters and benches of black and gold Italian marble from the Gulf of Spezia. Private booths then used for "coupon cutting" are finished in walnut. Foot by foot, the bank was the most expensive building constructed in the entire country in 1927. Part of the cost was mechanical: the massive vault at one end of the banking room was the latest thing in 1927 security. Bristling with bolts, locks, and alarms, it is made of reinforced concrete, boasts a circular steel door sixteen inches thick, and weighs twenty-five tons. A second story provided lockers, showers, and a dining room for bank employees and, never one to pass up an income opportunity, LG added offices to the mezzanine above the vault, which were snapped up by local insurance agents and dentists. (After a robbery at another Marquette bank, one such tenant came in handy: a crack shot, he was given a high-powered rifle and was ordered to stand by, between root canals, in case of trouble.)

A first-floor corner office now bears no trace of its original designation—the Women's Room. In 1927 it was assumed that ladies needed a private place to retire while their husbands contracted financial business, and many banks provided one. LG's featured a handy vanity and mirror, prettily upholstered armchairs, and shirred gold curtains. Even the wastebaskets were appropriately feminine, the *Mining Journal* noted at the time, cooing over carved walnut panels. "The fittings call to mind the delicacy of Watteau," its reporter opined, adding that the women's "lavatory is paneled in marble like a Roman bath."[17] In fact the ladies' and men's rooms were both lined with marble and were located in the bank's basement where, during a 1990s renovation, workmen made an odd discovery: buried beneath the building was a forty-foot-long railroad tank car full of heating oil. As the bank's furnace was coal burning the find is a mystery.

Removal was impossible, so the car was drained, filled with concrete, and left in situ.

Nine thousand citizens of Marquette (a majority of the town's population) trooped through the new bank on October 15, 1927, its opening day. Five thousand leather wallets were given away as favors, along with three thousand dime savings banks. Visitors were dazzled by the new temple of finance and by the hometown boy who had made it happen. "Louis G. Kaufman, Builder of Banks and Master of Finance Has Honored Home Town by Erection of Monument to Progress," the *Mining Journal* announced in extra-large type, above a workman-like poetic tribute to LG penned by a local teacher: "Marvelously beautiful it stands and exquisite in design: A dream, a vision realized in figured bronze and marble fine. All honor to the builder for he's given you and me a mighty inspiration through all the years that be."[18] Pages of "tombstone" ads followed, paid for by local firms that had contributed to the new structure (roofers, purveyors of building materials, etc.) and by many others eager to congratulate LG Kaufman upon his Marquette legacy, now set in stone. LG was, all knew, a man with endless patronage to distribute, able to elevate those he liked and inconvenience those he did not. Nobody wanted to miss a chance to be likable, and to shake the great man's hand, if only in print.

The night before the opening five hundred lucky citizens were invited to break bread with LG at a banquet in his honor. Planked whitefish—the Dover sole of the Great Lakes—headlined the menu, along with "Bankers Salad," with ice cream and cake to follow. The audience cheered as Mayor John Robertson read aloud telegrams of congratulation from swells in Chicago and New York. Then, twenty-six years after trustees of the First National Bank had resigned in disgust, unwilling to work with LG and his brothers, His Honor spoke to the new reality: "I take much pleasure," he intoned, "in paying tribute to a member of one of the most respected families in the history of Marquette."[19] When LG stood to thank the mayor and address his fellow diners the audience saw a man at the peak of his powers, with broad shoulders, a firm, determined chin, and heavy black hair with a distinguished touch of gray. In his powerful voice he called Marquette "the biggest little city in the world" (two years before Reno, Nevada, adopted that catchy slogan), attested to the "sterling character of the people who live here," and assured its citizens that "young men in Marquette have a better opportunity to achieve knowledge and success than those who live in New York, Chicago, and other large cities."[20] He himself, he did not need to add, was living proof that this was so.

Willard Whitman, superintendent of Marquette's school system, then rose to put the capstone on LG's local legacy. He reminded the audience that back in 1915 when the school board needed to buy land and clear houses to build a new high school, LG had sent it a check for $26,000. Delayed by World War I, construction of the new Graveraet High School, named for LG's mother and uncle, town pioneer Robert Graveraet, was only then nearing completion, and Whitman announced that its auditorium would be named for (and, he didn't have to add, paid for by) LG himself. The new Louis G. Kaufman Auditorium would have space for nearly one thousand audience members, professional lighting, and a "motion picture machine," not to mention heavy velvet stage and window curtains and a ceiling dome (enriched with paintings depicting the connection between education, culture, and industry), all designed to improve sound quality. They did: the resulting acoustics were said to be so good that a whisper on the stage could be heard in the second balcony.

Whitman then announced even bigger news: LG had just funded an endowment of $100,000 (about $1.5 million today) for the new Graveraet High School, to enrich the educational experience of the town's youth. As the *American Israelite* noted, it was the first endowment of any public high school in the country; it would be used to fund college scholarships for outstanding graduates and provide medals and cash prizes for "exceptional" seniors.[21] (Some medals were indicative of specific qualities important to their funder: one, for example, went to the boy who had best protected and defended younger, less robust students and had displayed "integrity, chivalry and forthrightedness [*sic*]."))[22]

LG's endowment would also fund a school band, an orchestra, and a music teacher from New York and would "bring to the children and people of Marquette some of the finer things in the world of education, travel and art." The finer things would be provided by a "Lyceum Series," which would pay for musicians, lecturers, writers, and other accomplished individuals to grace the stage of the Louis G. Kaufman Auditorium four to six times every year. The series, which lasted until 1945, did indeed bring the world to Marquette: presenters included radio personality Lowell Thomas speaking about Lawrence of Arabia, Amelia Earhart, the Vienna Boys' Choir, and photographer Margaret Bourke-White, along with scores of well-known explorers, dancers, and opera singers. For two decades local citizens queued for extra seats, students dressed up on Lyceum days, and the audience was shown to their places by proud ushers (female honor students in maroon skirts and white satin blouses).

A year after this ceremonial banquet, LG was invited to the new Louis G. Kaufman Auditorium to hear the Graveraet High School orchestra, band, and glee club perform in his honor. It was early in the school year and the students had had only two weeks to practice their numbers, but LG would soon be returning to New York, so their teachers took a chance and hoped for the best. They must have gulped a little when multiple members of Marquette's First Family—LG, Marie, Graveraet, Joan, and her husband, George Biddle, Young Kaufman's wife, and one of LG's sisters and her husband—all filed in and took their seats. "Such a program is a precarious undertaking," the *Mining Journal* admitted the following day before resorting to praising the students' ability to play and sing "with their hearts."[23] It is not known how the First Family felt about the missed notes and ragged timing but the paper praised the reaction of the Kaufman who really mattered: "One suspected," it wrote fondly of LG, "that because he is such a human 'just folks' kind of man for all of his financial wizardry, he got almost as much of a thrill out of the evening as the boys and girls did."[24]

6

THE SWEETS OF SUCCESS
Power, Money, and High Society

In the UP, New York City, and everywhere else, the 1920s was a good decade to be a Kaufman. The Great War had blurred the class structure of previous eras, and the rules of society had changed. For the first time a WASP pedigree and the possession of "old money" were no longer prerequisites for inclusion. Newly wealthy families with less than exalted backgrounds could now bring out their daughters as debutantes and join the right clubs alongside the toniest of *Mayflower* descendants. For Marie the timing could not have been better: she and LG were wildly rich and still in their prime and their older children were just reaching adulthood. If those children married well—and the Princess of Lake Geneva was determined that they should—their dodgy antecedents would finally be in the rearview mirror and there would be no social peak the family could not climb.

Private schools had already laid the groundwork for appropriate unions: the Kaufman children had attended exclusive Manhattan day schools and boarding schools, including Aiken Prep in the riding and hunting enclave of Aiken, South Carolina (known more for its social cachet than its academic rigor), and Fermata, its female finishing school complement, and they were already mixing with the "right" sort. For the girls, the debutante ritual was the next step up the ladder: the centuries-old practice of being introduced to society, organized to ensure that the children of the "right" British families met and married each other, had migrated across the Atlantic with the first settlers and had long helped to define an American social elite.

In the early 1920s, not only had that "elite" expanded, but American debs were suddenly in the spotlight: many postwar British families—short of money and marriageable sons—were forced to sit out the London Season, while in New York, an influx of new money was making balls grander and more frequent than ever. Marrying well was still the ultimate goal of the American deb, but as the season was now chronicled by newspapers and magazines coast to coast, celebrity was becoming an attractive by-product. A popular, well-dressed debutante could expect major media coverage on the day, all during the season, and for years thereafter, as the press tracked her social life along with those of Broadway ingenues and silent movie queens.

Ann (b. 1902), the first Kaufman daughter to benefit from the new order, was introduced to society at the Junior Assembly Dance at the Ritz-Carlton Hotel on December 3, 1921. Many of her fellow debs had been bidden to elegant pre-dance dinners, and she had had no invitations, but neither she nor Marie was discouraged. Ann's own ball was just around the corner, and it would make everything alright. Ann's money was new, her surname inconvenient, and her mother's connections midwestern, but these encumbrances were about to be neutralized in a rather inspired way. Hers would be a joint ball, shared with fellow debutante Diana Dalziel, a girl of fewer resources but impeccable lineage. Diana's mother, Emily Key Hoffman, was a descendant of both Francis Scott Key and Martha Washington and her father, British stockbroker Frederick Young Dalziel, was elegant and socially connected. With the Dalziels' invitation list—a who's who of society—and the Kaufmans' unlimited supply of money, Ann and Diana's ball would be one of the most important of the season.

It was not entirely a pairing of convenience: Ann and Diana were close friends who had met in New York after 1914 when Diana's family moved there from Paris (where Diana was born). "Anne [*sic*] is really very sweet and I'm awfully fond of her," Diana wrote in her diary in 1918. "She told me I was her best friend and she is really so sarcastic and fascinating . . . she did an awful lot for me as she took me to the theatre three times and I care for her a lot."[1] Ann's largesse would continue into the 1920s when Diana spent considerable time at Ann Kaufman's home in Palm Beach, but her young houseguest would later return the favor and then some: Diana accompanied Ann on many future shopping trips (one year, declaring their choice to be "the ultimate," the two girls bought and wore nothing but black), helping her friend hone an impressive fashion sense. She was well equipped to do so: for Diana Dalziel married Thomas Reed Vreeland in 1924, and as Diana Vreeland became editor of *Harper's Bazaar* in 1937, editor in chief of *Vogue* in 1962, a fashion icon to millions, and ultimately one of the most famous American women of the twentieth century. She remains a legend, venerated for her exceptional eye and outrageous "bon mots" and for her stewardship of the institution at the center of today's New York social calendar: the Costume Institute at the Metropolitan Museum of Art.

In 1921, on the evening of December 21, after an elaborate dinner party for forty at the Kaufmans' flat at 270 Park Avenue, Diana and Ann stood with Emily Dalziel and Marie Kaufman at the entrance to the ballroom of the Ritz-Carlton, ready to receive the first of eight hundred guests. In tribute to the season the ballroom and the hotel's restaurant (which the Kaufmans had also rented to accommodate a sumptuous midnight supper) were decorated with holiday flowers and greenery. The details of Ann's apparel are lost to the passage of time but her look, organized by Marie, was no doubt expensive and traditional. Diana's was not: her fringe-skirted dress was a thrifty copy of a design by French couturier Paul Poiret, and she had applied a liberal coating of calcimate (a kind of whitewash) to her face, shoulders, and arms to produce a dramatic complexion. "I was whiter than white," she later wrote in her autobiography (after shaving two years off her age by moving her ball forward to 1923). "My dress was white . . . I had velvet slippers that were lacquer red. I carried red camellias."[2] If Marie was startled by Diana's fashion-forward getup, the steady stream of Vanderbilts, Deerings, Drexel Biddles, Havemeyers, and Rhinelanders passing through the receiving line likely quieted all doubts.

The ball was a tremendous success. Images of Ann and Diana appeared in the *New York Herald* and *Tribune* the following day (other debs only got a mention in print), and Ann's society career was off to a brilliant start. She became a star of her season, earning full-page photos in both *Town & Country* and the horsier *Spur*, and was invited everywhere. Encouraged, Marie lost no time arranging Ann's next step on the social ladder: a presentation at Buckingham Palace. Once again, the timing was propitious: King George V had paused the presentation tradition during World War I and for several years thereafter, but in the spring of 1922 it was once again in full swing. Americans were welcome as long as they followed the strict dress code—white gown, hem less than five inches off the floor, train stretching no more than twelve feet behind the wearer's shoes, headpiece of three ostrich feathers, white gloves, floral bouquet—and were sponsored by women who had already been presented at court. Some girls had to scrounge a sponsor among the British gentlewomen in reduced circumstances who performed this service for a fee, but Ann was better equipped. Thanks to the power of the Chatham Phenix Bank (and perhaps

LG's oft-flaunted connections to Woodrow Wilson), Ann was sponsored by Mrs. George Brinton McClellan Harvey, the wife of the American ambassador to the Court of St. James.

On June 22, 1922, Ann and Mrs. Harvey slipped into a limousine and joined the long procession of motor cars snaking slowly up the Mall toward the palace. Crowds lined the route and many among them peered into the cars as they passed, loudly rating their passengers' looks and apparel. As the cars crawled past, bolder spectators even jumped on running boards to get a better look. Ann's pretty face and pricey gown of ivory mousseline de soie embroidered in pearls and diamanté and finished with a train of silver lace and velvet no doubt attracted approving nods from the sidelines. Inside her rolling fishbowl, she must have felt she had slipped into a fairy tale.

Once inside, however, her experience was likely short of enchanting. American debs of the 1920s waited hours for their turn to make their curtsy (members of the British aristocracy went first), crammed into crowded spaces that were uncomfortably hot or cold and offered nowhere to sit or powder one's nose. (A chamber pot behind a folding screen was the only amenity.) Feathers wilted along with spirits and trains were sometimes stepped on and torn. Finally, Ann's turn came: she advanced, handed her official "presentation card" to an official at the entrance to the Throne Room, heard her name announced and then Mrs. Harvey's. The two women glided to a spot directly in front of King George V, Queen Mary, and—the focus of every debutante's eye—Edward, Prince of Wales, later Duke of Windsor. It was showtime: Ann dropped a deep curtsy, Mrs. Harvey did the same several paces to the rear, and then, careful not to turn their backs on Their Majesties, they moved quickly on, making room for the next girl. The entire thing lasted less than three minutes.

Her presentation made little difference to Ann's standing in

British society, but that was fine. What mattered was the positive effect it would have on the "right people" in Oyster Bay, Palm Beach, and Manhattan. The Court of St. James was then considered the apogee of society on both sides of the Atlantic, and Ann's new association with it was duly noted among members of the American Social Register and by the press, which wholesaled it to a rapt American public. The Kaufmans' social star rose even higher when, the following spring, Marie too was presented at court. She went all-out for the occasion, laying on sparkle and important jewelry, and made her curtsy in white crepe, satin, and lace embroidered with rhinestones and finished with a diamanté belt and shoulder straps. Her train, which was lined with silver tissue, was joined to her shoulders with embroidered silver lace, and she topped off her ensemble with a pearl necklace, a wide diamond and platinum bracelet, and (in a clever nod to the three feathers of the debutante) an ostrich feather fan.

Although many newspapers noted the two presentations, neither the *London Times* nor the *New York Times* ran photos of Ann and Marie dressed for their occasions. That honor was conferred upon fifteen-year-old Joan Kaufman, who had come to London to ride in the 1922 International Horse Show at Olympia and was shown posing with her mount and looking adorably horsey in riding togs. A landmark of the London Season since 1907, the International was one of the most fashionable equestrian events in the world, and while the postwar shortage of males was likely responsible for Joan's inclusion and she won no events, her participation was noted on both sides of the Atlantic.

Spring 1922 was a season of social triumph for his wife and daughters, but LG did not witness Joan's turn in the ring nor Ann's curtsy to royalty. Although he went back and forth to Europe often during these years, he sat this one out, passing up the opportunity to support Ann and Joan, to get to know them better, and perhaps instill some fatherly wisdom. Why? We can only guess. Perhaps he was particularly busy at the bank and felt an Atlantic crossing would keep him away for too long. The Chatham Phenix had recently taken over yet another bank—the Union Exchange Bank this time—and he may have found it inconvenient to be absent. But it's also possible such a trip would not have occurred to him at all. Many wealthy 1920s fathers were barely involved in the raising of their daughters and, as we know, his own upbringing provided no other example. Whatever the reason, LG stayed in New York, and before he knew it his oldest daughter was married.

While in Paris with her mother the following spring, Ann eloped with Crawford Hill, the scion of a wealthy mining family whom she had met on an Atlantic crossing. Crawford's mother was Denver social arbiter Louise Sneed Hill, renowned in popular culture for snubbing the jolly parvenu and *Titanic* survivor, the Unsinkable Molly Brown. Ann soon found herself in the same boat: icily unwelcoming to new money and not partial to the Chosen People, Louise disapproved of Crawford's choice and had forbidden him to marry Ann for at least a year and he had agreed. Then, as soon as his mother was safely aboard the *Aquitania* en route to New York, he married Ann in Paris in a private ceremony. Louise was beyond furious when the news reached her and, publicly distancing herself from her new in-laws, she telegrammed the press that Crawford was "disgraced" and no longer part of her family: "Absolutely I have disowned him . . . and as long as I live I never expect to speak to his wife." Louise told the gaggle of reporters that met her at the pier in New York, "I do not care to discuss my reasons."[3] Anti-Semitism was likely one of them: Ann would always be known in the Hill family as "the little Jewish girl from New York," and Louise would remain implacably distant from her daughter-in-law throughout her son's decade-long marriage.[4]

LG and Marie (who attended the wedding, such as it was) said nothing publicly except to provide the cover story that it had been very small because the bridegroom's family was in mourning. But given Crawford's financial and social bona fides, the Princess of Lake Geneva was likely delighted. With LG, the picture is slightly murkier: after Ann and Crawford left to honeymoon in the South of France, Marie went blithely off to London for her presentation but LG, who had planned to join her in Europe, was said to be "detained" in New York and did not make the trip. This time his absence may have been more calculated: it is unclear whether Ann knew her grandfather was Jewish and therefore understood the source of Louise Hill's dislike. Did LG hesitate to deal with difficult questions about her disapproval? Or worse, did he fear his presence (and name) would highlight Ann's social "unsuitableness" and precipitate further unpleasant press sallies from Ann's mother-in-law? It's impossible to say. We only know that he stayed home and that the Hill connection added to the Kaufman family's social luster.

Only a dozen years out of Marquette, Louis and Marie Kaufman were now fully integrated into the wealthiest, most social set in America. They were rich—seriously rich—thanks to LG's machinations on behalf of General Motors and to the exponential growth and success of the Chatham Phenix Bank. In 1911 when LG took the helm of that new composite bank its resources had been just $22 million. By 1925, the year it became the Chatham Phenix National Bank and Trust Company (the first national bank in New York City to be so designated), those resources had ballooned to $300 million, and the Chatham Phenix had become one of the ten largest banks in the country. Deposits and loan income were only half the story: under LG's supervision the bank had subsumed and taken over the resources of more than a dozen local financial institutions. The list of banks the Chatham Phenix had "merged with" and obliterated include the Century Bank, the Consolidated National Bank, the National Reserve Bank, the Mutual Alliance Trust Company, the Nineteenth Ward Bank, the Twelfth Ward Bank, the Gansevoort Bank, the Security Bank, the Monroe Bank, the Jefferson Bank, the Van Norden Trust Company, the People's Bank, the New York County National Bank, and the Metropolitan Trust Company.

Fueled by LG's success and Marie's intrepid social climbing, by the mid-1920s the Kaufman family had intermarried with Biddles and Hills, shared a ball with Dalziels, been presented at court, entertained du Ponts, and worked their way into the wealthy social set that crossed on the *Majestic, Aquitania, Olympic,* and *Queen Mary* each spring, spent the season in London, then followed a prescribed social round at their multiple dwelling places in summer, fall, and winter. After the season, when friends dispersed to Newport, Oyster Bay, and the Adirondacks, the Kaufmans entertained at Granot Loma before returning to New York in autumn to attend debutante balls, enjoy the nightlife of Jazz Age Manhattan, and oversee the accelerating mating dances of their children. Then, early in the new year, they and almost everyone else in their set headed south to Palm Beach.

Palm Beach, known familiarly in LG's household as "Palm Bitch," had been the undisputed winter home of the social moneyed set since about 1910. The Kaufmans arrived there in the late 1910s, established themselves at the Breakers, the hotel owned by oil tycoon and Palm Beach pioneer Henry Flagler, and began to insinuate themselves into the local social hierarchy. They had little trouble. People of "mixed" ancestry were accepted in the Palm Beach of the 1920s, and new money was fine as long as there was plenty of it. (In the 1950s this social dynamic changed and with Jews no longer welcome in certain circles, Jews and gentiles began to socialize in the "separate but equal" manner that still exists today.) The Kaufmans jumped into this open, palm-shaded society with both feet: they hosted all-night dances and sunrise breakfasts on rented houseboats and gave lavish parties at the Breakers. In 1920, now sure of their social ground, they began the search for a permanent local home.

They found it in the Villa Sonia, a large Dutch Revival–style house overlooking Lake Worth, the town's inland waterway. The size and location were perfect and so was the provenance: the house, on the Lake Trail at Sunset Avenue, was currently owned by Jews but it had been built by popular racing impresario Colonel E. R. Bradley and was located just north of his eponymous Beach Club, a private gaming establishment and Palm Beach landmark much frequented by Vanderbilts and Kennedys. In 1920, in the largest real estate transaction recorded in Palm Beach that year, $100,000 changed hands and the Kaufmans became the new owners of the Villa Sonia.

Thus equipped they began to entertain at scale: the Villa Sonia boasted a capacious dining room, a two-story "great room" filled with wicker and teak furniture, and plenty of guest rooms, and these were soon augmented with three adjoining guest cottages, purchased between 1920 and 1923 and christened El Bella Vista, Vista del Lago, and El Nido. (These purchases gave LG control of an entire block of Sunset Avenue, with the exception of a villa belonging to a certain Mr. Benjamin Clayton, whom he was apparently unable to shift.) His villa's commodious waterside lawns were also put to good use: in March 1923 the Kaufmans hosted seventy people for dinner and another eighty for dancing on a large, enclosed dance floor on the lakeshore, then did it all again with a second group of guests two weeks later. On each occasion a red carpet covered the patio that led to the dance floor. In return the Kaufmans were asked everywhere and partied with A-listers like Lawrence Copley Thaw, Violet Deering (whose Miami mansion Viscaya is now a museum), and Mrs. Randolph Hearst (who became a

The Villa Sonia in Palm Beach, ca. 1925. Collection of Peter Kaufman.

more frequent companion after Mr. Hearst began to spend most of his time with the actress Marion Davies). Minor European royalty were also part of their coterie: "At Palm Beach . . . no one is in the spotlight more than Mr. and Mrs. LG Kaufman," reported the *Detroit Free Press*, in a paean in newsprint to life at the Villa Sonia: "The Kaufmans apparently have assembled that rarity in household arrangements—the perfect servant force . . . they frequently ask eight or ten guests to their home, the Villa Sonia. Recently, they numbered among their house guests a Russian prince, an Italian princess and a Russian Count."[5]

The "perfect servant force" (which Marie likely achieved by cannibalizing the staff of 270 Park Avenue and Granot Loma and transporting them south by private train) was only one of the attractions of the Kaufmans' menage: they commissioned a houseboat, painted green and orange and shaped and decorated like a sixteenth-century Spanish galleon, and moored it in Lake Worth. One of only three private houseboats operating in Palm Beach at the time, it was an enviable piece of social kit—perfect for small dinners and dances like one they hosted for their daughter Joan during her debutante year, featuring a Hawaiian orchestra and dancers from the Ziegfeld Follies. It was on this houseboat in 1924 that composer Vincent Youmans played LG and Marie a new song he had just written for an upcoming Broadway musical. It was "Tea for Two," one of the most famous show tunes ever written.

Other watercraft were also part of the Kaufmans' entertaining arsenal: although they did not have their own yacht (they were often reported to be commissioning one but never actually

The Kaufmans' houseboat moored in Lake Worth, Palm Beach, ca. 1925. Collection of Peter Kaufman.

did) they frequently chartered others' for trips to the Florida Keys and other destinations, and they had a good eye for luxury and quality. In 1928 they rented the *Sequoia* (the American presidential yacht from the 1930s to the 1970s), which could seat twenty-two for a formal dinner, and they later chartered William Vincent Astor's sleek, black *Nourmahal*, considered the finest private yacht of its era, filled it with family and friends, and cruised off Southampton, New York.

Back on land, the Kaufmans' Palm Beach days were spent at the Everglades Club, founded in 1919 by sewing machine heir Paris Singer, and at the Bath and Tennis Club, syndicated by LG's friend and Chatham Phenix board member E. F. Hutton and his in-law Anthony Biddle in 1927. (LG would be a lifelong member of both clubs and a savior of one: when the Everglades faced bankruptcy during the Depression he was part of a small group that bought the club and kept it going.) An avid golfer, LG was also a member of the exclusive Seminole Golf Club, also founded by E. F. Hutton. Friendly and easygoing, he was popular among his fellow members and his fishing skills, honed since his childhood in the UP, made him a valued sporting companion. Among the Palm Beach set he was famous for having landed a fifty-pound grouper while cruising on Charles Dillingham's yacht off the Florida Keys. Marie was admired for her elegant wardrobe of well-cut, unusually patterned silk dresses and for her prowess at social dancing. Dancing was part of most evening entertainments in Palm Beach, dancing contests were common at local charity events, and Marie was often asked to help pick the winners. On one such occasion when attendees had donated $1,000 each to watch a Charleston contest pitting chorus girls against debutantes, Marie likely had to recuse herself as two of her daughters were in the running. A chorus girl won the grand prize that night but Joan and Ann—apparently chips off the maternal block—came second and third.

This triumph, and all other aspects of the Kaufmans' life in Palm Beach, was chronicled incessantly by the local society rag, the *Palm Beach Post*. LG and Marie's arrivals to and departures from "the Colony," the names of their houseguests, and their attendance at social events made the paper on an almost daily basis, along with northern news of their coming-out balls, presentations at court, and the society weddings of their children. Relentlessly adhering to the formula "if you can't say something nice say nothing at all," the *Post* never alluded to the parade of unsuitable partners, divorces, and other unfortunate behaviors that were fast becoming part of Kaufman family life. The same could not be said for other members of the Fourth Estate: the papers that had printed every word Louise Sneed Hill had to say about the unsuitability of Ann Kaufman covered all aspects of Graveraet Kaufman's elopement with Follies girl Mae Daw the following year and panted for news it would cause a similar family rupture. LG, no stranger to the art of handling the press, spoiled the fun: "They had been engaged for months," he smoothly informed every reporter who asked for comment. "They had our complete consent . . . Miss Daw is a sweet girl."[6]

Graveraet's other behaviors were harder to neutralize: although only a lowly assistant cashier at the Chatham Phenix, he had been equipped with a stenographer, a valet, and a chauffeur and proved unable to keep the proper distance from any of them. In 1926 he became romantically involved with the stenographer, promised to marry her, and then eloped with Mae Daw instead. His valet regaled the *New York Daily News* with the gory details, emphasizing his own role as go-between and pocketing a juicy fee for the information: the stenographer then brought suit against Graveraet for breach of promise, demanding $100,000, and even after the Kaufmans settled out of court for $15,000 and the stenographer and valet both left the family's employ, the story continued to have "legs" and to highlight Graveraet's less attractive characteristics. "His great idea always seemed to be to impress his inferiors that he was Graveraet Kaufman, the son of a millionaire," sniffed the jilted stenographer, going on to praise the millionaire himself, whose behavior (if not his parenting) she found exemplary. "The elder Mr. Kaufman is extremely courteous toward his employees," Miss Fee reported. "He holds the door open for the humblest little girl typist as gallantly as though she were Mrs. Vanderbilt."[7]

Courtesy and gallantry came naturally to LG, along with an ability to put people—all kinds of people—at their ease. He did not lord it over his children, servants, employees, and fellow townspeople, or constantly remind them of his power over them. Although in his business life he was all about control—often exerted from behind the scenes—and he had expertly corralled the rich and powerful on behalf of Mayor Hylan, power for power's sake was not his modus operandi. Nor was distance and hauteur: unlike Marie, who instructed, corrected, or ignored anyone of a lower station, LG was the man who sat and watched Nestor Kallioinen work, the "natural parent" to children and grandchildren, the millionaire his hometown newspaper knew as a "just folks kind of man."

He was also a family man for whom money was no object when tragedy threatened. In the early fall of 1928, his son Young Kaufman, now rising quickly in the ranks of the Chatham Phenix, had left his pregnant wife, Patricia, at Granot Loma and returned to work in New York. Patricia went into labor, the baby proved to be in distress, and the remoteness of the UP and the limitations of early air travel (there was only one air passenger terminal in the country in 1928) made the danger very real. Acting with concern and dispatch, LG sent a plane to pick up a Chicago physician and the pilot landed his Fairchild monoplane (and the doctor) safely on a Marquette golf course. (When he attempted to take off again, however, he grazed a tree, nosedived into the ground, but survived.) Meanwhile, the distraught young husband chartered a plane at Curtiss Field on Long Island and raced toward Chicago, hoping to connect with a "flying boat" that would take him as far as Milwaukee. Alas, none of these emergency flights were successful. Mechanical issues forced Young's plane down at Cleveland, it took him two more days to get to the UP by train, and he arrived too late: the baby did not survive, and Young was not there to comfort his wife during labor or to see his daughter before she died. As always, dozens of newspapers reported every detail of this aeronautical saga—but not always correctly. The ever-vigilant *American Israelite* got the Chicago doctor right but mistakenly named LG, the most important (and most Jewish) member of the Kaufman clan, as the patient.[8]

The *American Israelite* had its facts straight in one important particular: its article went on to identify LG as a "ardent numismatist," noting that his coin collection had recently been on public display in New York.[9] Indeed, LG had become a macher in the numismatic world—although not in the usual way. His collection had originated with mining tycoon Edward N. Breitung in the second half of the nineteenth century, passed at his death to his wife, Mary, and after 1893 became the property of her second husband, Nathan Kaufman, who added considerably to its riches. After Nathan's death Mary had retained ownership of the collection, but when she died in 1923 it reverted to Nathan's estate. It was then (by some unknown mechanism Nathan's heirs would later call illegal appropriation) that it became the property of Louis Graveraet Kaufman.

LG took his inheritance seriously and, just as he had once studied nightly to absorb the principles of banking, he educated himself about the world of coin collecting. He read widely, took advice from dealers, became a member of the American Numismatic Association, and is assumed by those in the trade to have been the "wealthy Michigan banker" to whom, in the late 1920s, prominent Milwaukee coin dealer Hubert Polzer supplied many important examples. LG spoke proudly about his collection, in person and in print, and like many numismatists of his era presented coins as gifts—including to the young winners of debate contests held in Marquette. In 1925 when the Chatham Phenix annexed the Metropolitan Trust Company, the elegant lobby of its marble-fronted building at 716 Fifth Avenue became a public showcase for his coins, complete with an expensively printed catalogue signed with a flourish in LG's old-fashioned hand. Three years later the same coins made their way to Brooklyn where, as part of a National Thrift Campaign organized to encourage Americans to invest in safe securities, they were exhibited in the windows of Namm's Department Store. (This "Thrift" campaign was unsuccessful, as the rampant investing on margin that fueled the crash of 1929 continued unchecked.)

Visitors to both exhibitions saw only half of LG's collection—the coins he had designated "Dollars of the World." These "dollars"—sixteen hundred of them—had apparently been an interest of Edward Breitung's, and it's easy to see why Nathan and LG felt the same fascination: all were about the size of a U.S. silver dollar and contained about the same amount of silver, but none had been made in America. Instead they were issued by 429 other countries, states, provinces, principalities, cities, religious bodies, and organizations around the world, beginning in 1486 when Sigismund, Archduke of Austria, struck the first "dollar-sized" coin. Some in the cache were related to American history, including a "Blood Money" coin minted in 1778 and used to pay the Hessian troops hired by King George III to help put down the American Revolution, a coin struck in Amsterdam in 1601 by the government that sent explorer Henry Hudson to the New World, and a coin minted in Spain in 1504 in honor of the discovery of America. Others were notable for their origins or decoration, including a coin struck by Napoleon in 1815 after his return from Elba, an English coin from 1658 bearing an image of Oliver Cromwell, and an 1865 coin from the Swiss canton of Schaffhausen depicting William Tell's son with an apple on his head.

The second part of the collection (which would later prove far more valuable) was all-American: included in this roster of 1,530 coins was one of every size and date struck by every U.S. Mint between 1794 and 1942 (the year of LG's death)—and that was just for starters. The group also included rare nineteenth-century American gold pieces and silver dollars struck by non-U.S. entities like the Lesher Dollar minted in Colorado in 1900 by the Free Silver Movement without government sanction. The collection was rich in private and territorial gold pieces, copper coins, rare Colonial coins, Confederate coins, and Civil War tokens—copper, nickel, or white metal discs stamped with patriotic symbols and/or the names of the businesses, accepted as Union currency during the Civil War.

In 1927 LG's American coins too went on display—but not in New York. As part of the construction of the new First National Bank of Marquette, LG had ordered a series of custom wall safes and locked vitrines installed in the "Directors' Room," a plush office space opposite the "Women's Room," and just before the grand opening he quietly filled them with his 1,500 American coins. It was a bit of a stealth move, and as the local press said little about the collection's presence, few of the residents of Marquette who toured the bank on opening day in 1927, or who banked there for the next half a century, realized that one of the country's most important numismatic caches was only a few steps away. LG's "Dollars of the World" were later installed on the bank's mezzanine and remained on display there until their sale, with little fanfare, in the 1950s. In the 1970s, an auction of the American coins in the Directors' Room would generate considerably more money and attention.

Neither part of LG's coin collection attracted much attention from Marie Kaufman. While she and LG collaborated on the design and furnishing of Granot Loma and the American and European paintings and antique European furniture that filled their many residences, their other collecting interests diverged. LG concentrated on coins, purebred farm animals, and local banks he could add to the ever-expanding Chatham Phenix, and Marie—perhaps because her father had been in the jewelry business—became a major collector of important jewels. Jewelry was Marie's passion and calling card: so famous was her glittering trove that by the 1920s reporters routinely commented on the specific pieces she was wearing on any given evening. Her collection was considered one of the most important in the country (rubies, diamonds, and pearls predominated) and so valuable that a male retainer from Granot Loma accompanied her on every journey, serving as a de facto bodyguard and ensuring that no baubles went missing.

Marie's other collecting interest was equine: she had always been "horsey"—she rode at Granot Loma, took a box at the National Horse Show at the 94th Street Armory in New York City, and encouraged her daughters' equestrian talents—but in 1927 she upped the ante and became a player in the sport of kings. It cost about $50,000 a year to maintain and race a single horse ($780,000 today), but that presented no problems for Marie, especially as she could move her entourage and her horses from racetrack to racetrack by private car. She established Loma Stables and, displaying a shrewd eye for equine talent, immediately purchased a yearling called Twink. By 1928 she was in the money. The two-year-old Twink was celebrated as "one of the best juveniles of the year."[10] And, with Racing Hall of Fame jockey Laverne Fator aboard, he romped to victory in the Albany Handicap, the Grand Union Hotel Stakes in Saratoga, and the Waldon Handicap at Pimlico.

As the country descended into financial misery, Marie ascended in her rarified new world. The sporting columns began to refer to her as "a woman of the turf" and to mention her in company with Mrs. Payne Whitney, Mrs. Graham Fair Vanderbilt, and other well-born and well-known owners.[11] After Twink she acquired On Post (winner of the Walden Handicap at Pimlico in 1931) and finally Tick On, the horse that would put Loma Stables on the map. Sixteen hands high, jet black, and temperamental, Tick On was the son and grandson of serious racehorses and his breeding was coming to the fore. As a two-year-old he won so many races that in 1931 Loma Stables was listed as one of the sport's leading money earners, standing twenty-first in the nation. Marie splashed out, securing winter quarters at New York's Belmont Park, boarding her breeding stock on a farm in Kentucky, and hiring Max Hirsch, one of the most successful trainers in racing history, to take her promising horse in hand. It all paid off, and in 1932 Tick On was entered for the Kentucky Derby.

The fifty-eighth running of this iconic race was not as iconic as some in its history—several important horses had scratched, the Depression was deepening and bets totaled less than in any year since World War I, and the rainy weather was not propitious. But when the Kaufman family arrived at Churchill Downs in their private car they found an unexpectedly large crowd of forty thousand assembled to witness what was shaping up to be a three-horse race. The favorites were Stepenfetchit, owned by Mrs. John Hay Whitney; Burgoo King, owned by their friend and Palm Beach neighbor Colonel E. R. Bradley; and Tick On, owned by Mrs. Louis Graveraet Kaufman. Tick On's glossy coat and elegant lines had caused much positive chatter in the press and among the crowds, and during a prerace workout he had thrilled onlookers by running the track in near-record time. By Derby Day he was *the* favorite, at odds of two to one, and it seemed as if a Kaufman win was in the bag.

But on the day Tick On spoiled his own party: he was so fractious at the starting gate that the race had to be delayed for sixteen minutes and when it finally began, he broke in the middle of the field and was shut off at the first turn. The Kaufmans watched with shock and dismay as their horse finished sixth behind four others and the winner, Burgoo King. Hoping Tick On had just had an off day, Marie tried again and entered him in the Preakness that same month, but while he did better, finishing only a head behind winner Burgoo King, the magic had vanished. Tick On made less than $10,000 each year in 1934, 1936, and 1937, and Marie stopped hoping. Loma Stables existed until 1939, but after the Derby Day debacle it faded, following a downward trajectory that seemed sadly appropriate. While the Kaufmans would not face the penury that overwhelmed so many during the 1930s, the fracturing of the family and everything LG had long taken for granted had begun.

7

THE BEGINNING OF THE END

For Louis Graveraet Kaufman the Chatham Phenix National Bank and Trust Company was more than a métier and moneymaking machine. It was his creature, his raison d'être, his alter ego. He had created it in his own nimble, successful image, grown it to fifty times its original size, and used it to make history. The Chatham Phenix was the first bank with branches in New York City and the first national bank in New York to incorporate the designation "trust company" into its title. It had sold the most war bonds during World War I. It was clearly the best. The demise—even the diminution—of such a financial masterpiece seemed impossible to LG; it was like imagining his own death. "We have sought to make the Chatham Phenix a monument . . . that will last for all time," he told the *Wall Street Journal* in 1927. "You can say from me that the Chatham Phenix is more than a bank: it is a trust, a stewardship, and long after I am gone it will still be doing business under its own name."[1] That name was sacrosanct: while LG had deprived twenty-one other banks of their historic monikers—sloshing them ruthlessly into the giant mixing bowl of the Chatham Phenix and proudly adding their defunct charters to the walls in his private office—that was as it should be. His bank had been the big dog in those transactions and those other banks had been, well, dog food—something the Chatham Phenix would never be.

Two years later this point of view would prove monumentally inconvenient: in the spring of 1929, just a few months before the worst stock market crash in history, the California-based Bank of America proposed a merger with the Chatham Phenix. The West Coast bank was headed by Amadeo Giannini, a brilliant, up-from-nothing wunderkind much like LG himself, and onlookers loved the Horatio Alger-ness of it all when it was announced that there would soon be a bicoastal consolidation of the two institutions. LG would be at the helm as president and chief executive where he would reign over assets of nearly $1 billion—a major step up from his already lofty perch. But as soon as merger discussions got serious a problem arose: the two banks were of roughly equal size and when LG insisted that, of course, the new entity would be called the Chatham Phenix, he discovered that Giannini was equally insistent that it be called the Bank of America. No amount of talking could break the deadlock and the following month Wall Street awoke to the news that the merger was off. In the years to come LG would have reason to contemplate this road not taken as from the sidelines he watched the Bank of America survive the Depression, grow exponentially, and earn Amadeo Giannini a permanent place in banking history.

But in 1929 LG simply shrugged off the merger misfire and moved confidently on. Who needed the Bank of America? The Chatham Phenix was rocking the financial markets of the Roaring Twenties and he was about to embark upon a project that would ensure him a place in American history. The opportunity had come to him through the Chatham Phenix Corporation, a bank offshoot he'd established to provide capital to developers in the red-hot New York real estate market of the 1920s. A developer by the name of Lloyd de L. Brown had soon come calling. Brown had his eye on a crackerjack of a site—two acres at the corner of Fifth Avenue and 34th Street. The land was currently occupied by the Waldorf Astoria Hotel, but the neighborhood around the venerable *hôtellerie* (which, coincidentally, was built of ruddy Marquette sandstone) was becoming increasingly commercial. Its owners wanted to sell up and build a new hotel further uptown. All Brown had to do was turn the Waldorf Astoria into a pile of sandstone and presto! One of the largest, best-located building sites in all of Manhattan would be his. Brown scurried to the Chatham Phenix Corporation and borrowed an estimated $15 million to secure the Fifth Avenue acreage, planning to erect a large office and loft building there.

Brown's contract called for three payments, and he made the first two with no issues, but on June 1, 1929, just as talks were opening between the Bank of America and the Chatham Phenix, he defaulted on the third and the rights to the Waldorf Astoria site reverted to his creditor, the Chatham Phenix Corporation. Suddenly LG had control of the most coveted site on the island of Manhattan. It was twice as big as others occupied by Midtown towers and part of it was zoned for a building of unlimited height. Rather than let others make the fortune it represented LG decided to develop the parcel himself and formed a syndicate of wealthy friends to share the financial load. Edgar Bloom (president of Western Electric), Edward F. Hutton (chairman of Postum Cereal), Ellis P. Earle (president of Nipissing Mines), and Frank Phillips (president of Phillips Petroleum) came on board and bought the lot from the bank. Lloyd de L. Brown had secured the services of veteran architects Shreve, Lamb, and Harmon (two of its partners had worked for the famous Gilded Age architects Carrère and Hastings) for the building he had hoped to erect, and LG's group decided to retain this team for the large office and showroom tower they now planned. But before the new blueprints were completed, LG was contacted by an old colleague with an unexpected proposition.

It was John J. Raskob, the financial Svengali of DuPont

de Nemours, Inc., who came knocking at LG's door. The two men were not close personal friends, but they respected each other's business acumen and had worked together in several capacities. In particular, Raskob had been helpful to LG at the time of the take-back of GM for William Durant in 1915. It was Raskob who, foreseeing the coming of the auto age and its benefits for the DuPont Corporation, had advised his boss Pierre du Pont to accept banker Storrow's offer and join the board of General Motors, break the tie between the pro- and anti-Durant factions, and put LG's man back in control. As a GM board member, LG had continued to work with Raskob during the years he ran the huge automotive corporation for the du Ponts, and Raskob had also spent time on the board of the Chatham Phenix, along with Samuel and Pierre du Pont.

When the two men sat down together in the early summer of 1929, the fifty-year-old Raskob was, for the first time in many, many years, out of a job. The previous year he had backed his friend, former New York governor Al Smith, for president and in doing so had become persona non grata at GM. (Its president, Alfred P. Sloan, was a staunch Hoover man.) The politically incorrect Raskob had been forced to depart, albeit with a haul of valuable GM stock. Raskob had thought to leverage his auto industry experience and join Walter P. Chrysler's company and had even begun talks with that entity, but then negotiations had unaccountably stalled. Humiliated, Raskob had watched as a preening Walter P. announced the construction of a grand, record-breaking seventy-seven-story Manhattan office building named for himself, while Raskob remained unhappily sidelined. His buddy Al Smith had failed in his presidential bid and was now hurting for money and badly in need of a sinecure. This level of failure was new to John J. Raskob, and he didn't like it one little bit.

And then Raskob heard that his old comrade in arms Louis

Graveraet Kaufman now controlled the old Waldorf site at Fifth Avenue and 34th Street and he had an idea: his brainstorm would, at a stroke, put Walter P. Chrysler in his place, employ Al Smith, provide Raskob with the project of a lifetime, and help LG monetize his real estate windfall. He called on LG and laid out his plan: together, John J. Raskob and Louis Graveraet Kaufman were going to build the tallest building in the world.

There are no records of this pivotal meeting but it's not hard to imagine Raskob's pitch: the economy was booming and in the world of Manhattan real estate the sky was literally the limit. The two men worked well together, and the new project would be something of a reprise of their General Motors gambit with Pierre du Pont (who was already on board) providing some of the money and Raskob in charge of operations. Al Smith, a popular figure with New Yorkers, would make the perfect front man for the project. The new skyscraper would not only be a huge moneymaker but blow past Walter P.'s Chrysler Building on its way up to the sky and catapult its builders into the history books. LG listened with interest. Why should he give up the name "Chatham Phenix" to join forces with the Bank of America when his bank could finance this record-setting building and make the name even more important? He was fifty-nine years old, rich beyond his wildest dreams, his professional life ticking along on autopilot. Here was a chance to open a new chapter, work in his preferred way—uber-connected and behind the scenes—and leave behind another monument that would stand forever. He was in.

And it was at that moment that Louis Graveraet Kaufman became the father of an architectural icon. As Jason M. Barr, author of *Cities in the Sky: The Quest to Build the World's Tallest Skyscrapers*, writes of the genesis of America's favorite skyscraper: "The pivotal figure was Chatham Phenix National Bank president Louis Kaufman, without whom the Empire State Building would never have gone forward. If he had decided to let the whole thing go, who knows what would have happened to the site, but instead this one banker was excited to try his hand at Manhattan real estate."[2]

With LG on board things happened very quickly. LG's original building syndicate was dissolved (although, as many of its members were directors of the Chatham Phenix and related companies, they would end up investing in the new project anyway) and the 34th Street site became the property of a new syndicate, Empire State, Inc., comprised of LG, Chatham Phenix real estate expert Robert C. Brown, Ellis Earle, John J. Raskob, and Pierre du Pont. For noncommercial window dressing the group added two well-known New York philanthropists, Michael Friedsam and August Heckscher, to their roster. Al Smith was engaged as president at a salary of $50,000 a year, and the architects Shreve, Lamb, and Harmon got started on yet another set of plans.

By July 1929, LG and Raskob were corresponding daily, figuring and refiguring operating expenses, calculating depreciation, and discussing janitorial services and other building-related issues in what seemed to be impressive detail. Their letters bristle with facts and figures, but looking closely it's clear that neither Raskob—who had spent his career in gunpowder and autos—nor the financier/banker LG was much experienced in real estate. Nor could either of them have known that their profit predictions—based on the expectation that the 1931 real estate market would be as buoyant as that of 1929—would be spectacularly wrong. No matter: that summer everyone involved was having a wonderful time. Al Smith and a team from Shreve, Lamb, and Harmon traveled to Granot Loma (no doubt in one of LG's plush private cars) ready to unroll enticing sets of blueprints and share specifics that would keep their moneyman excited and engaged. Fortunately, the excitement turned out to be mutual. The visitors from New York were gobsmacked by the endless vistas and rolling breakers of Lake Superior and by the giant log lodge perched on its shore. Al Smith regarded LG with new interest and respect and presented him with an autographed photo of himself.

At the end of August, two months before the stock market crashed, Raskob wrote the letter that made the project real: marked "personal" and beginning "Dear Lou," the three-page missive laid out the financial underpinnings of the unprecedented build about to be undertaken. Raskob and Pierre du Pont would supply half of the $10 million in working capital the project required and LG "and certain other gentlemen" would supply the other half. (Those "other gentlemen" would later prove to have been the Chatham Phenix Allied Corporation, another Chatham Phenix spin-off, leaving LG and his bank on the hook for the entire $5 million.) The building was to be eighty stories high—comfortably above the Chrysler Building's "record" specs—and projections for future income, assuming a vacancy rate of 10 percent or less, were excellent. Following a long paragraph detailing Al Smith's $50,000 salary, Smith's right to 5 percent of the building's common stock, and exactly when that stock would be vested, Raskob addressed himself to the man who was making it all possible: "I appreciate the opportunity you have given us in this matter," he wrote, "and particularly in the privilege of being associated with you and your group in the doing of something big and really worthwhile. I am sure it will be the most outstanding thing in New York and a credit to the city and state, as well as to those associated with it."[3]

The next day Al Smith went before the press and made an official announcement: he was, he informed the jostling crowd of young men packing notepads and flash equipment, now the president of a company that was about to build a skyscraper the likes of which the world had never seen. It would stand one thousand feet high—higher than any existing building or any under construction—contain three million square feet of floor space, and house more than sixty thousand persons—more than the population of many counties in his own New York State—on any given day. The architects would be Shreve, Lamb, and Harmon and, the former governor concluded coyly, knowing all would recognize the reference to his former gubernatorial role, the new edifice was to be called the Empire State Building.

As New Yorkers contemplated the enjoyable prospect of "a race to the sky" above Fifth Avenue between the Chrysler Building and the Empire State Building, LG and Raskob began a search for the final members of their team. Five contractors would be asked to make their pitch in Al Smith's office in the Biltmore Hotel but the outcome was never in doubt. Starrett Brothers and Eken, the last team to present, was already the clear favorite. William Starrett had served as head of the Construction Section of the War Industries Board and Paul Starrett had built Manhattan's Main Post Office for the famous architectural team of McKim, Mead and White. Together they had built the seventy-story Bank of Manhattan Building—the tallest New York City building then standing—and so could boast the most experience in skyscraper engineering. When they appeared in Smith's office there were minor questions lobbed about and some jockeying over fees, but the meeting soon concluded with handshakes all around. By mid-September the contractors Starrett Brothers and Eken were in place and about to begin the construction of LG and Raskob's record-breaking build. Not mentioned in any other accounts of the Biltmore meeting was an important reason the Starretts had the inside track on the Empire State Building: they were already working for Louis Graveraet Kaufman. Around the time the Starretts were strutting their stuff in Al Smith's office they were putting the finishing touches on the elegant apartment building they had constructed for him at 625 Park Avenue, on the northeast corner of 65th Street.

In 1928 the Kaufmans had needed a change: like the area around the Waldorf Astoria, the neighborhood surrounding their flat at 270 Park Avenue was growing less fashionable. The luxury residential action was now north of 60th Street—especially on Park Avenue where, thanks to the electrification of the trains that ran beneath it to and from Grand Central (no more steam venting required), its central mall had been covered and planted to form a true "boulevard." Apartment buildings were going up on every corner and the once smutty stretch was fast becoming a glorious fenestrated canyon all the way to 96th Street. Anxious to cash in on the boom (and to provide himself with a fabulous new apartment), LG asked the Chatham Phenix's real estate expert Robert C. Brown to find him a Park Avenue site upon which to build. The search had proved harder than either man had expected, and it was the Starretts—the Starretts who were now finishing LG's new edifice bang on time—who had finally pointed an increasingly frantic Brown toward a rare available parcel. LG was grateful: as far as he was concerned, the Starretts were his guys and the right team to build the Empire State Building.

While LG expected to make a tidy annual profit from his new apartment house, he may have had another motivation for venturing into residential real estate. In 1928 even wealthy, well-connected people of Jewish ancestry were rejected when they attempted to purchase apartments on the most fashionable stretches of Park Avenue, and LG's name did not do him any favors. Most of the rejected gave up and bought across Central Park on the more welcoming Central Park West, but a few took matters into their own hands. In 1927 Jesse Isador Strauss, the president of Macy's Department Store, bought land on Park Avenue near 70th Street and (with the help of the Starretts) erected 720 Park Avenue, a luxurious apartment house in which he and his wife, his extended family, and selected Jewish friends could live. It is more than possible that, having made multiple fruitless attempts to buy a cooperative apartment in existing Park Avenue buildings, LG followed suit. He commissioned 625 Park the following year and, as in Strauss's case, much of his extended family moved there along with him. It was a safe harbor for the Kaufmans and certainly no hardship. Even the Princess of Lake Geneva could not fault the beauty and luxury wrought by the Starretts, nor the classical elegance of the design provided by its architect.

James Edwin Ruthven Carpenter Jr. was a graduate of the prestigious École des Beaux Arts in Paris, a former apprentice in the offices of McKim, Mead and White, and the architect of dozens of high-end apartment houses on Park and Fifth Avenues. LG was consistent in his choices: like the architect of Granot Loma, Benjamin Marshall of Chicago, Carpenter came from a well-to-do family, moved in the same social circles as his clients, was about the same age as LG, hailed from the middle of the country (Tennessee), and was business-savvy—often acting as developer as well as architect on projects.

He was also a major innovator: known as the "father of the modern large apartment," he had pioneered the revolutionary "off the foyer" layout that changed the look and functionality of luxury New York spaces forever.[4] After 1912, instead of presenting the usual enfilade of large rooms and a rabbit warren of smaller ones, all Carpenter apartments featured a grand entrance gallery around which all reception spaces—drawing room, dining room, library, study—flowed as gracefully as in an elegant country house, while private and service areas remained discreetly "invisible." His innovation was swiftly appropriated by his younger and more famous competitor, Rosario Candela, and every one of the 123 classic Park and Fifth Avenue buildings

*625 Park Avenue in New York City, 2023.
Photograph by Ann Berman.*

designed by these two architectural giants features apartments organized the Carpenter way.

Exterior-wise, Carpenter skewed minimal and elegant. The building he designed for LG (still as beautiful as it was in 1929) is an elongated limestone echo of a Renaissance palace with restrained classical decoration, including ornamental stonework just below its top floor. This sly architectural punctuation separates the spectacular triplex penthouse Carpenter created for LG and Marie from the other apartments—still grand but only single story—below. The Kaufman triplex was, and remains, a true mansion in the sky. Its first level, the building's entire top floor, originally featured a twenty-eight-foot-long entrance gallery, a grand semicircular staircase, a thirty-foot-long drawing room, a dining room, a library, six bedrooms, six maid's rooms, a servants' hall, six and a half baths, a kitchen, and a laundry room—twenty-eight rooms in all. At the top of a curving staircase, a duplex penthouse set back behind lush planted terraces provided eight more rooms, including another major entrance gallery and a sixty-eight-foot-long ballroom. LG and Marie took possession of the triplex in the fall of 1929. Marie brought roomfuls of classic antique furniture—mostly dark woods, often finished with marquetry—from 270 Park and installed them against a muted background of plaster moldings, classical woodwork, cream carpets, and marble floors. The three youngest Kaufman daughters, Juliet, Marie Louise, and Jane, moved into the penthouse with their parents, while four of their married siblings were ensconced with their spouses and children in full-floor apartments below.

The stock market crashed on October 24, 1929, but as that financial avalanche began its terrible descent, the Kaufmans did not appear to hear its rumble. Life in the triplex went on unchanged and, as breadlines began to form in the streets, Marie began to plan a grand debutante ball for her daughter Juliet.

Unlike Ann's, this one would be "at home." Who needed the Ritz when you had your own ballroom? On the evening of January 3, 1931, the entrance gallery on the first floor provided the perfect space for Juliet—resplendent in white georgette and tulle studded with diamantés—to receive her hundreds of guests. The celebrants then circulated through Carpenter's gracefully connected rooms before drifting up the curving staircase to dance in the penthouse or to sit out (for private, frosty minutes) in its surrounding gardens. Downtown, Juliet's brother Young and his wife, Patricia, were indulging in elaborate entertainments of their own: the following month the pair rented an old carriage house at 3 MacDougall Alley and hosted a "barn dance" for the smart young married set. Guests sporting ancient frock coats, overalls, and ruffled gingham were greeted in a hayloft before sliding down a hay chute to dance to a band that tootled Gershwin tunes from seats in an old wagon.

On one of his terraces high above Park Avenue LG set up a large standing telescope and looked south every morning through its lens to the site where the Empire State Building was rising at a record four and a half stories a week. Although the market had crashed a month after Al Smith's announcement of the coming of the building, LG and Raskob did not pull the plug. Raskob, in fact, had upped the ante. In late 1929, Empire State, Inc., purchased a seventy-five-hundred-square-foot lot abutting the old Waldorf site and with this extra space available he ordered the planned height of the new building to be increased to a whopping eighty-five stories. The additional height was critical in Raskob's eyes, as Walter P. Chrysler had recently (and clandestinely) added the famous Art Deco spire to the apex of his skyscraper, increasing its height and bringing the stats of the competing builds uncomfortably close. Fearful Chrysler might pull another rabbit out of his hat and somehow add even more height to his building before the Empire

State Building was finished, Raskob took a page out of Chrysler's book and called for the installation of a two-hundred-foot dirigible mooring mast (a wildly impractical piece of kit that was never successfully used) atop *his* new building. In the end, the Empire State Building would soar a record 1,250 feet tall, eclipsing the Chrysler Building by 266 feet and Raskob would win his race to the sky.

But extra floors and mooring masts did not come cheap. Raskob, du Pont, LG, and the Chatham Phenix had supplied the first $10 million for the project and Empire State, Inc., had secured a $27.5 million mortgage from the Metropolitan Life Insurance Company. But by April 1930 it was clear more money was needed and to raise it, the Chatham Phenix Allied Corporation, another bank offshoot organized by LG just before the crash and capitalized at $50 million, offered Empire State, Inc., second-mortgage debentures (a kind of bond). The bonds were purchased in the same proportions as the original capital raise with Raskob and du Pont each buying a quarter and the Chatham Phenix Allied Corporation responsible for the other half. As the Chatham Phenix Bank, the Chatham Phenix Corporation, and the Chatham Phenix Allied Corporation were interlocking directorates—entities run by LG and the same selected group of directors—no one objected to these serial investments in a single risky project. No one suggested that putting the bank and its investors on the hook for half of all private capital raised to build the tallest building in the world just after a major financial crash was not the most prudent thing to do.

The Empire State Building rose faster than any major building in history. By the autumn of 1930 most of the structural steel was in place and LG no longer needed a telescope to see his nascent skyscraper looming over the city. On September 9 Al Smith laid the 4,500-pound cornerstone (containing photos of LG and the other officers, architects, and builders) and, having leased the entire eightieth floor, Raskob, du Pont, and LG began to plan an elaborate suite of offices for themselves, complete with paneled walls, wood-burning fireplaces, and elaborately carved mantelpieces. The building was finished over the winter and suddenly it was opening day, May 1, 1931. The entire city seemed to pause: in Depression-era New York City the Empire State Building's sleek silhouette and impossible height were rare reasons to celebrate and New Yorkers made the most of them. Newspapers covered the opening from every possible angle and people gathered in the streets on the day, necks craned as they gazed up at the beautiful new building that towered above their city like Mount Olympus. The ceremony began: policemen held back excited crowds as Al Smith's grandchildren cut a ribbon at the Fifth Avenue entrance. New York governor Franklin Delano Roosevelt pronounced himself "a little awestruck" by the building's height and, from his desk at the White House in Washington, D.C., President Hoover pressed a special key that turned on the building's lights.[5]

But behind this scrim of celebration all was not well. When, after the ceremony, Al Smith took two hundred VIP guests off to a celebratory lunch, the owners of the tallest building in the world were not among them. Only Robert C. Brown was present. Raskob had left town and was steaming toward Italy on the SS *Augusta*, and there is no evidence that LG or Pierre du Pont was anywhere near Fifth Avenue and 34th Street on the big day. It would not have been a happy place to be. What should have been predicable was now abundantly clear: the Empire State Building was a financial disaster. While a huge drop in the price of labor and materials had allowed construction to come in well under budget, profit projections had been based on that 90 percent occupancy rate. In May 1931 the building was 75 percent *empty* and, given the state of the economy, no one expected that figure to improve any time soon. Elevators soon stopped running from the forty-first floor to the seventy-ninth, where not a single space was rented, interiors remained unfinished, and bare light bulbs hung like nooses above concrete floors. New Yorkers who paid with precious nickels to see the view from the building's observation platform made some difference to the bottom line, but not enough. Each night its lights blazed from top to bottom but the brightness was a mirage. The Empire State Building was hemorrhaging money and sliding quickly into debt. Dubbed the "Empty State Building," it was both the pride of New York City and a symbol of its economic pain.

That pain, heretofore unknown to Louis Graveraet Kaufman, finally breached his fortress of money and power. He was still a wealthy man, but his other self, the Chatham Phenix National Bank and Trust Company, was in mortal danger—hemorrhaging from wounds he himself had inflicted. The Empire State Building had become a serious drag on his bank's resources, sucking cash and credit as he and his partners struggled to keep the towering building out of bankruptcy. By some accounts another $22 million ($370 million today) was advanced by Raskob, du Pont, LG, and the Chatham Phenix during its construction and as much as half of that came from the Chatham Phenix and its interlocking satellite corporations. Soon those entities were robbing Peter to pay Paul in a series of increasingly desperate, under-the-radar transactions in an effort to keep the machinery in motion. The scope of the disaster was becoming clear and LG's board of directors, some of whom had also invested personally in the Empire State Building, felt misled by LG and were deeply unhappy about the effects of the project on the Chatham Phenix and their own bottom lines.

It was a bad time to have made a bad call. The Depression was deepening and, as at many other banks in the country, deposits at the Chatham Phenix were falling steadily. In January 1931, as an apparently unperturbed LG had watched the glittering crowds dancing at Juliet's penthouse ball, the troubling numbers would have been on his mind. That winter he may still have hoped that the problem would be temporary, but by the summer he knew better: deposits at the Chatham Phenix were now down a whopping $111 million, the Empire State Building was nearly bankrupt, and the financial dominoes in his life were starting to fall. In August 1931 the Chatham Phenix Allied Corporation was "acquired" by the Atlas Utilities Corporation in a sweep of ten distressed entities and the papers began reporting a "whispering campaign pertaining to one of New York's leading institutions, the Chatham Phenix Bank," hinting at a serious collapse.[6] A lawyer for the Chatham Phenix brandished a financial statement attesting to its healthy liquid position, but his documents convinced nobody. The following month retail distribution of Chatham Phenix Corporation bonds were halted. LG knew what came next. There was no other way.

If Harvey D. Gibson (1882–1950), the president of the Manufacturers Trust Company of New York, was familiar with Louis Graveraet Kaufman's up-from-the-sticks backstory, he might have mused on its similarity to his own. Newspapers that had once marveled at LG's exotic midwestern roots and unlikely elevation to the presidency of the Chatham Phenix were now chronicling Gibson's rise from his birthplace in North Conway, New Hampshire, and his assumption in 1917, at the age of thirty-four, of the presidency of the Liberty National Bank in New York. As the Chatham Phenix had done a decade earlier, Gibson's bank had grown steadily larger through takeover and merger, and in January 1931 he had become the president of the Manufacturers Trust, which, with no giant liabilities like the Empire State Building, was doing just fine. From his perch Gibson was now negotiating more takeovers—taking his pick among the copious litter of distressed New York banks humbled by the Depression. It wasn't long before he turned his attention to the struggling Chatham Phenix. In January 1931 the Chatham Phenix's deposits had been $17 million *more* than the Manufacturers Trust Company's, but by November of that year they were $31 million *less*, and Gibson moved in for the kill. LG's board of directors, angry about the Empire State Building, seeing no better option, and anxious to protect the value of their own shares, agreed to a "merger" with the Manufacturers Trust Company.

LG's own Chatham Phenix shares were in play, but when he and Gibson met to discuss terms, money was not the main issue on his mind. The resources of the Chatham Phenix were still $236 million and as Manufacturers Trust's resources were only $358 million, LG hoped they were similar enough to assure him a place in the new bank's power structure and, more importantly, some leverage in the question of its name. He quickly learned that a leadership position would not be forthcoming. When the management roster of the "merged" bank was announced in December 1931, Harvey D. Gibson was president and CEO while LG, whose name appeared in small type in a long list of board members, was designated only as "Head of the Executive Committee." With its announcement of the merger, the *Brooklyn Standard Union* ran a telling montage: below a large photo of Gibson in a snappy cardigan and tie, the editors appended a small, outdated portrait of LG in a dark suit fashionable around 1910. It looked less like a merger announcement than a death notice.[7]

For a while Harvey Gibson remained cagey about the name of the new bank, telling LG only that several names were under consideration and repeating many times that the one chosen would be different from that of either "partner." He was no fool, had likely divined LG's weak spot, and realized that, as long as the older man had any hope that the name "Chatham Phenix" would figure in the new bank's title, he would cooperate willingly in the processes of extinction. When all such details had been tidied the ax fell: the name of the new "merged" bank, Gibson told the papers, would be the Manufacturers Trust Company, adding smoothly that "the conclusion became obvious that no better standard could be found under which the enlarged bank resulting from the merger could carry on . . . and it seemed more prudent to retain the established name than to construct a composite name or adopt a new one." "Thus," wrote the *Boston Globe*, recording LG's sorrow and humiliation in black-and-white, "the name of the Chatham Phenix National Bank and Trust Company will pass out of existence."[8]

Financially, Gibson's deal was as good as could have been expected and LG and other Chatham Phenix stockholders now owned part of one of the biggest banks in New York. But while LG had seen his bank's size as nearly equivalent to Gibson's, the Manufacturers Trust president had calculated their size ratio at approximately two to one in his bank's favor. Gibson's original stockholders retained holdings of 1.1 million shares in the newly enlarged bank while "newcomers" like LG divided 546,750 shares among themselves. (LG's portion is unknown, but as the Chatham's Phenix's president he likely claimed a substantial slice.) The shares were worth owning: the newly enlarged Manufacturers Trust was almost obscenely vibrant in a year in which more than two thousand American banks failed and, as LG must have noted grimly, boasted a whopping sixty branches.

But these were of no more interest to him than the rest of Harvey Gibson's empire. He could exert no real influence from his makeshift perch on the executive committee and there was no joy in interacting with former Chatham Phenix directors who had once answered only to him (and blamed him for the debacle of the Empire State Building). He waited until June 22, then resigned his executive committee post on the face-saving pretext that he was too often out of town to give it his full attention. He kept his seat on the Manufacturers Trust board and his son Young was made a vice president. The bank later became Manufacturers Hanover Trust Company, then Chemical Bank, and today is part of JP Morgan Chase.

Toppled bank presidents were thick on the ground in 1932 and the resignation of even one of the most famous and longest-serving in New York attracted little attention. But amid a scattering of press reports announcing LG's decision to "step down" from the merged entity, a writer from the *Daily Oklahoman* paused to note the human and historical implications of the event: "The resignation of Louis G. Kaufman as chairman of the Executive Committee of the Manufacturers Trust Company removed temporarily from the active ranks of Wall Street bankers an engaging personality," the reporter wrote, going on to identify LG as "the Father of Branch Banking" and noting that he had "been so proud of his Michigan hometown" that he had been granted permission to be the first man in the country to head two national banks at once.[9]

LG now retreated to that Michigan town, and to the president's office in that other bank. In Manhattan he had no work to do and nowhere to be except his ridiculous office in the Empire State Building—the colossus that dominated the skyline from every location, reminding him constantly of the decision that had hollowed out his world. Marquette was a better world. There, the death of the Chatham Phenix was of only passing interest and Louis G. Kaufman was still First Citizen and the wealthiest man in town. Nor was there danger that the First National Bank would go the way of the Chatham Phenix. Like all banks in Michigan, it would close its doors twice in 1933—once when the governor declared a "bank holiday" to prevent a panicked run on the state's banks and once when Franklin Roosevelt did the same, nationwide—but the

Depression was relatively muted in the UP and throughout the 1930s LG's conservatively run institution continued to chug along nicely. LG sank into life in the Upper Peninsula as if into a warm bath. His 1932 summer sojourn stretched into the autumn and then later still.

LG's life might well have gone a different way: he was only sixty-two years old, still wealthy, and a director of General Motors, the Chicago and Erie Railroad, and the Manufacturers Trust Company. He could have lived the life of a retired New York bank president—attending board meetings, lunching with friends at Midtown clubs, writing his memoirs in his penthouse study. But with the demise of the Chatham Phenix something appeared to shift in LG. His exile seemed emotional as well as geographical. He fled from his past, likely explaining his extended residence in the UP as a "health" issue, and cut daily ties with the business world of Manhattan. When John J. Raskob wrote not to LG for advice about how to save the ever-endangered Empire State Building but to LG's banker son Young, as if he was corresponding with the caretaker of an elderly person, he thanked Young for the partridges LG had sent to him and then wrote of his old colleague: "If that's the kind of living your father is enjoying in the wilds of Michigan one cannot blame him for not wanting to come home. I hope your father . . . will soon be restored to his former good health and vigor. Please remember me to him."[10]

Most members of the Kaufman family (including Marie) did not join LG in Michigan and if they were aware of the sea change in their patriarch's psyche they gave no sign. Their servants, private cars, budgets, and annual activities remained in place (Tick On ran in the Kentucky Derby six months after LG lost the Chatham Phenix) and their lives went on, chronicled as usual like royalty in Depression-era newspapers. In September 1931, for example, as LG's beloved bank was crumbling and Harvey Gibson was about to make his move, the *New York Daily News* found Marie on the town—solo—dancing at a private Manhattan club, and marveled at "the slim, youthful woman in the beaded black gown who was tangoing so beautifully and so enthusiastically at the Brook last night" before adding the obligatory mention of the evening's rock selection: "Mrs. Kaufman has a beautiful collection of rubies," the reporter confided, "and last night wore a half dozen handsome diamond and ruby bracelets."[11]

Those bracelets likely had another outing when Marie and Juliet crossed the pond in May 1933 for the London Season and Juliet made her curtsy to royalty at the Court of St. James, but this time jewelry wasn't the focus of the American press. It was in the coverage of this event that the legend of Otto Young's $1 million handouts to Marie Kaufman's children suddenly resurfaced, publicly, and with a bang: "She is literally a Million Dollar Baby," the *New York Daily News* wrote of Juliet in May 1933, "for each time an infant arrived at the Kaufman home the delighted maternal grandpa used to send his daughter a check for $1 million."[12] It was the first public airing of this unsubstantiated chapter of Kaufman family lore that even today exists in many versions. Some of Marie and LG's descendants believe that Otto Young provided the millions, while others have it on good authority that the money came from LG himself who, upon their arrival, gifted each of his children with $1 million. It's also possible that the fortune Otto Young left to his grandchildren in his convoluted, generation-skipping will somehow morphed into a myth of those individual millions for Marie's children.

Whatever the truth of the matter, how in 1933 the *Daily News* suddenly came upon this sexy Kaufman backstory is an interesting question. The answer may lie with the PR firm Publicity Associates founded by the famous Belle Moskowitz.

Moskowitz was a fantastically gifted political operative who had served as Al Smith's chief strategist during his campaign for the New York governorship in 1923 and again when he ran for president in 1928. After his presidential loss she opened Publicity Associates (she was the first woman to found such a concern), and when Smith was tapped to front the Empire State Building, she headed up the building's PR plan. It was she who branded the Empire State Building in the public imagination, commissioning the unemployed Louis Hine to take his iconographic photos of construction workers living and working high in the air, she who arranged for Al Smith to be photographed at the top of the building with celebrities like former heavyweight champion Max Schmeling and aviatrix Amelia Earhart. (It was likely due to Miss Moskowitz that Schmeling visited Granot Loma and that Earhart joined the list of presenters in LG's Lyceum Series.) Belle would have been well-known to the Kaufman family, along with her son Josef Israels, who carried on her work at Publicity Associates after her death in 1933, and who may have been hired by Marie Kaufman that year to spruce up the family image. The timely reference to those millions would have distracted from the prurient interest in the Kaufman children's lengthening parade of unsuccessful marriages and reminded the post–Chatham Phenix public that she, Marie, had come from great wealth and that the Kaufman family was still rich, still American royalty.

If so, the gambit was a huge success. The new sobriquet appeared in nearly every tabloid story about the family from that day forward and those stories became ever more frequent although, inevitably, not all "Million Dollar Baby" stories were happy ones. Many newspapers took note when, in the spring of 1934, LG Kaufman Jr. left his estranged wife, Dorothy Dilley Kaufman (reportedly because she had taken a role in *Hot and Bothered* on Broadway against her husband's wishes), in New

York with their young son LG Kaufman III and decamped to his father's UP kingdom. As the months wore on LG Jr. is said to have drunk more and more heavily with local cronies. Finally, after a long night out he contracted pneumonia and became seriously ill. Informed of her husband's grave condition, Dorothy Dilley Kaufman did what emergency travelers to Granot Loma always did—she took to the air. Reporters charted the progress of the musical star as she took off from Newark, New Jersey, and raced toward the UP, arriving in time to be with her husband in his last hours. LG Kaufman Jr. died on August 27, 1934, at the age of twenty-eight.

It was a shocking loss. Marie coped by losing herself in plans for her son's funeral, making elaborate arrangements for the service, the cortege, and the burial in the Kaufman family mausoleum. She is said to have ridden on horseback behind the hearse on the way to the cemetery and to have instructed the undertaker to lay her son out in one suit for the funeral, then dress the body in different clothes for the interment. For LG, who had lived with his son at Granot Loma during the preceding spring and summer, grief must have been mixed with unaccustomed guilt. Preoccupied by the seismic change in his own life and his subsequent flight and used to leaving the supervision and guidance of his children to his wife, he may have failed to pay attention to his son's mood or movements. Now LG Jr. was gone, and many of his other children's lives were unstable. The marriages of Ann, Joan, and Young had failed or were failing and Graveraet (he of the 1926 breach of promise suit) had recently been sued for failing to pay for $20,000 worth of jewelry purchased for women who were not his wife. Maternal supervision had worked so well for LG and his siblings in nineteenth-century Marquette. Did Juliet's son wonder what had gone wrong in this generation, and what he should have said or done to set his offspring on the right paths?

If so, there is no evidence that he found an answer or that he changed his behavior toward his adult brood. Nor, apparently, were there new parental suggestions from Marie, whose perennial advice—marriage to a wealthy, socially appropriate partner—seemed only to push her offspring in the other direction. The list of imprudent Kaufman marriages lengthened: after her debutante ball at 625 Park and presentation at court Juliet married Giovanni De Manio, a waiter and reception clerk at the Grosvenor House Hotel in London. As Juliet was expecting when she tied the knot (her son Peter was born eight months later), her parents made the best of it and formally announced the marriage in the always accommodating *Palm Beach Post*. The *Post* informed its readers that the couple had been wed in an Anglican church, and that the groom had attended an English public school and was the son of Count Jean Baptiste de Manio, the famous Italian aviator.[13] Not quite: Giovanni's late father had indeed been a famous flyer, but he and Juliet had married in a registry office, "Jack" De Manio had failed to graduate from any school, his sketchy title had not been used since his grandfather's time, and (a sigh here from LG) his family was hard up for funds. This marriage too did not last: as Jack De Manio later wrote in his breezy 1970 biography *Life Begins Too Early*, he'd been quite glad when World War II started as "I was fed up with the hotel business . . . and even more fed up with my first wife."[14] He and Juliet spent most of the war years apart and divorced in 1945.

In 1936, Marie Louise celebrated her debutante season with another elegant ball at 625 Park Avenue, the last her mother would plan there. The lovely deb received her guests in clouds of white tulle, the guest list was heavy with blue bloods, and the triplex was a bower of roses. But like Juliet, Marie Louise did not choose a spouse from among the well-born men her mother paraded before her. She eloped the following year with Carl

Tonella, the son of a Marquette undertaker with no professional prospects. This was a bridge too far: Marie was horrified by the groom's provincial origins and family métier and LG, no doubt annoyed to be presented with yet another impecunious son-in-law, backed her up. No nuptial announcement was forthcoming and the papers had a field day with the idea that a "Million Dollar Baby" would actually have to work for a living.[15] In the end Marie Louise managed to avoid that terrible fate: she became pregnant, family relations thawed a bit, and the young couple was installed at Granot Loma, conveniently near the senior Tonellas and far from the Kaufmans in Palm Beach. The young couple divorced two years later.

As the 1930s wore on the unfortunate marriages of his children were not the only problems on LG's mind. Bad financial news from New York continued to make its way north into the pine forests of the UP. The Empire State Building was still largely empty and leaking money at such a rate that LG and his partners were in constant danger of losing it. Al Smith was sent to beg Franklin D. Roosevelt to move government agencies from as far away as Philadelphia into the empty building. The president did so, but the rental income they produced was a drop in the bucket of bottomless need. A 1936 payment of $500,000 to the building's mortgage holder secured a lower interest rate (Met Life was determined not to be lumbered with a giant unprofitable skyscraper), but the discount offered only minor relief. There were numerous capital calls to stockholders (including LG) and so many "reorganizations" and behind-the-scenes financial machinations that the value of the building's bonds and notes became "essentially fictions agreed upon by the partners and investors."[16]

That reality was likely top of mind when, in May 1937, LG was summoned to Washington, D.C., to testify in front of the recently organized Securities and Exchange Commission (SEC).

Determined to avoid another crash, Senators Carter Glass and Henry Steagall had authored a bill regulating the banking system, the failure of which was believed to have contributed to the financial debacle. The hearing to which LG was called was not part of a criminal case (all actions under scrutiny took place before the passage of the Glass-Steagall Act made them illegal) and the SEC was more interested in the sins of the late Chatham Phenix than those of the current Empire State Building, but LG knew that the ill-fated connection between his bank and the giant skyscraper would be thoroughly aired in the process. It was: eager to recap the dangers of financially incestuous "interlocking directorates" like the Chatham Phenix National Bank, the Chatham Phenix Corporation, and the Chatham Phenix Allied Corporation, the general counsel of the SEC's investment trust got right to it and asked his witness about his bank's decision to fund the Empire State Building during one of the worst years of the Depression and the dicey methods by which that "funding" was achieved.

Taking LG back to 1931, the painful year in which his bank faltered and Harvey Gibson swept in and obliterated his legacy, the general counsel elicited LG's testimony that the Chatham Phenix Allied Corporation had bought $5.9 million worth of second-mortgage debentures to fund the building, purchased with 468,000 shares of the Chatham Phenix Bank, which then had a value of only $1.5 million.[17] (The bank lost $4.5 million on that transaction and outside investors like Phillips Petroleum ultimately lost over $9 million on their investment in the building.) The counsel then asked why, after the real estate market collapsed in 1929, an investment trust company was justified in investing so heavily in second-mortgage bonds to finance the construction of the tallest building in the world. LG gave his torturer no satisfaction. Speaking about terrible decisions he knew had hastened the demise of his beloved Chatham Phenix, he responded crisply that the trust had considered the Empire State Building "a splendid investment."[18] He did not add that the shortfall had diluted his own interest and that he now owned only thirty-five thousand shares, or about 10 percent of the building. He was then forced to admit that his ownership in the building currently had no value, but with a flash of the optimism that had characterized so much of his career, he added that he remained hopeful about the future.[19]

But in 1937 there was precious little to be hopeful about: even LG's beautiful apartment building at 625 Park Avenue was in distress. Many wealthy renters of luxury apartments had lost their fortunes and stopped paying the rent upon which the building's upkeep and profit depended, and as it was hard to find others to take their places, rents were lowered and new tenants came and went, producing a sad change in ambiance. While the management was "selective" about tenants, Marie Kaufman no longer knew whom she might meet in the elevator and LG could never be sure the building would be in the black at the end of the month. It had become another cash suck and an unhappy reminder of the glamorous, sure-footed Manhattan life he had once lived, but he was stuck with it. For who would buy a struggling Park Avenue apartment building—even one with a fabulous triplex atop—in the worst economy in the nation's history?

It took a minute, but salvation came in the form of a Jewish Polish–born cosmetics tycoon. In 1940 Madame Helena Rubinstein returned to New York from wartime Paris where she had been living in a luxurious penthouse on the Île Saint-Louis, determined to replicate its charms on the Isle of Manhattan. Hearing of the penthouse at 625 Park Avenue (which the Kaufmans, due to LG's almost total absence from New York, had recently vacated in favor of a smaller, less elegant rental at 420 Park Avenue), she took one look and wrote breathlessly to her son that she had "fallen in love with a castle in the air."[20] Her real estate agent counseled against the rental, warning that the penthouse would require a huge staff to run, privately fearing the Jewish émigré would be refused as a tenant. Rubinstein was indeed turned away—an ironic state of affairs given the likely genesis of 625 Park and its current financial plight—so Rubinstein solved her problem, and LG's, by buying the entire building.

No deus ex machina appeared to rescue LG's sprawling concrete mansion in Short Hills, New Jersey. Once so central to Kaufman family life, the house had played an increasingly smaller role as the children grew older and gravitated to the more social precincts of Manhattan and Palm Beach. By the early 1930s LG had retreated to Granot Loma, the family was spending only Christmas and the occasional weekend in Short Hills, and the mansion stood empty for months at a time, watched over by the chauffeur living above the garage, an English caretaking couple, and one or two other servants. Then, sometime in 1937, these retainers were abruptly dismissed, and the fifty-room house—still completely furnished with Persian rugs, antique furniture, and gold bathroom fixtures—was simply abandoned. "Windows were being broken," a neighbor later recalled after referencing the great wealth of the Kaufman family, the local belief that LG's father "was a German immigrant who went to Michigan and married an Indian squaw," and, inevitably, the Million Dollar Babies. "There was quite a bit of vandalism taking place after they left, let the servants go. . . . It got to a point where one morning we missed our milk . . . and come to find that a hobo was living up there."[21] In the evenings teenagers came looking for the "wine house" and partied in its abandoned wine cellar.

Finally so many neighbors were complaining about the abandoned house that the town gave LG an ultimatum: hire guards to secure the site, sell the house, or tear it down. A sale was attempted, but while the garage and a smaller house on the property found buyers, the main house languished on the market and in 1939 demolition finally began. Due to its unusual materials and construction the process took nine months to accomplish and, in the end, remained incomplete: mountains of concrete chunks and pillars spiked with reinforced iron were not carted away but simply buried on-site, surprising the property's future owners with the vast scope of the Brutalist ruins beneath their lawns.

It was a sad ending and hard to parse. In Short Hills people whispered that LG and Marie had abandoned the house out of shame after being denied membership in an exclusive local club (Cheap John's Jewishness was once again the culprit), but that seems a stretch. Even if such a membership was withheld it would have happened back in the 1910s when the Kaufmans first moved to Short Hills, not twenty-five years later when Short Hills was only an occasional destination. LG's decision not to hire guards and secure the property remains a mystery, as he could certainly have afforded to do so. "The crash didn't affect Grandfather that much," recalls Daisy Eimen, noting that chauffeurs, chefs, waitresses, laundresses, and maids were employed at Granot Loma and Villa Sonia into the early 1940s.[22] Indeed, the summer the house was abandoned Marie and her youngest daughter, Jane, toured Europe for months and sailed home on the *Queen Mary*. Nor was Jane's debutante ball, held that fall at the fashionable Sherry-Netherland Hotel, less than the usual extravaganza: the ballroom was a mass of flowers and Jane wore the usual tulle—bouffant this time—accessorized with a muff of gardenias.[23] Perhaps simple exhaustion led LG to abandon his Short Hills property, exacerbated by grief over his son's death, disappointment in his other children, and the wish to leave the past behind. His bank was lost, the Empire State

Building was still struggling, and perhaps he had neither the interest nor energy to deal with a giant concrete white elephant in suburban New Jersey.

He was nearly seventy now and was likely suffering from the heart condition that would soon end his life. His days were quieter—in Palm Beach there were fewer fishing trips and more time spent with friends and family at the Bath and Tennis and Everglades Clubs, and only the occasional investment, like the one he made with E. F. Hutton, helping to finance a cluster of spec houses near the Seminole Golf Course. He carried extra weight around his middle and his strong features sagged, but his hands were still strong and well-shaped and he still dressed carefully, favoring intricately patterned shirts and neckties by Charvet or Sulka. When he passed he left a faint scent of Florida Water in the air. In the evenings he could be found on the terrace of the Villa Sonia enjoying the sunset (he had always been partial to sunsets) with a drink in his hand (he liked a drink or two, even three), enjoying a quiet moment alone before joining the guests Marie had assembled in the villa's guest rooms and cottages.

A man called Alexander Dallas Bache Pratt (1883–1947) was often among them. The fifty-something Pratt was a few years younger than the Princess of Lake Geneva and everything she admired. He was the son of "Commodore" Dallas Bache Pratt of the Social Registers of New York and Newport and the nephew of Charles Pratt of Standard Oil, a Princeton graduate and yachtsman, and a clubman down to the tips of his expensive shoes. Pratt had been married twice, first to Beatrice Benjamin Cartwright, a granddaughter of Henry H. Rogers of Standard Oil, and then to socialite/actress Katherine Harris (who may have introduced Pratt to Marie and to Granot Loma during the party days of the Roaring Twenties), but by the late 1930s he had been single for a decade and a half and had become Marie's frequent escort. The newspapers in New York and Palm Beach that published lists of guests at tony dinner parties and balls slotted his name automatically just below Marie's when they weren't boldly reporting that "the charming Mrs. L. G. Kaufman in chic black print accented with priceless

*Louis Graveraet Kaufman at Palm Beach, ca. 1935.
Collection of Peter Kaufman.*

pearls and rubies was with the distinguished looking Alexander Dallas Bache Pratt of the Social Register."[24]

Some members of the Kaufmans' circle no doubt believed that Pratt and Marie were more than dancing partners and they may well have been (they would marry after LG's death), but whatever the arrangement actually was, it seemed to suit everyone. LG was rumored to have his own extracurricular interest in Marquette (although there is no hard evidence that this was so) and at this stage of their lives both partners may have found it expedient to incorporate "friends" into their ménage and carry civilly on. LG and Marie had always had different temperaments and interests and as they got older they may have felt freer to indulge them. Divorce, as their children had amply demonstrated, was messy and unnecessary. They had come a long way together and shared seven children and many grandchildren. Their marriage would endure until LG's death.

They were together at Granot Loma in July 1939 when their daughter Jane was married. As the New York triplex was no longer an option, hers was the first (and only) Kaufman wedding held in Marquette. The ceremony was at St. Paul's Episcopal Church with a reception at the lodge to follow, and as the groom, Edward Ellsworth Harding III, was a socially appropriate University of Pennsylvania graduate, a pleased Marie had planned a blowout family event. All of the Kaufman children—save Londoner Juliet De Manio—were present. Ann Kaufman (now married to Richardson Dilworth of Philadelphia) was matron of honor in delphinium blue chiffon and a leghorn hat, Young and Graveraet Kaufman served as ushers, and a small Dilworth and Biddle niece and nephew charmed as flower girl and page. Marie Louise, Joan, and LG Jr.'s widow, Dorothy Dilley Kaufman, arrived from California in thoroughly modern fashion. All now lived on the West Coast and, instead of poking along in a private railcar, they had snagged a lift to Marquette in a gleaming Lockheed monoplane registered to Harold Vanderbilt and piloted by wedding guest Russell Thaw. (The pilot was as glamorous as the plane: he was the son of Evelyn Nesbit, the "girl in the red velvet swing" over whom her millionaire husband, Harry K. Thaw, had famously shot architect Stanford White back in 1906.) After a stop in Omaha, the Lockheed touched down at the new Marquette County Airport in just three and a half hours.

News of the arrival of the powerful plane and its glamorous cargo rippled through the town. Jane's marriage was big news in Marquette and, especially after so many years of Depression drabness, nobody wanted to miss the fun. Arriving at St. Paul's with Jane on the day, LG waved to excited crowds gathered to ogle the wedding party and their guests and to catch glimpses of the nave, elaborately decorated with delphiniums, greenery, and white candles. It was Jane's wedding, of course, but it was also his day—a chance to bask in his local celebrity and, not incidentally, an immersive experience in history and belonging. Walking Jane down the aisle of his childhood church under the benevolent stained-glass gaze of his mother, he would have felt truly and comfortably at home. The town had formed him and nurtured him, and when life had become difficult, Granot Loma had received and soothed him. Whatever losses he had suffered, this place remained to him—would sustain him.

Jane became Mrs. Edward Ellsworth Harding III, and when the Lockheed was on its way to New York City and the other wedding guests departed LG resumed his UP life as a monarch in a kingdom organized around one man. Each day he breakfasted in solitary splendor, comfortable in a white terry-cloth robe, in the huge dining room overlooking the lake, then dealt with his mail, delivered in a padlocked sack by the milk truck from Loma Farms on its return journey from Marquette and presented by his butler, Remy. The sack also contained his preferred selection of newspapers—the *Daily Mining Journal*, the *Milwaukee Journal*, the *New York Herald Tribune*, and the *New York Journal American*. Like many men of his age and financial bracket LG skewed conservative. In spite of Roosevelt's attempts to help the failing Empire State Building, he had not been a fan of the New Deal, nor of the taxes required to support it.

After being helped to dress by Barney, his longtime valet, he might be driven to Marquette, where he would drop in at the First National Bank and Trust Company; he was still the president, even if some of the day-to-day oversight had passed to others. He'd make a few phone calls (there was still no phone at the lodge), then pause to admire his coin collections in the Directors' Room and on the balcony, and chat graciously to customers and employees on his way out. Driving home, he might direct his chauffeur to make a stop at Loma Farms. Now operated by a skeleton crew of only thirty-five, its "scientific farming" programs were over, but vegetables, hay, and oats were still grown there and its rich, unpasteurized milk remained a local favorite. Standing in the farm office lined with blue ribbons won a decade before, LG might inquire about a particular cow's output or a change in the milking regimen. Having dismissed W. W. Blake Arckoll back in 1936 he now took a more hands-on interest in milk production and had sold his Guernsey herd and replaced it with Holsteins in an effort to lose less money per bottle. The change had had little effect and champagne remained cheaper than Loma Farms milk.

Other days LG visited the workshop of rustic craftsman Nestor Kallioinen. In the years since LG moved north the two men, born the same year, had become good friends—to the end LG had kept a photo of Nestor in his Manhattan apartment. LG repeatedly offered to set him up in a New York shop so that his rustic furniture could find a wider audience, but

Nestor always declined and remained stubbornly local. As the years passed LG was grateful: he sat in his friend's workshop for hours at a time, watching as Nestor prepared stumps and branches and magically transfused nature into chairs and head-boards. Other afternoons LG was outside, tramping his forested acres in search of game for the larder, or trolling for fish on the big lake, dragging a series of lures behind a slowly moving boat. He sat in the stern watching the lines while Jack Martin—a young man who had started as a laborer at Loma Farms and had morphed into Granot Loma's jack-of-all-trades—drove LG's green clinker-style inboard. Martin also served as Marie's escort/bodyguard on trips to New York and Palm Beach, a job that would bring him into close proximity with the Kaufman family and, ultimately, change his destiny.

Children, in-laws, and grandchildren came to Granot Loma and formed parties of which LG was always the center. The grown-ups still ate separately—dressing up to do so—but LG, who seemed more comfortable with his grandchildren than many of the other adults, would sometimes look in on the chil-dren's early supper and confide that the protein on the menu was "bear meat" his chef had marinated for over a week until it tasted just like beef. Then it was cocktail time, everyone's favorite part of the day: leaving the lodge's resident nannies in charge, he and the other grown-ups would make their way, drinks in hand, to LG's private office—a space that was off limits at other times of the day. When all were assembled, LG would perch behind his massive inlaid desk, martini in hand, and as the alco-hol flowed, so did the anecdotes. (Marie, who had heard her husband's stories and had a few of her own, held a rival soiree in her large, mirrored bathroom, propping a frosted ice bucket atop the closed commode.) Laughter rippled through log-lined spaces as LG found his rhythm and took his listeners on a jour-ney into his past. As he talked, they saw the boy who was the first to go barefoot every spring; the young banker who had caught the eye of Elbert Gary; the talented financier who had finessed branch banking, helped reorganize GM, and financed the Empire State Building.

Not everything was cocktail talk: the Semitic origins of Cheap John, whose personality had lifted LG and whose surname had obstructed his path, were not part of the story LG wanted to tell, nor was the fact of his mother's Indigenous ancestry. Early lessons held fast. His mistakes—in business, as a husband, as a father—were also off limits. It was all a long time ago and the world had moved on. Dinner was served and afterward, as others played backgammon, LG sat near the radio straining to hear the war news over the scratchy UP airways. He had been with the mayor of New York on a boat in the harbor when the troops came home from World War I; where would he be when this one ended? He turned off the radio and, in the silence, heard the familiar sound of the waves breaking on the rocks below. The day was over.

The heart attack struck on March 8, 1942. It was high season in Palm Beach and LG, along with Marie, Ann, Young, and Joan and their families, was at the Villa Sonia. LG was rushed to Good Samaritan Hospital but too much damage had been done and he died there on March 10, 1942. His body was put onto a private train car and the family immediately began the long trip north to Marquette. There was no time to spare. Marie had scheduled the funeral for 3:00 p.m. on March 13 at St. Paul's, only three days after his death.

When her son died in 1934 Marie had produced an elaborate funeral, meticulously planned down to the last detail. Her husband's send-off would be a hastier affair. By the time LG's old friends and colleagues—fellow directors from GM and the Chicago and Erie, Raskob and the du Ponts, bankers from his Chatham Phenix days, and so on—learned of his death, it was too late to make the trip to Marquette. Was Marie's speedy dispatch a way to save face? A decade had passed since the loss of the Chatham Phenix and her husband, sequestered in the UP, had been all but forgotten in the canyons of New York. It would have been embarrassing to give a party and have nobody come. The obituaries had been unremarkable and brief—scant paragraphs with many of LG's accomplishments omitted (although the *Palm Beach Post* did mention all of his club memberships). In the absence of eminent friends and colleagues from the East, Marie's roster of nineteen pallbearers—actual and honorary—was downscale, local, and not familial—neither of LG's surviving sons, his surviving brother, Harry, nor any of his sons-in-law were on her list. LG's coffin was borne in and out of St. Paul's by his valet, his private secretary, a local Masonic leader, the editor of the *Mining Journal*, and various officials of the First National Bank.

Although these choices reflected Marie's disdain for Cheap John's other children and her disappointment in many of her own, in an important way LG's pallbearers were appropriate as they represented a place that he had loved and that had loved him. On March 13, 1942, behind the front pews occupied by Marie and six of her seven surviving children and their families (Juliet was again absent), the church was packed to the rafters. The turnout wasn't fueled only by public gratitude for the bank, the high school, and the endowment. Marquette had admired and respected Louis Graveraet Kaufman, and he was a part of the town to the very end. His passing brought Marquette to a standstill: the morning of the funeral the Graveraet High School flag was lowered to half-mast and its students observed two minutes of silence in LG's honor, before being dismissed at noon. All of the banks closed early. The town's love surrounded its favorite son until the very end: when the funeral cortege reached Park Cemetery and LG was laid to rest in his grand mausoleum, it was to the accompaniment of the hymn "Abide with Me" played on trumpet, trombone, and horn by the Graveraet High School brass quartet.

That evening, when the family drove home through the blustery March woods to Granot Loma, nothing there at the great lodge had changed but everything was different. For years this place had been LG's sanctuary and kingdom and in it he had been the sun around whom all life had revolved. What was Granot Loma now? His valet now had no one to dress, his chauffeur no one to drive, and the family members who had flocked to his court would soon scatter to the winds. His children grieved for their father and for all that had been, now that the king of the Upper Peninsula was dead.

EPILOGUE
After LG

Louis Graveraet Kaufman had risen from the Upper Peninsula of Michigan like an unlikely comet and soared over Jazz Age America in a trail of money and celebrity. But the magic did not last. The Chatham Phenix National Bank and Trust did not survive him, and his children founded no businesses or made any history of their own. By the end of his life much of what he had had already crumbled, and after his death the "Westerner" who had conquered the New York banking world, changed the trajectory of GM, financed the Empire State Building, and built the country's most spectacular Adirondack-style lodge disappeared from the record with thoroughness and speed.

Marie married her former dancing partner two years later and while the social exploits of Mrs. Alexander Dallas Bache Pratt continued to be noted in the society pages in New York and Palm Beach, they ceased to be associated with the man who had made them possible. Now when LG's name appeared in print it was in the tabloid press, where accounts of his children's marital mishaps and of his family's intergenerational squabbles were ever more frequent.

This "news" did LG's memory no credit: as if vying to marry men who would cause the Princess of Lake Geneva the most angst, her daughters continued to choose partner after partner from precincts far from the Social Register. Marie retaliated emotionally and financially (and often publicly) and the cycle continued in a dizzying whirl, sordid and sometimes comical. For example: after divorcing the undertaker's son her mother had so deplored, Marie Louise eloped with a commercial pilot. She soon wanted a divorce but her mother refused to send her hard-up daughter the requisite funds, so the undertaker's son financed the split, and Marie Louise married him a second time. The tabloids loved the "can't make this up" marital career of her older sister Joan, who divorced twice then married a cowboy—twice. She met him in Reno, divorced him after three months, and boarded a plane for the East. The cowboy booked a seat and when the flight reached a refueling stop the pair got off and married again. (A horrified Marie facilitated their second divorce.) Not to be outdone, little sister Jane jilted a Marie-approved fiancé and ran away with the Jewish Hollywood writer Sidney Sheldon. In the end, the eight Kaufman siblings would marry a total of twenty-eight times.

LG's last will and testament had added fuel to these family fires. He left the lion's share of his fortune (estimated to be about $180 million, or over $3 billion today) to Marie, and Marie alone. Where his children had hoped to see their names listed, his will included the following life-changing sentence: "My children will be sufficiently provided for under the terms of the last will of their maternal grandfather and for that reason I am making no provision for them."[1] It must have been a terrible shock: Otto Young had indeed left a fortune to be divided among his many grandchildren, but as LG had certainly known, distribution of the spoils would not happen until Marie died (an event that would not occur for another fourteen years). His children had been brought up in luxury, were unused to economizing, and many of them had never earned a dollar. Now those not in Marie's good graces had only the annual interest payments from their grandfather's trust (and the occasional solvent partner) to support them.

Why had LG made such a decision? We do not know. Perhaps he had had concerns about the behavior and financial acumen of his offspring and Marie had argued for herself as financial controller. The couple may have hoped that leaving her in charge would be a good way to keep his money out of the hands of fortune hunters and to help Marie guide their children toward better life choices. Instead the will created financial hardship and hard feelings.

Marie's wedding to Alexander Dallas Bache Pratt, held at her Manhattan apartment in 1944, was a showcase of family dysfunction: only Ann Dilworth and Lieutenant Young Kaufman, then a naval officer—Marie's two most conventionally and infrequently married children—were present. Later, when some of the no-shows (or perhaps those not invited) were driven by exigency to borrow against their shares of the Otto Young trust (transferring huge tranches of their expectations to third parties for a fraction of their worth), Marie retaliated by halting their annual interest payments. True penury ensued: Graveraet brought suit against his mother, desperately seeking to have the ban reversed. The son who had once had his own chauffeur, valet, and stenographer now could not pay his grocery bill or the rent on his room at the New York Athletic Club.

With all funds concentrated in Marie's hands Granot Loma also suffered: Mr. and Mrs. A.D.B. Pratt preferred to summer in Newport and Southampton, and after Pratt's death in 1947 Marie established herself at the Hôtel de Paris Monte-Carlo. The giant lodge limped on without servants or a maintenance staff, although one key employee was still in residence in a new capacity. After divorcing her fourth husband in 1946, Joan Kaufman cast her eye upon the (married) former bodyguard

Granot Loma after LG's death. Courtesy of Superior View Photography, Marquette, Michigan.

and boat driver Jack Martin. Jack was soon divorced, Joan and Jack married in 1947 (it would be the last marriage for both) and moved into the lodge, and Jack became Granot Loma's caretaker—a one-man band fighting decaying logs and weather damage on a tight budget. Loma Farms, now run by Young Kaufman, was soon off his docket: that year Michigan passed a law decreeing that milk sold in the state must be pasteurized and as Granot Loma's milk had never been profitable and Marie had no interest in paying for upgrades, the family did not invest in the necessary equipment. The farmhands were let go and the cows sent to auction. The farm, LG's pride and joy, had outlasted him by only five years.

In the triplex atop 625 Park Avenue no one remembered the man who had commissioned its splendors. Now renowned as the residence of Madame Helena Rubinstein, it was a showcase for her big personality and cutting-edge art. In the restrained, classic rooms where LG's debutante daughters had danced through the night, members of the avant-garde drank and argued among works by Picasso, de Kooning, and Salvador Dalí, Venetian shell furniture, and Madame's fabulous Lucite bed. Thirty blocks south in the lobby of the Empire State Building, office workers and commuters hurried past the commemorative plaque (Art Deco, so unfashionable) bearing LG's name. Postwar America was booming, so was occupancy at the Empire State Building, and nobody wanted to look back to the Depression era—including Marie, who, thanks to her late husband, now owned a piece of one of the most profitable office buildings in the world. When the Empire State Building was sold in 1951 for a whopping $51 million she netted around $3.7 million ($37 million today) for her stake. As the building changed hands for that record price, it was not the vindication of her late husband's hopes that sprang to mind. "We are selling the Empire State Building," her granddaughter remembers Marie sighing. "Now I'll have no place to store my furniture."[2]

The furniture was stored at Granot Loma and Marie was soon thousands of miles away, ensconced in a palatial suite in the Hôtel de Paris Monte-Carlo. When her daughter Ann and husband Richardson Dilworth (now mayor of Philadelphia) visited her there in 1956 that Gilded Age hotel was newly gilded, having just hosted the wedding of Grace Kelly and Prince Rainier, and Marie was no doubt enjoying its centrality among the beau monde. Ann, who had married two wealthy, socially prominent men and divorced only one, was still her favorite daughter, and Dilworth was the one son-in-law of whom she thoroughly approved. Marie enjoyed the visit only to be told she had nearly lost the favored pair. Just as LG had been in the wrong place at the wrong time when the Wall Street bomber struck in 1920, Ann and Richardson Dilworth had sailed home from that European visit on the *Andrea Doria*. They too had survived: but when the *Doria* collided with the *Stockholm* near Nantucket around

11:00 p.m. on July 25, 1956, Dilworth refused to leave the ship until all of the other passengers were safe and had to push Ann forcibly into a lifeboat as she refused to go without him. The ship was listing 40 degrees when the mayor finally was rescued by the *Île de France* around 5:30 the following morning.

A month later Marie took ill in her suite and died there at the age of seventy-nine. Her will was a testamentary showcase of her disappointments and prejudices: Ann inherited a good chunk of her $136 million estate, while Graveraet, Young (rather mysteriously), Juliet, and Jane were left nothing at all. Marie Louise got the LA house in which she lived, and Joan got Granot Loma. Ten grandchildren inherited millions and six others were pointedly ignored. A codicil echoed a familiar refrain: "I wish emphatically," Marie had written, "that nothing is to be inherited from my estate by any of my sons in law, daughters in law, or relatives outside of those specifically named."[3] She left instructions that her body be cremated in Europe and her ashes scattered there, and so was not brought home to the Marquette mausoleum to lie beside her son and her husband of forty years. Family members sued and squabbled over the will (and Marie's jewelry) and sold what remained of LG's empire: the Villa Sonia, which was bulldozed to make way for a Palm Beach apartment building, and, ending six decades of Kaufman control, the family's interest in the First National Bank and Trust Company of Marquette.

At Granot Loma Joan and Jack Martin lived in the aging, coal-guzzling lodge only in summer and spent winters in the manager's house at Loma Farms. The empty lodge attracted trespassers and thieves and many valuable things disappeared during the 1950s and 1960s. Still, the couple loved the place and would never sell it, even when a celebrity came calling: in the summer of 1977 Joan had died and Jack had inherited Granot Loma when a five-car entourage came racing up the driveway. His guest was world heavyweight champion Muhammad Ali, who was in Marquette for a boxing exhibition. (Always a crowd-pleaser, while giving a speech for the occasion, Ali heard someone refer to Marquette as "the land of Superior," grabbed the microphone, and shouted to the crowd: "Muhammad Ali is the greatest and you all are the superiorist.")[4] Ali had his own log house in Michigan and, having heard that Martin owned the country's largest domestic log structure, he was determined to have a look.

The champ was instantly enchanted with Granot Loma and intrigued by its moneymaking potential (he imagined filming commercials there and opening a training camp on the offshore island), and he began to badger a startled Martin to sell the lodge, repeatedly sweetening the pot and finally offering the elderly man $20 million in small, unmarked bills. But to no avail. Like LG before him, Martin wanted to spend his last years in the woodland kingdom on the lake. Plus, the elderly Martin was a man with the prejudices of his time: he was not keen on the idea of so many young Black boxers coming to live at the lodge and patronizing restaurants and shops in Marquette. He steadily refused, depriving Granot Loma (and therefore LG) of a moment in the national spotlight.

The name Louis Graveraet Kaufman did make history the following summer when his American coin collection was offered at auction. Marie had sold the "Dollars of the World" collection back in 1952, but before her death she gave the American coins to LG's Marquette foundation, and they had been left on display in the Directors' Room at the First National Bank. It was 1976 before anybody thought about their value and commissioned an appraisal. The result was a happy shock and the ensuing sale at Chicago's Palmer House Hotel on August 4–5, 1978, was a sensation. The contents of the vaults and cases the people of Marquette had seen every day for decades turned out to be

Muhammad Ali at Granot Loma, 1977. Courtesy of Superior View Photography, Marquette, Michigan.

"one of the largest and most varied collections of United States coins privately held in the world," and its sale was a "numismatic Super Bowl" full of rare examples—some previously unknown to the market.[5] Many of the 1,530 lots soared past their estimates. An 1855 Territorial gold piece brought $115,000, and an 1825 half eagle displaying a rare nineteenth-century numismatic shortcut—a "5" stamped over the "4" in the date—brought a whopping $140,000 (more than $627,000 today). The sale put the Kaufman name permanently on the numismatic map—the only place beyond the UP that it has retained any recognition. (Nathan Kaufman's heirs contested the sale on the grounds that the coins had never been legally transferred to LG, but the statute of limitations had long expired, and their suit was unsuccessful.)

The sale added $2.25 million to the Louis G. Kaufman Endowment Fund. Although its signature Lyceum Series ceased to operate in 1945, it has continued to provide scholarships to promising Marquette students and to support local educational and recreational programs; as of this writing it remains one of the largest and most influential philanthropic funds in Marquette County, with assets of over $3.5 million. Overseen (at this writing) by Young Kaufman's son who lives in the area and other prominent members of the community, it provides annual grants of over $150,000 supporting college scholarships, free school breakfasts and lunches, services for disabled children, local cultural organizations, and more.

It operates in a town that retains the ruddy Victorian charm of LG's childhood but is now a popular destination for hipsters, who flock there for mountain biking, breweries, and food trucks. In Marquette, the building that once housed Sam Kaufman's haberdashery shop is now a trendy hair salon, although LG's grand Beaux Arts bank still looks much as it did in 1927. The Anishinaabe (who are among the 240,000 Indigenous people living in Michigan today) are part of this picture: their language, Anishinaabemowin, is being taught to a new generation of UP residents, and tribal members practice the crafts and skills of their ancestors, study at Northern Michigan University, and work at local cultural centers and in the community at large.

When Jack Martin died in 1982, he left Granot Loma almost as its original owner had known it—Indigenous artifacts and all. When it was offered for sale the photos in the prospectus showed a gently decaying time capsule of LG's life and times. But this remnant would soon be swept away: in 1987 Lucien T. "Tom" Baldwin bought Granot Loma for $4.5 million and although his restoration of the lodge was careful and impressive and he made few changes to its original architecture and interiors (Granot Loma was designated a National Historic

Landmark in 1991), he also cleaned house with a thoroughness that stymied me when I began the research for this book. Baldwin kept only a few items, like a visitors' book full of boldfaced names, LG's oversized Granot Loma checkbook, and the plans for the Empire State Building (left behind after the architects' cheerleading trip), while closets full of the family's Jazz Age clothes, the period contents of medicine cabinets and cupboards, the original plans for the lodge, children's toys, other personal possessions, and family papers, possibly including personal letters, were tossed. Sadly, nothing was offered to family members or to the local historical society, thus depriving future researchers of important clues about the Kaufmans and life at Granot Loma.

Salable items were dispersed at auction: antique European furniture that once graced the Kaufman house in Short Hills and at 625 Park (including an inlaid English chest sold for $3,650) was flogged to eager buyers. The auction catalogue listed family photographs, the Halmi pastel of Joan Kaufman, a brass telescope (I like to think it was the one through which LG watched the Empire State Building rising), the cranky crank telephone from the depot, and examples of Nestor Kallioinen's fabulous rustic furniture. Bidders carted away china and sterling silver, the copper animal weathervanes that had swiveled atop the barns at Loma Farms, piles of milk crates bearing the farm's logo, and sixty blankets and rugs made by Indigenous communities. I would have given anything to have seen these items in situ.

LG's descendants mourned the loss of Granot Loma as a repository of family memories, but their connection was, and remains, more visceral. Impelled by cultural or genetic imperative, many of LG's grandchildren and great-grandchildren have built log and stone palaces of their own, including elaborate examples in the Poconos and in the UP. One great-grandchild felt a different compulsion. Wendy Stocker, Ann Kaufman Dilworth's granddaughter, was brought up as "the best of Social Register Philadelphia" but soon became aware of something compelling and unspoken in her family background. In the 1960s she found herself announcing "I am Jewish" in response to anti-Semitic banter at her exclusive boarding school and she later hired a genealogist to identify unacknowledged "cultural traces" in her beloved grandmother. Wendy believes the irony, whimsy, and humor she loved in Ann Kaufman Dilworth were a direct inheritance from Ann's father, LG, and the Jewish side of her family. She has embraced her history and developed close social and cultural connections to the Jewish community.[6]

Thus far interest in Louis Graveraet Kaufman's life and times has been confined to his descendants and the population of Marquette. This is unfortunate and also shortsighted: for unlike other one-generation wonders who made fortunes of only brief significance, LG built, or helped shape, important structures and institutions that remain part of our landscape. These connections have long gone undocumented. But without Louis Graveraet Kaufman, branch banking, General Motors, and the Empire State Building would not have developed as they did, or perhaps even exist, and his other signature real estate is part of the cultural record. A century after it rose the Empire State Building still defines New York City's skyline and identifies the city on the world's television and movie screens. LG's triplex atop 625 Park Avenue is still considered one of New York's greatest prewar apartments, and Granot Loma the country's most spectacular example of Adirondack-style architecture. LG's most personal build, it continues to stand tall on the rocky shore of a timeless lake. No longer a destination for Jazz Age revelers nor a refuge for a lion in winter, it remains a fitting monument to its creator, Louis Graveraet Kaufman.

ACKNOWLEDGMENTS

Many people contributed their skills, knowledge, and support to the writing of this book, and I am glad to have this opportunity to thank them.

The deft editing and quiet encouragement of my editor Marie Sweetman of Wayne State University Press made this a better book and kept me going when the going got rough, and her colleagues deserve endless credit for their good work and patience with their tech-challenged author.

I am grateful to the members of the Kaufman family for their time and willingness to share their memories, documents, and photographs. Many thanks to Deborah Bishop, Daisy Eimen, Chesley Lydekker, Clare Kaufman, Mike Hill, Colin Berens, and Tamia Karlinski. Special thanks to Wendy Stocker, and to Peter Kaufman and the late Audrey Kaufman for their hospitality and friendship. Thanks, too, to Lisa Immordino Vreeland, who shared the diary of her grandmother-in-law, Diana Vreeland, the legendary *Vogue* editor.

Many librarians, authors, academics, and experts generously shared their resources and knowledge with me. My first shout-out must be to Beth Gruber, research librarian at the Marquette Regional History Museum. Thanks, too, to Linda Gross, reference librarian of the Hagley Museum and Library, Rose Guerrero, research director of the Historical Society of Palm Beach, and Lynn Ranieri, formerly of the Milburn-Short Hills Historical Society. You all made my job so much easier.

Many thanks are due to my other Upper Peninsula sources—

historical photography guru Jack Deo, author Tyler R. Tichelaar, and Dr. Russell Magnaghi of Northern Michigan University. Elsewhere, Jeff Groff, estate historian of Winterthur Museum, Garden and Library, author Michael Veitch, architectural historian Andrew Alpern, and numismatic expert Robert Bill Bair provided useful background information about Kaufman's projects and possessions. Jason Barr of Rutgers University–Newark demystified the convoluted history of his most famous project, the Empire State Building, and Eugene White of Rutgers University and Sean Vanatta of the University of Glasgow provided explanations of the history of branch banking that were intelligible even to this neophyte.

Closer to home, I would like to thank writer Joanne Kaufman, who lent a friendly yet critical eye to my manuscript, and Kitty McGraw Berry, who hosted me in the Upper Peninsula. And I am eternally grateful to my husband, Dan Feld, who rejoiced at my discoveries, tuned out my grumpy complaints, and saw me through to publication.

AUTHOR'S NOTE

My research for this book began in Michigan's Upper Peninsula. While in the Lower Peninsula (and everywhere else in the country) the name Louis Graveraet Kaufman was met with blank stares, in Marquette people were pleased that someone was finally paying attention to their hometown hero. The library of the Marquette Regional History Center has been collecting material about LG and his family for years, and in its files I found copious material related to the history of Marquette, Robert Graveraet, Peter White, Edward Breitung, Sam and Juliet Kaufman (including letters written by Sam and Juliet in the 1870s found in the walls of a local house the Kaufmans once occupied), the First National Bank of Marquette, Graveraet High School, and Granot Loma. Crucially, the library also contains college papers and other unpublished documents written about LG and Granot Loma in the 1970s and 1980s, which include interviews with people who knew him and remembered the construction of the lodge.

Of course, my research also took me further afield: I consulted online newspaper archives and the scrapbooks of newspaper clippings in the collection of a Kaufman descendant. Between 1910 and 1930, the era of LG's financial and social ascent, there were thousands of daily newspapers in America. He and his family were in the papers almost every day, in New York City and in syndicated papers around the country. These articles allowed me to chart LG's progress as he made his way to the top of the banking world, and to know where he and his family were (London, Palm Beach, New York, northern Michigan) at any given time and what they were doing. This coverage was also a barometer of how LG and his family were perceived by the world in which they lived. It was thrilling to realize how well-known LG had been—between 1910 and 1930 his had been a household name. Plus, as LG was quoted in many of these articles, they were a window into the man I wanted so much to know, revealing something of his speaking style, opinions, beliefs, and concerns.

I went to Flint, Michigan, to consult the Kettering University (GM) Archives. Letters and business documents there, and in the DuPont Archive in Wilmington, Delaware, contributed to my understanding of LG's work with William Durant and John J. Raskob, and of the personal relationships between the men as well. *They Told Barron*, a book written during LG's lifetime, provided clues about his branch banking scheme and take-back of GM and, importantly, how he had wanted those events to be seen by his peers. Privately printed documents about Birch, Michigan, and Short Hills, New Jersey, and a typed account of life at Granot Loma written by one of LG's grandchildren provided fascinating information about Kaufman family life, as did documents and photographs in the collection of another grandchild. Interviews with grandchildren, great-grandchildren, and selected non-family members provided information about LG's and Marie's personalities, opinions, and lifestyles. Articles, books, online documents, catalogues, and other relevant materials enriched my knowledge of the world LG came from and the one in which he lived.

Unfortunately, and surprisingly, there are no extant Kaufman family letters, or none that have yet been found, even though LG and Marie moved frequently between states and continents and lived at a time when long-distance phone calls were uncommon. Due to this lack, I have made occasional educated suppositions about aspects of LG's life, supported by a wealth of information gathered from the above-mentioned sources. Because of that trove, we know how he was shaped by his ancestry, how he lived his life, what he did and did not do, said and left unsaid. This knowledge helps us understand how he thought and felt and, ultimately, how he shaped his times, and ours. Now that he is no longer lost to history, I hope future researchers will add to that understanding, and to the remarkable legacy of Louis Graveraet Kaufman.

NOTES

Chapter 1

1 Tyler R. Tichelaar, *Kawbawgam: The Chief, the Legend, the Man* (Marquette, MI: Marquette Fiction, 2020), 66.

2 Ralph D. Williams, *The Honorable Peter White: A Biographical Sketch of the Lake Superior Iron Country* (Cleveland: Freshwater Press, 1905), 25.

3 Williams, *The Honorable Peter White*, 37.

4 Williams, *The Honorable Peter White*, 35–36.

5 Alvah L. Sawyer, *A History of the Northern Peninsula of Michigan and Its People: Its Mining, Lumber and Agricultural Industries* (Chicago: Lewis Publishing Company, 1911), 220.

6 Frank B. Stone, *Philo Marshall Everett: Father of Michigan's Iron Industry and Founder of the City of Marquette* (Baltimore: Gateway Press, 1997), 91–92.

7 Stone, *Philo Marshall Everett*, 93.

8 Williams, *The Honorable Peter White*, 23.

9 Williams, *The Honorable Peter White*, 23.

10 Williams, *The Honorable Peter White*, 26.

11 Williams, *The Honorable Peter White*, 40.

12 Robert Graveraet to Pierre Boisdoré Barbeau, January 10, 1855, "Graveraet Biographical File," Kaufman Family Letters, J. M. Longyear Research Library, Marquette Regional History Center.

13 *Detroit Free Press*, June 15, 1861.

14 *Lake Superior Journal*, May 9, 1860.

15 *Lake Superior Journal*, March 6, 1863.

16 Sally M. Walker, *Deadly Aim: The Civil War Story of Michigan's Anishinaabe Sharpshooters* (New York: Henry Holt, 2019), 7.

Notes

17 Walker, *Deadly Aim*, 68.

18 Walker, *Deadly Aim*, 110.

19 *Detroit Free Press*, July 20, 1864.

20 *Lake Superior Journal*, October 6, 1865.

21 *Mining Journal*, October 31, 1874.

22 *Mining Journal*, December 19, 1874, 3.

23 Juliet Kaufman to Samuel Kaufman, June 23, 1876, "Kaufman Family Letters: 1876–1878," Kaufman Family Letters, J. M. Longyear Research Library, Marquette Regional History Center.

24 *Mining Journal*, February 8, 1879, 1.

25 Samuel Kaufman to Ike Neuberger, July 4, 1876, "Kaufman Family Letters: 1876–1878," Kaufman Family Letters, J. M. Longyear Research Library, Marquette Regional History Center.

26 Shinny is a sort of pickup game of ice hockey.

27 *Brooklyn Daily Eagle*, June 11, 1916, 17.

28 Ernest Rankin to Harry Livingston Kaufman, November 27, 1959, "Kaufman Biographical File," Kaufman Family Letters, J. M. Longyear Research Library, Marquette Regional History Center.

29 Rankin to Livingston Kaufman, November 27, 1959.

30 *Marquette City Directory*, 1889, 129.

31 *Mining Journal*, February 10, 1894, 10.

32 Peter White to Samuel Kaufman, May 30, 1895, "Kaufman Biographical File," Kaufman Family Letters, J. M. Longyear Research Library, Marquette Regional History Center. Published in the *Daily Mining Journal* as an ad on May 29, 1896, https://uplink.nmu.edu/node/23443.

33 Ralph Williams to Peter White, December 25, 1901, Peter White Papers, 1848–1915, Box 12, Bentley Historical Library, University of Michigan, Ann Arbor.

Chapter 2

1 *Marquette Times*, July 1, 1893.

2 *Sault Ste. Marie Evening News*, May 6, 1895.

3 Deborah Bishop, interview with the author, December 21, 2018.

4 The Gilded Age palace was reconfigured and reimagined many times: it fell on hard times in the 1950s and 1960s, becoming a boardinghouse, a warehouse, and a French restaurant. A developer divided the house into condominium apartments and installed a swimming pool and a circular bar that revolved 360 degrees on its roof. Fortunately, the house later found owners who appreciated its Beaux Arts architecture and history and in 2017 Younglands, now known as Stone Manor, became a single house again and its original interiors were lovingly restored.

5 C. Fred Rydholm, *Superior Heartland: A Backwoods History*, 2 vols. (Marquette, MI: C. F. Rydholm, 1989), 1:328.

6 John Munro Longyear, "Reminiscences" (unpublished manuscript, 1912), typescript, J. M. Longyear Research Library, Marquette Regional History Center.

7 Rydholm, *Superior Heartland*, 1:325.

8 Longyear, "Reminiscences."

9 Rydholm, *Superior Heartland*, 1:326.

10 Longyear, "Reminiscences."

11 *Commercial West*, January 6, 1923.

12 Rydholm, *Superior Heartland*, 1:328–29.

13 *Washington Times*, December 25, 1910, 11.

14 *Chicago Examiner*, December 1, 1908, 2.

15 *Detroit Free Press*, June 16, 1908, 12.

16 William Howard Taft to Louis Graveraet Kaufman, June 6, 1908, private collection of Peter Kaufman.

17 Unsigned to Mrs. G., September 13, 1957, Granot Loma Pamphlet File, Kaufman Family Letters, J. M. Longyear Research Library, Marquette Regional History Center.

Chapter 3

1 *Detroit Free Press*, October 30, 1907, 8.

2 Ida M. Tarbell, *The Life of Elbert H. Gary: The Story of Steel* (New York: D. Appleton, 1925), 96.

3 Newspaper clipping from a scrapbook in the private collection of Peter Kaufman. Many of the clippings in Peter Kaufman's scrapbooks lack the name and/or exact date of publication.

4 "The Chatham and Phenix National Bank of New York," *Bankers Magazine* 84 (1912): 369.

5 Roger M. Andrews, "From Messenger Boy to President of a $75,000 Bank," *Clover-Land*, April 1916, https://lib.nmu.edu/voices/documents/cloverland/Volume1-4_Apr.pdf.

6 *Brooklyn Daily Eagle*, February 13, 1927, 82.

7 Lynne Ranieri, "Local History: The Founding Family of Short Hills," *Patch*, September 21, 2009, https://patch.com/new-jersey/millburn/local-history-the-founding-family-of-short-hills.

8 *Brooklyn Daily Eagle*, June 11, 1916, 17.

9 *New York American*, October 13, 1915.

10 Clarence W. Barron, Arthur Pound, and Samuel Taylor Moore, *They Told Barron: The Notes of Clarence W. Barron* (New York: Harper & Brothers, 1930), 30.

11 Barron, Pound, and Moore, *They Told Barron*, 31.

12 Louis G. Kaufman to John Skelton Williams, September 10, 1915, private collection of Peter Kaufman.

13 *New York Times*, August 25, 1915, 5; "New Giants of Wall Street," *Brooklyn Daily Eagle*, June 11, 1916.

14 *Seattle Daily Times*, September 8, 1915.

15 *Post-Crescent* (Appleton, WI), December 5, 1931, 10.

16 Bernard A. Weisberger, *The Dream Maker: William C. Durant, Founder of General Motors* (Boston: Little, Brown, 1979), 174.

17 Weisberger, *The Dream Maker*, 175.

18 Richard M. Langworth and Jan P. Norbye, *The Complete History of General Motors, 1908–1986* (New York: Beekman House, 1986), 56.

19 Elsa Maxwell, "Come to My Party," *Woman's Home Companion*, March 1954.

20 Axel Madsen, *The Deal Maker: How William C. Durant Made General Motors* (New York: Wiley, 1999), 160.

21 Alfred D. Chandler and Stephen Salsbury, *Pierre S. Du Pont and the Making of the Modern Corporation* (New York: Harper & Row, 1971), 437.

22 *Flint Daily Journal*, September 17, 1915, 18.

23 *New York Sun*, December 8, 1915.

24 William C. Durant to Louis G. Kaufman, August 10, 1916, 1974.002.039, 1915–1916, W. C. Durant Collection, Kettering University Archives, Flint, Michigan.

25 *New York Sun*, January 14, 1917.

26 *Lamb*, September 2, 1916.

27 Kaufman to Durant, December 7, 1916, W. C. Durant Collection, Kettering University Archives, Flint, Michigan.

28 Kaufman to Durant, July 15, 1916, W. C. Durant Collection, Kettering University Archives, Flint, Michigan; Durant to LG, August 10, 1916.

29 Barron, Pound, and Moore, *They Told Barron*, 100.

30 "Who's Who in Finance," *New York Herald*, March 5, 1918.

31 Grover Whalen, secretary of the Mayor's Committee of Welcome for Home-Coming Troops, to Louis Graveraet Kaufman, April 30, 1918, private collection of Peter Kaufman.

32 "Liberty Bonds the Safest of All Investments Known," *New York Sun*, April 14, 1918, 38.

33 *New York Tribune*, June 6, 1919, 1.

34 *American Business & National Journal*, January 19, 1922.

35 *Town Topics*, November 1918.

36 "Rajah Stabs Queen as Artists Cavort," *New York Herald*, February 2, 1919, 10.

37 Tamia Karlinski, interview with the author, July 2019.

38 *Lamb*, September 2, 1916.

39 *Marquette Monthly* (May 2017): 20–21.

Chapter 4

1 *Social Register Observer* (Winter 2007): 34.

2 C. Fred Rydholm, *Superior Heartland: A Backwoods History*, 2 vols. (Marquette, MI: C. F. Rydholm, 1989), 1:477.

3 Kathleen Ryan O'Day, "Granot Loma: A Legend in Our Time" (unpublished manuscript, April 16, 1986), typescript, J. M. Longyear Research Library, Marquette Regional History Center.

4 Marshall and Fox ledger, private collection of Peter Kaufman.

5 Marshall and Fox's plans for Granot Loma, private collection of Peter Kaufman.

6 Rydholm, *Superior Heartland*, 1:487–88.

7 "No Expense Spared in Granot Loma Construction," *Mining Journal*, July 16, 1983.

8 National Register of Historic Places Report 1991, Granot Loma, Section 8, 1, https://s3.amazonaws.com/NARAprod storage/opastorage/live/47/3400/25340047/content/electronic -records/rg-079/NPS_MI/91000330.pdf.

9 Daisy Eimen, interview with the author, January 16, 2019.

10 Janny Scott, *The Beneficiary: Fortune, Misfortune, and the Story of My Father* (New York: Riverhead Books, 2019), 43.

11 Jeff Groff, telephone interview with the author, July 13, 2020.

12 Matthei Howe, "Loma Farm Is Complete: Project Proves Value of Livestock Breeding," *Mining Journal*, December 11, 1928.

13 Louis Hill, descendant of L. G. Kaufman, "Seven Summers at Granot Loma," September 25, 1991, private collection of Peter Kaufman.

14 "Kaufman Tells Real Purpose of Loma Farms," *Mining Journal*, August 18, 1930.

15 "Farmers of Peninsula Gather at Loma Farms Tomorrow," *Mining Journal*, August 15, 1930, 7.

16 Howe, "Loma Farm Is Complete."

17 *Detroit Free Press*, August 17, 1930.

18 *Mining Journal*, August 19, 1930.

19 "Farmers of Peninsula Gather at Loma Farms Tomorrow."

Chapter 5

1 Louis Hill, descendant of L. G. Kaufman, "Seven Summers at Granot Loma," September 25, 1991, 10, private collection of Peter Kaufman.

2 C. Fred Rydholm, *Superior Heartland: A Backwoods History*, 2 vols. (Marquette, MI: C. F. Rydholm, 1989), 1:560.

3 Rydholm, *Superior Heartland*, 2:1441.

4 Jane Kaufman Boyce to Rosemary Michelin, August 9, 1988, Granot Loma Pamphlet File, Kaufman Family Letters, J. M. Longyear Research Library, Marquette Regional History Center.

5 Betty Waring, *Golden Memories of Birch* (Marquette: Self-published, 1991), 30.

6 *Detroit News*, June 13, 1984, 11E.

7 Lucius Beebe, *Mansions on Rails: The Folklore of the Private Railway Car* (Berkeley, CA: Howell-North, 1959), 279.

8 *Detroit News*, June 13, 1984.

9 Beebe, *Mansions on Rails*, 199.

10 *Montgomery Advertiser*, July 28, 1928, 4.

11 *Detroit News*, June 13, 1984, 11E.

12 Supplemental Trust Indenture, dated February 26, 1951, private collection of Peter Kaufman.

13 *San Antonio Light*, June 17, 1928.

14 Mary Ellen Peterson, interview with the author, July 23, 2019.

15 Deborah Bishop, interview with the author, December 21, 2018.

16 Kaufman Family and Granot Loma, Granot Loma Pamphlet File, Kaufman Family Letters, J. M. Longyear Research Library, Marquette Regional History Center.

17 Matthei Howe, "Women's Room in Bank Building Artistic, Comfortable," *Mining Journal*, October 14, 1927.

18 *Mining Journal*, October 14, 1927, 1.

19 "Louis G. Kaufman Honored by Marquette Complimentary Banquet Attended by More Than Five Hundred Citizens," *Mining Journal*, October 15, 1927, 1.

232 Notes

20 "Louis G. Kaufman Honored."
21 *American Israelite*, October 27, 1927.
22 *Mining Journal*, May 22, 1928.
23 *Mining Journal*, September 22, 1928, 3.
24 *Mining Journal*, September 22, 1928, 3.

Chapter 6

1 Diary of Diana Dalziel, June 23, 1918, private collection of Lisa Vreeland.
2 Diana Vreeland, George Plimpton, and Christopher Hemphill, *D.V.* (New York: Da Capo Press, 1997), 27.
3 *Oakland Tribune*, June 10, 1923, 1.
4 Marilyn Hill, interview with the author, August 19, 2019.
5 *Detroit Free Press*, March 14, 1926, 68.
6 *Chillicothe Constitution Tribune*, December 20, 1924, 6.
7 *New York Daily News*, March 16, 1926, 167.
8 *American Israelite*, October 4, 1928, 3.
9 *American Israelite*, October 4, 1928, 3.
10 *St. Louis Globe Democrat*, November 11, 1928, 15.
11 *Syracuse Herald*, March 31, 1929, 141.

Chapter 7

1 *Wall Street Journal*, May 28, 1927.
2 Jason M. Barr, *Cities in the Sky: The Quest to Build the World's Tallest Skyscrapers* (New York: Scribner, 2024), 35–36.
3 John J. Raskob to Louis G. Kaufman, August 28, 1929, File 1225, John J. Raskob Papers, Manuscripts and Archives, Hagley Museum and Library, New Castle County, Delaware.
4 Christopher Gray, "The Architect Who Shaped Upper Fifth Avenue," *New York Times*, August 26, 2007.
5 John Tauranac, *The Empire State Building: The Making of a Landmark* (New York: Scribner, 1995), 228.
6 *Evening Star* (Washington, D.C.), August 27, 1931, 15.
7 *Brooklyn Standard Union*, December 4, 1931, 7.
8 *Boston Globe*, December 18, 1931, 46.

Notes 233

9 *Daily Oklahoman*, June 23, 1932, 16.

10 John J. Raskob to Young Kaufman, October 11, 1933, File 1226, John J. Raskob Papers, Manuscripts and Archives, Hagley Museum and Library, New Castle County, Delaware.

11 *New York Daily News*, September 6, 1931, 82.

12 *New York Daily News*, May 21, 1933, 40.

13 *Palm Beach Post*, March 7, 1935, 7.

14 Jack De Manio, *Life Begins Too Early: A Sort of Autobiography* (London: Hutchinson, 1970), 59.

15 *Scranton Republican*, September 30, 1936, 2.

16 John J. Raskob Papers 0473, 12, Manuscripts and Archives, Hagley Museum and Library, https://hagley-aspace-pdf.s3 .amazonaws.com/0473.pdf.

17 *Miami Herald*, May 14, 1937, 14.

18 *Wall Street Journal*, May 14, 1937, 10.

19 *Cincinnati Enquirer*, May 14, 1937, 19.

20 Helena Rubinstein, *My Life for Beauty* (New York: Simon and Schuster, 1966), 91.

21 "An Interview with Mrs. Kirk (Polly) McFarlin of 24 Delwick Lane," *Thistle* (Millburn-Short Hills Historical Society Newsletter, NJ) (Fall 2004): 16–18.

22 Daisy Eimen, interview with the author, January 16, 2019.

23 *New York Daily News*, November 25, 1937, 411.

24 *Miami Herald*, February 21, 1939, 10.

Epilogue

1 Louis Graveraet Kaufman, dated April 20, 1940, records of the Marquette County Clerk, Probate Court.

2 Deborah Bishop, interview with the author, December 2018.

3 *New York Daily News*, August 30, 1956, 509.

4 *Escanaba Daily Press*, July 11, 1977, 15.

5 *New York Times*, August 4, 1978, A9; *Detroit Free Press*, July 30, 1978, 8A.

6 Wendy Stocker, interview with the author, May 29, 2021.

BIBLIOGRAPHY

Archival Sources

Durant, William. Papers. Kettering University Archives, Flint, Michigan.

Kaufman, Peter. Private Collection.

Kaufman Family Letters. J. M. Longyear Research Library, Marquette Regional History Center.

Raskob, John J. Papers. Manuscripts and Archives, Hagley Museum and Library, New Castle County, Delaware.

Vreeland, Lisa. Private Collection.

White, Peter. Papers. Bentley Historical Library, University of Michigan, Ann Arbor.

Newspapers and Periodicals

American Banker
American Business & National Journal
American Israelite
Bankers Magazine
Boston Globe
Brooklyn Daily Eagle
Brooklyn Standard Union
Chicago Examiner
Chillicothe Constitution Tribune
Cincinnati Enquirer
Commercial West
Daily Oklahoman
Detroit Free Press
Detroit News
Escanaba Daily Press

Evening Star
Flint Daily Journal
Lake Superior Journal
Lamb
Marine Review
Marquette City Directory
Marquette Times
Miami Herald
Mining Journal
Montgomery Advertiser
New York American
New York Daily News
New York Herald
New York Sun
New York Times
New York Tribune
Oakland Tribune
Palm Beach Post
Post-Crescent
San Antonio Light
Sault Ste. Marie Evening News
Scranton Republican
Seattle Daily Times
Social Register Observer
St. Louis Globe Democrat
Syracuse Herald
Town Topics
Wall Street Journal
Washington Times

Catalogues

Corning Museum of Glass. *Tiffany's Glass Mosaics in a Changing Consumer Landscape, May 20, 2017–January 8, 2018*. Edited by Kelly A. Conway, Lindsy Parrott, and Morgan T. Albahary. Corning, NY.

Iron Bay Auction. *The Kaufman Collection at Auction: The Treasures of Granot Loma Farm.* July 7–8, 1990.

Rare Coin Company of America. *The N. M. Kaufman Collection and Other Important Consignments at Unrestricted Public Auction Sale.* August 4–5, 1978. Chicago.

Unpublished Sources, Reprints, and Theses

Bertschinger, Walt, and Tom Vomastek. "The Kaufman Family and Granot Loma." Unpublished manuscript, 1979. J. M. Longyear Research Library, Marquette Regional History Center.

Cambensy, Sara. "A History of the Graveraet School: Pictures, Stories, Articles, and Writings." Unpublished manuscript, n.d. Author's possession.

Christ Church of Short Hills. "The Stained Glass Windows of Christ Church of Short Hills: Their Backgrounds, Secrets and Donors." Unpublished pamphlet, February 2009. Author's possession.

Hill, Louis. "Seven Summers at Granot Loma." Unpublished manuscript, September 25, 1991. Typescript. Private collection of Peter Kaufman.

Kaufman, Peter. "Peter Kaufman Remembers Granot Loma." Unpublished recording, n.d. DVD.

Longyear, John Munro. "Reminiscences." Unpublished manuscript, 1912. J. M. Longyear Research Library, Marquette Regional History Center.

O'Day, Kathleen Ryan. "Granot Loma: A Legend in Our Time." Unpublished manuscript, April 16, 1986. J. M. Longyear Research Library, Marquette Regional History Center.

Peck, Robert. "The Cult of the Rustic in Nineteenth Century America." Master's thesis, University of Delaware, 1976.

Rankin, Ernest H., and Jesse P. Williams. "The Graveraet/Harsen/Kaufman Families." Unpublished biographical note. J. M. Longyear Research Library, Marquette Regional History Center.

"The Ritz-Carlton Hotel of New York." Classic Reprints, 1919. Pranava Books, India.

Magazine Articles

Alpern, Andrew. "Madame's Mansion: Helena Rubinstein Reigned at 625 Park Avenue." *Avenue Magazine*, October 2001.

Andrews, Roger M. "From Messenger Boy to President of a $75,000 Bank." *Clover-Land*, April 1916. https://lib.nmu.edu/voices/documents/cloverland/Volume1-4_Apr.pdf.

"Article 18." *E-Sylum: An Electronic Publication of the Numismatic Bibliomania Society*. August 30, 2015.

Bair, Robert, Jr. "Legendary Collector." *The Numismatist*, August 2015.

Berman, Ann E. "Granot Loma in Michigan: A Classic American Retreat on the Shores of Lake Superior." *Architectural Digest*, May 1995.

Chabot, Larry. "The Day Muhammed Ali Came to Town." *Marquette Monthly*, November 2002.

Charnes, K. C. "Granot Loma: Michigan's Log Masterpiece." *Log Home Guide for Builders and Buyers*, Summer 1987.

"A Country House in Reinforced Concrete." *International Studio*, October 1909.

"For Generations to Come." *Marquette Monthly*, September 1995.

Hauptman, Laurence. "Into the Abyss." *Civil War Times*, February 1997.

"An Interview with Mrs. Kirk (Polly) McFarlin of 24 Delwick Lane." *Thistle* (Millburn-Short Hills Historical Society Newsletter, NJ) (Fall 2004): 13–20.

Maxwell, Elsa. "Come to My Party." *Woman's Home Companion*, March 1954.

Netto, David. "Is This Park Avenue Penthouse the Best Apartment in New York?" *Town & Country*, May 2017.

Wahlberg, Holly. "Rustic Luxury in the Upper Peninsula." *Michigan History Magazine*, September–October 2016.

Online Sources, Blogs, and Podcasts

"Best Friends: Jewish Society in Old Palm Beach." *Palm Beach Social Diary,* January 28, 2020. https://www.newyorksocialdiary.com/best-friends-jewish-society-in-old-palm-beach/.

"Cambridge University Press Roundtable on Anti-Semitism in the Gilded Age and Progressive Era." Moderated by David S. Koffman. *NEW: The Journal of the Gilded Age and Progressive Era* (2020): 1–33. doi:10.1017/SI537781420000055.

"Company K of the First Michigan Sharpshooters." American Indians and the Civil War: An American Indian's Perspective. https://benaysnativeamericans.weebly.com.

Findagrave.com.

Genealogytrails.com.

Hamp, Patricia. "1st Michigan Sharpshooters Company K-Red Book." June 16, 2011. https://linguistadores.com/Native%20Americans.1st-Michigan-Sharpshooters-Company-K-Red-Book.ashx (URL unavailable).

Harrison, Jon. "May 9 1864: Company K Faces Action at Battle of Spotsylvania Court House." *Red Tape* (blog). Michigan State University Libraries, May 9, 2018. https://blogs.lib.msu.edu.

Mifamilyhistory.org. https://peoplefinder.info/collaborations/mifamilyhistory.

Newspaperarchive.com.

Newspapers.com.

Northern Michigan University. "Recorded in Stone: Voices on the Marquette Iron Range" (website). Central Upper Peninsula and Northern Michigan University Archives. https://lib.nmu.edu/voices/.

Ranieri, Lynne. "Local History: The Founding Family of Short Hills." *Patch*, September 21, 2009. https://patch.com/new-jersey/millburn/local-history-the-founding-family-of-short-hills.

State of Michigan. "Native American Cultural Trail Deepens Historical Perspective on Mackinac Island." https://content.govdelivery.com/accounts/MIDNR/bulletins/1892dff.

"The Story of Company K: Native Americans from Michigan Who Saw Tough Action in the Civil War." *Stateside*. Podcast audio, August 23, 2017. https://www.michiganradio.org/offbeat/2017-08-23/the-story-of-company-k-native-americans-from-michigan-who-saw-tough-action-in-the-civil-war.

Tichelaar, Tyler R. *My Marquette* (blog). Tylertichelaar.wordpress.com.

Informational Interviews with the Author

Bair, Robert. Numismatic expert. 2020.

Barr, Dr. Jason. Professor, Rutgers University. February 15, 2021, to May 13, 2021.

Bishop, Deborah. December 21, 2018.

Bruegl, Heather. Historian and Indigenous consultant. December 2023.

Clawson, Dr. Mary Ann. Expert on freemasonry and professor emerita, Wesleyan University. August 18, 2020.

Eimen, Daisy. January 16, 2019.

Falk, Cynthia. Author of *Barns of New York*. July 7, 2020.

Flannery, Cathy, and Katherine Thomson. Researchers for *Women He's Undressed*, a documentary about Orry-Kelly. January 13, 2020.

Gleason, Pam. Editor and publisher of *The Aiken Horse*. November 16, 2020.

Groff, Jeff. Estate Historian, Winterthur Museum. July 13, 2020.

Hill, Jessie. December 26, 2020.

Hill, Marilyn. August 19, 2019.

Jacob, Dr. Margaret. Expert on freemasonry and history professor at UCLA. August 4, 2020.

Karlinski, Tamia. July 2019.

Kaufman, Clare, and Louis Graveraet Kaufman III. February 2021.

Kaufman, Peter. Marquette, Michigan, 2019–20.

Kobrin, Dr. Rebecca A. Professor, Columbia University. February 20, 2020.

Krueger, Kurt. Dealer in coins and Civil War tokens. January 8, 2021.

Lydekker, Chesley. January–March 2021.

Okrent, Daniel. Author of *Last Call*. August 26, 2020.

Peck, Robert. Author of "The Cult of the Rustic in Nineteenth Century America." June 9, 2020.

Peterson, Mary Ellen. July 23, 2019.

Richardson, Kristen. Author of *The Season: A Social History of the Debutante*. November 12, 2020.

Schock, David. Filmmaker, *The Road to Andersonville*. October 2019.

Stocker, Wendy. May 29, 2021.

Vanatta, Dr. Sean. Visiting assistant professor, New York University. New York City, February 21, 2020.

Veitch, Michael. November 5, 2020.

White, Dr. Eugene N. Professor, Rutgers University. New York City, February 15, 2020.

Books, Journal Articles, and Reports

Alpern, Andrew. *Apartments for the Affluent: A Historical Survey of Buildings in New York*. New York: McGraw-Hill, 1975.

Alpern, Andrew, Rosario Candela, and J.E.R. Carpenter. *The New York Apartment Houses of Rosario Candela and James Carpenter*. New York: Acanthus Press, 2001.

Arculus, Paul. *Durant's Right-Hand Man*. Victoria, BC: Friesen Press, 2011.

Barr, Jason M. *Cities in the Sky: The Quest to Build the World's Tallest Skyscrapers*. New York: Scribner, 2024.

Barron, Clarence W., Arthur Pound, and Samuel Taylor Moore. *They Told Barron: The Notes of Clarence W. Barron*. New York: Harper & Brothers, 1930.

Bascomb, Neal. *Higher: A Historic Race to the Sky and the Making of a City*. New York: Broadway Books, 2004.

Beebe, Lucius. *Mansions on Rails: The Folklore of the Private Railway Car*. Berkeley, CA: Howell-North, 1959.

Benston, George J. *The Separation of Commercial and Investment*

Banking: The Glass-Steagall Act Revisited and Reconsidered. New York: Oxford University Press, 1990.

Bernard, George S. *The Battle of the Crater in Front of Petersburg. July 30, 1864. A Memorable Day in History*. Petersburg, 1890.

Binzen, Peter, and Jonathan Binzen. *Richardson Dilworth: Last of the Bare-Knuckled Aristocrats*. Philadelphia: Camino Books, 2014.

Brinks, Herbert J. *Peter White: A Great Men of Michigan Book*. Grand Rapids, MI: W. B. Eerdmans, 1970.

Carr, Shelby, and Thomas J. Noel. *The Queen of Denver: Louise Sneed Hill and the Emergence of Modern High Society*. Charleston, SC: The History Press, 2020.

Chandler, Alfred D., and Stephen Salsbury. *Pierre S. Du Pont and the Making of the Modern Corporation*. New York: Harper & Row, 1971.

Cleland, Charles L. *Rites of Conquest*. Ann Arbor: University of Michigan Press, 1992.

Cotter, Arundel. *The Gary I Knew*. Boston: Stratford Company, 1928.

Cray, Ed. *Chrome Colossus: General Motors and Its Times*. New York: McGraw-Hill, 1980.

Czopek, Chris. *Who Was in Company K: Reliable Facts about the Native American Soldiers in Company K, 1st Michigan Sharpshooters, during the Civil War, 1861–1865*. Lansing, MI: Red Oak Research, 2015.

De Manio, Jack. *Life Begins Too Early: A Sort of Autobiography*. London: Hutchinson, 1970.

———. *To Auntie with Love*. London: Hutchinson, 1967.

Diner, Hasia R. *Roads Taken: The Great Jewish Migrations to the New World and the Peddlers Who Forged the Way*. New Haven: Yale University Press, 2015.

Downs, Gabriel N., and Michael C. Downs. *Marquette: The Images of America Series*. Charleston, SC: Arcadia Publishing, 1999.

Durant, William C. *In His Own Words: The Unedited Memoirs of William C. Durant*. Flint, MI: Kettering University, 2008.

Falk, Cynthia G. *Barns of New York: Rural Architecture of the Empire State*. Ithaca: Cornell University Press, 2012.

Farber, David R. *Everybody Ought to Be Rich: The Life and Times of John J. Raskob, Capitalist*. Oxford: Oxford University Press, 2013.

Federal Reserve Bank of St. Louis. *Branch Banking in the United States. Material Prepared for the Information of the Federal Reserve System*. Federal Reserve Committee on Branch, Group and Chain Banking, 1931.

Gilborn, Craig A. *Adirondack Furniture and the Rustic Tradition*. New York: Abrams, 1987.

Gosling, Lucinda. *Debutantes and the London Season*. Oxford: Shire Publications, 2013.

Gustin, Lawrence R. *Billy Durant: Creator of General Motors*. Ann Arbor: University of Michigan Press, 2008.

Herek, Raymond J. *These Men Have Seen Hard Service: The First Michigan Sharpshooters in the Civil War*. Detroit: Wayne State University Press, 1998.

Hopkins, Alfred. *Modern Farm Buildings*. New York: Robert McBride, 1920.

Kaiser, Harvey H. *Great Camps of the Adirondacks*. Boston: D. R. Godine, 1982.

Kawbawgam, Charles, Charlotte Kawbawgam, and Jacques LePique. *Ojibwa Narratives of Charles and Charlotte Kawbawgam and Jacques LePique, 1893–1895*. Recorded with notes by Homer H. Kidder. Edited by Arthur P. Bourgeois. Detroit: Wayne State University Press, 1994.

Koffman, David S., Hasia R. Diner, Eric L. Goldstein, Jonathan D. Sarna, and Beth Wenger. "Roundtable on Antisemitism in the Gilded Age and Progressive Era." *Journal of the Gilded Age and Progressive Era* 19, no. 3 (2020): 473–505.

Langworth, Richard M., and Jan P. Norbye. *The Complete History of General Motors, 1908–1986*. New York: Beekman House, 1986.

Longtine, Sonny. *UP People: Incredible Stories about Incredible People*. Marquette, MI: Sunnyside Publications, 2017.

MacManus, Theodore F., and Norman Beasley. *Men, Money, and Motors: The Drama of the Automobile.* New York: Harper & Brothers, 1929.

Madsen, Axel. *The Deal Maker: How William C. Durant Made General Motors.* New York: Wiley, 1999.

Mayor, Archer. *The Huron Mountain Club: The First Hundred Years.* Marquette, MI: Huron Mountain Club, 1988.

Morris, S. Brent. *The Complete Idiot's Guide to Freemasonry.* New York: Alpha Books, 2006.

Nyquist, Michael S. *The Samuel Robert Kaufman Family of Marquette.* Self-published, 2023.

O'Leary, Ann Stillman. *Adirondack Style.* New York: Clarkson Potter Publishers, 1998.

Pelfrey, William. *Billy, Alfred, and General Motors: The Story of Two Unique Men, a Legendary Company, and a Remarkable Time in American History.* New York: AMACOM Books, 2006.

Pennoyer, Peter, and Anne Walker. *The Architecture of Warren & Wetmore.* New York: W. W. Norton, 2006.

Perry, Elisabeth Israels. *Belle Moskowitz: Feminine Politics and the Exercise of Power in the Age of Alfred E. Smith.* Boston: Northeastern University Press, 2000.

Pound, Arthur. *The Turning Wheel: The Story of General Motors through Twenty-Five Years, 1908–1933.* New York: Doubleday, Doran, 1934.

Pugh, Martin. *"We Danced All Night": A Social History of Britain between the Wars.* London: Bodley Head, 2008.

Richardson, Kristen. *The Season: A Social History of the Debutante.* New York: W. W. Norton, 2020.

Ridley, Jasper. *The Freemasons: A History of the World's Most Powerful Secret Society.* New York: Arcade Publishing, 1999.

Rubinstein, Helena. *My Life for Beauty.* New York: Simon and Schuster, 1966.

Rydholm, C. Fred. *Superior Heartland: A Backwoods History.* 2 vols. Marquette, MI: C. F. Rydholm, 1989.

Sawyer, Alvah L. *A History of the Northern Peninsula of Michigan and Its People: Its Mining, Lumber and Agricultural Industries.* Chicago: Lewis Publishing Company, 1911.

Schwinn, Ed, and Jim Davis. *Stone Manor: Otto Young, the Younglands & Stone Manor.* Delavan, WI: Self-published, 2016.

Scott, Janny. *The Beneficiary: Fortune, Misfortune, and the Story of My Father.* New York: Riverhead Books, 2019.

Seltzer, Lawrence Howard. *A Financial History of the American Automobile Industry: A Study of the Ways in Which the Leading American Producers of Automobiles Have Met Their Capital Requirements.* Boston: Houghton Mifflin, 1928.

Shier, Quita V. *Warriors in Mr. Lincoln's Army: Native American Soldiers Who Fought in the Civil War.* Bloomington: True Directions iUniverse, 2017.

Sloan, Alfred P., and Boyden Sparkes. *Adventures of a White-Collar Man.* New York: Doubleday, Doran, 1941.

Sparling, Earl. *Mystery Men of Wall Street: The Power behind the Market.* New York: Greenberg, 1930.

Starrett, William Aiken. *Skyscrapers and the Men Who Build Them.* New York: Scribner, 1928.

Stone, Frank B. *Philo Marshall Everett: Father of Michigan's Iron Industry and Founder of the City of Marquette.* Baltimore: Gateway Press, 1997.

Stuart, Amanda Mackenzie. *Empress of Fashion: A Life of Diana Vreeland.* New York: Harper, 2012.

Tarbell, Ida M. *The Life of Elbert H. Gary: The Story of Steel.* New York: D. Appleton, 1925.

Tauranac, John. *The Empire State Building: The Making of a Landmark.* New York: Scribner, 1995.

Tichelaar, Tyler R. *Iron Pioneers: A Novel.* Book 1 of the Marquette Trilogy. Marquette, MI: Marquette Fiction, 2006.

———. *Kawbawgam: The Chief, the Legend, the Man.* Marquette, MI: Marquette Fiction, 2020.

———. *My Marquette: Explore the Queen City of the North, Its History, People, and Places with Native Son Tyler R. Tichelaar.* Marquette, MI: Marquette Fiction, 2011.

246 Bibliography

Treloar, Wilbert H. *Cohodas: The Story of a Family*. Marquette: Northern Michigan University Press, 1977.

Vetich, Michael. *Summit of Champions: Thoroughbred Racing in Saratoga Springs, 1901–1955*. Saratoga Springs: Advantage Press, 2013.

Vreeland, Diana, George Plimpton, and Christopher Hemphill. *D.V.* New York: Da Capo Press, 1997.

Wagner, Geraldine B. *Thirteen Months to Go: The Creation of the Empire State Building*. San Diego: Thunder Bay Press, 2003.

Walker, Sally M. *Deadly Aim: The Civil War Story of Michigan's Anishinaabe Sharpshooters*. New York: Henry Holt, 2019.

Waring, Betty. *Golden Memories of Birch*. Marquette, MI: Self-published, 1991.

Weisberger, Bernard A. *The Dream Maker: William C. Durant, Founder of General Motors*. Boston: Little, Brown, 1979.

Westfall, Carroll William. "Benjamin Henry Marshall of Chicago." *Chicago Architectural Journal* 2 (1982): 8–27.

White, Eugene Nelson. "Banking and Finance in the Twentieth Century." In *The Cambridge Economic History of the United States*. Vol. 3. Edited by Stanley L. Engerman and Robert E. Gallman. Cambridge: Cambridge University Press, 2008.

———. "Banking Innovation in the 1920s: The Growth of National Banks' Financial Services." *Business and Economic History* 13 (1984): 92–104.

———. "The Political Economy of Banking Regulation, 1864–1933." *Journal of Economic History* 42, no. 1 (1982): 33–40.

Williams, Ralph D. *The Honorable Peter White: A Biographical Sketch of the Lake Superior Iron Country*. Cleveland: Freshwater Press, 1905.

Willis, Carol. *Form Follows Finance: Skyscrapers and Skylines in New York and Chicago*. New York: Princeton Architectural Press, 1995.

Willis, Carol, and Donald Friedman. *Building the Empire State*. New York: W. W. Norton, 1998.

ABOUT THE AUTHOR

ANN BERMAN is a writer and cultural journalist who has contributed to *The Wall Street Journal*, *Town & Country*, *Architectural Digest*, *Forbes*, *Martha Stewart Living*, and many other publications. She has also contributed to a number of books.